SNOOZE

THE BEST OF OUR MAGAZINE

SNOOZE
THE BEST OF OUR MAGAZINE

CONCEIVED AND CREATED BY

ALFRED GINGOLD AND JOHN BUSKIN

WORKMAN PUBLISHING, NEW YORK

Library of Congress Cataloging-in-Publication Data
Gingold, Alfred.
    Snooze: The Best of Our Magazine.
    1. Parodies. 2. New Yorker (New York, N.Y. :
1925)
I. Buskin, John. II. Title.
PN6231. P3G56 1986   051   86-40198
ISBN 0-89480-118-X (pbk.)

Cover and book design:
David Kaestle and David Vogler

Cover illustration:
Warren Sattler

Workman Publishing Company, Inc.
1 West 39 Street
New York, New York 10018

Manufactured in the United States of America
First printing October 1986
10 9 8 7 6 5 4 3 2 1

For Rose and Roxy

ACKNOWLEDGMENTS

Abra Bigham, David Buskin, Pamela Buskin, Oliver Buskin, Ross Charap, H. D. Ehrlich, Judy Fireman, David Freeman, Rose Gingold, Wayne Kirn, Sally Kovalchick, Richard Leiberman, Bob Leitman, Nathaniel Lubell, Jefferson Morley, James Raimes, Helen Rogan, Faith Sale, Lynn Strong, David Vogler.

With special thanks to Peter Workman.

OUR CONTENTS

ANNALS OF GREY FLANNELS

THE WORLD OUTSIDE OUR OFFICE

WE PACK OUR BAGS

RECHERCHÉ REPLAY

WE BREAK OUR LEG

FOOTAGE AFOOT

THE VIRTUOSO LISTENER

AFTERWORD

OUR APPENDIX

•   •

FOREWORD

CALL me Eustace. It's my name. How they all laughed when I suggested the dandy on our first cover be called Eustace, too! Mr. Shhh would have been too polite to laugh, but he was not there in those days. I was.

By the time this collection appears, I will be gone from the shabby office where, for more than sixty years, I've invested my life's blood in every part of our magazine from night-club listings to book reviews, from Newsbreaks to Notes and Comment, certain that, one day, my contribution would be recognized and I would be appointed editor.

It was not to be.

Instead, my years of service have been rewarded with the odious task of assembling this anthology. The truth is that no one else wanted the job, although they all said that I must do it, that I was the only one who could do it. This last, at least, is so.

Harold C. Russ, or perhaps Rouse, was our first editor; his signature consisted of a hastily scrawled "R" and his voice was a piercing yawp frequently impossible to understand, so his name remains a mystery whose possible solution is suggested by the varied spellings that follow. During the magazine's formative years, we all worked together as equals. It must be said that my own ideas were more influential than most and that the number of hours I spent at the office was not equalled by Royce himself, but in all other respects our staff worked together with the fine grace of a lacrosse team moving the puck downcourt.

What energy we all had then! One memorable evening, a group of us were asked to leave a speakeasy when a spirited disagreement over a Talk of the Town piece—as I recall, a brief chat with Lucius Beebe's shoe repairman—proved too much for the small jazz band blaring at the other end of the room. Reason prevailed, in the form of my opinion (that our readers had no interest in cobblers), and the piece never ran. I suggested in its place one of my own, about the cufflink-buffer at Cartier, but the space was given over to one of Jim Thumper's deft (if primitive) dog drawings. Thumper was a much nastier man than his work would suggest, but I acquiesced to his usurpation of my piece's space as I did to a thousand other wrongs inflicted by writers, editors, even art people, believing that my turn would come when Rass stepped aside.

Ruh's receptivity to my advice stood him in good stead, and he frequently thanked me for urging that the magazine cover events and people outside New York City. "Goddamn it, Eustace," he said to me as we toasted V-J Day in a crowded Schrafft's near the office. "If you hadn't twisted my arm, we'd've missed the Second World War!" Our cultural coverage expanded along with our journalism, and soon the magazine was reporting on dog shows, quilting bees, foreign movies, smoky little piano bars, and more.

12

By the end of the forties, ours was no longer a provincial humor magazine with a small, effete readership; rather, it had become the nation's brightest showcase of fiction, factual writing, humor, poetry, and "drawings" (Riis's curious euphemism for cartoons). Our magazine was now the periodical I'd always dreamt it could be.

Reese's death was, of course, a complete shock to him, to me, and to the rest of our staff, but not nearly as much of a shock as the appointment of his successor, Mr. Shawm, or perhaps Schwa, a gentleman of profound talents and even profounder silences. (His signature consists of a neatly lettered "W.S." and his voice is so quiet that it is frequently overwhelmed by the ticking of his wristwatch, so his name remains a mystery whose possible solution is suggested by the varied spellings that follow.)

How the magazine changed after the ascent of Shmuh! Gone were the convivial staff lunches, which frequently ran well into cocktail hour and engendered some of our best column fillers. Under Shwoo, we stayed in our increasingly dingy offices, contemplating the magazine's mission and becoming graver by the hour. The magazine acquired a pronounced political conscience, commitments to the work of a wide range of excellent—or, at least, very serious—writers, and a proclivity for exploring subjects like the antimacassar industry, yucca, or two weeks in the life of a violist at lengths that make some readers tear up their copies of our magazine into tiny strips and burn them in the wastebasket.

This collection brings together more than the best of our six decades; it contains the best of what might have been. Even our very oldest and most devoted readers will not recognize everything in this volume, for I have included material we ought to have run but which, owing to internecine frictions or the immutable stupidity of some of our higher-ups, we did not. Two standards and two alone were used in considering articles, stories, drawings, and listings for inclusion in "Snooze": the first, my own judgment; the second, whether or not I've still got my copy—a condition that has limited the range of choice more than somewhat, since several crates of my belongings were "inadvertently" lost the last time our offices were painted. I suspect the machinations of one of our younger editors, jealous of my stature at our magazine.

The theft, if it was theft, was not necessary. My rivals have won. I am leaving. But I leave behind this, my monument, a celebration of the magazine to which I have given the best years of my life (and many other years as well)—the best of the magazine that, from its Jazz Age beginnings to its Space Age present, readers have always relied upon for a good read, a good laugh, and a good snooze.

E.T.
West 43rd Street

CHAPTER ONE

THE

YEARS

WITH

US

Family Tales

*T*HIS *chapter brings together several perspectives on the thick crust of legend, myth, and rumor that has grown around the magazine. Included herein is a look at what lunch was really like at the Algonquin Round Table; E. B. Quite's finest dilation on rural themes, full of the flinty, plain-spoken tone and effortlessly far-ranging insights that so irked many of his admirers; Robert Densely at his densest in his previously unpublished, lone foray into sports reportage; and S. J. Perlmutter's memoir of a strenuous afternoon in Stamford with our first editor, Roim.*

Here, too, is a brace of articles that are classics of their kind. Mr. DePinna's obituary is a shining example of our magazine's ultimate salute to one of its own. Obituaries are the only feature of the magazine written by our current editor, Mr. Shih. While all of us who toil here share the grief he so eloquently expresses in them, we must also confess to some relief that his temperament inclines him toward a form so unsuitable for expansion into more than one installment. James L. Stevedore's brief disquisition with pictures is, to the informed eye, an exquisite filling of some unexpected lacunae in the steady flow of prose from our Talk reporters' pens.

LETTUCE, ANYONE?

(1928)

[The Hotel Algonquin, just down the street, has always found favor with employees of our magazine, largely because it is close enough to our offices for even the most distracted staffer to find without having to call our switchboard for directions—a proximity especially vital to us of the Lost Generation. This 1928 Talk piece conveys a keen sense of what it was like to dine with the most terribles of the day's enfants. As a Talk story it ran with no byline, of course. It was written by, and is now attributed to, the versatile Alexander Woolcott Gibbs, who managed—by dint of careful timing, a light hand with his makeup brush, and the ability to change clothes in seconds—to convince the world that he was two entirely different people.]

W E'D had enough of the daily grind for one morning and headed over to a nearby hotel dining room where the drinks are cold, the soup is hot, and the badinage is as fresh as the fruit cup. Raymond, our regular waiter, acknowledged our arrival with discreet salutations and escorted us to our usual table, around which, already seated and nursing tea-cups, were two of our favorite lunch-time companions: tart-tongued, bespectacled dramatist-critic-director George S. Kupperman and the formidably witty, stylish poet-critic-short-storyist Dorothy Perky. The noise level in the dining room diminished measurably as Raymond pulled out our chair for us and we espied a camel's-hair overcoat neatly folded on it.

"Trying to save the tip again, eh, George?" we joshed, brushing the coat to the floor as prelude to seating ourselves and asking rhetorically, "Mind if we join you?"

"Why? Are we coming apart?" queried the poker-faced playwright, rising

to the bait. Around us, diners put down their implements and chewed slowly so as not to miss the floor show. We chuckled and patted George lightly on the shoulder. He recoiled violently and slapped our hand away. "Don't touch me! Just don't touch me! I don't like it when people touch me!" he barked. Nonplussed, we stared at George with something like concern. His demeanor returned instantly to his habitual one of edgy repose.

"Touchy, isn't he?" said Dorothy soberly, gimlet eyes a-twinkle.

"Pardon me, George—for living!"

We quieted down and, amenities done, set about ordering food and drink. No sooner had we asked for a Waldorf Salad with extra walnuts than a pair of hands covered our eyes while a teasing voice asked, "Ever have a Honeymoon Salad: lettuce alone, without dressing?" Even Raymond laughed at that, in his gracious, muted fashion, and we knew without looking that towering over us was the acerbic and extremely tall Forrest Sher-

norm Blaggnes

16

wood, celebrated author of "The Petrified Robert." He smiled amiably at the gawking onlookers, took a seat, and ordered a cup of tea on the rocks while George, moving quickly in the vain hope that he would not be noticed, scribbled notes on a pad which he then crammed back into his inside jacket pocket. He was too slow for Dorothy.

"What do you do with all the jokes you write down, George? Save them for your plays or use 'em in chat as if you'd just thought 'em up?"

"Shut your face, Dot," countered George. "Women should be obscene and not heard."

"Frankly, George," rejoined the redoubtable Perky, "the first time I heard that joke, I laughed so hard I fell out of my cradle."

"Listen, Dot," riposted Kupperman, his usually soft voice just loud enough to carry over the snowballing giggles of the other diners. "Would you like to lose ten pounds of ugly fat? Cut off your head!"

At that moment, Marc Donnelly entered. Donnelly is Kupperman's collaborator; together, they're responsible for Broadway successes like "Animal Feathers," "Of Thee I Came to Dinner," "Come Back, Little Merton," and "The Dark at the Top of the Beggar on Horseback." With Donnelly were Irving West Berlin, the composer, and Paolo Fleischmann, yeast kingpin and patron of the arts. We noticed them first, and greeted them with a bantering "Marc, Irving, Paolo— fancy meeting you here!"

Irrepressible Dorothy pretended she didn't know them. "Good God, they must be letting anyone in here now!"

"I'll say," added George. "You fellows sure you're in the right place?"

For a long moment, all speech and even the tinkling of ice and silverware ceased. Waiters stood unmoving, holding aloft their cargoes of steaming food

and dirty dishes. Together, we waited for Donnelly's reply. Donnelly did not disappoint. Holding up the three middle fingers of his right hand, he looked Kupperman straight in the eye and asked levelly, "George, can you read between the lines?"

"He got you that time, Four-eyes!" cried Dot Perky, tears literally running down her well-foundationed cheeks into her tea-cup, which she spiked from time to time with the contents of a flask hidden in the fur muff she affected even indoors. "Marc, Irving, Paolo—what a lovely name, Paolo—sit down and join us, we're coming apart."

After a breezy roundelay of ordering, another to change the orders, and another round of tea while waiting for our food, lunch was served. During the moment of silence while the assembled company dug in, we yielded to an impulse and, pointing our index finger squarely at the yolk of the poached egg that lay atop Forrest Sherwood's corned-beef hash, deftly pierced it, splashing thick, yellow fluid on the tablecloth and pushing most of the hash into Sherwood's bony lap. As he looked down in dumb-struck surprise, we inquired intently, "You going to eat that?"

Pandemonium ensued. Sherwood flung the rest of his corned-beef hash at us but missed and instead hit Raymond, who was approaching the table bearing Irving West Berlin's Chicken à la King. The paprika-flecked, chunky white goo hydroplaned off its toast-point bed in a single bolus and landed, *splat*, on Paolo Fleischmann, who entered the fray with a fusillade of yeast packets which he pulled from every pocket on his person in perplexing plenitude. Dorothy Perky had fallen quiet for a moment yet was still, undeniably, awake. Calmly, she spooned the mint jelly that garnished her lamb chops into her hand and turned to George

Kupperman, who was attempting to dissociate himself from the brouhaha by feigning absorption in his cuticles. "Say, George," Dorothy said evenly, "do you know what Cleopatra said to the Sultan of Turkey when he asked her for a match?"

"No, I don't. What did she say?"

"Your fez and my asp!" Dorothy fairly shouted, simultaneously smearing the green stuff across Kupperman's thick glasses. The momentarily blinded George retaliated with the first weapon at hand and overturned the table, which rolled over Dorothy, Irving, Paolo, ourselves, and a small, elderly woman who'd been trying to slip past us and who babbled, as she struggled to extricate herself, that nothing like this ever happened in Dubuque.

By now, lunch hour was nearly over and our high spirits settled as we got ready to go. Raymond and the large staff of Panamanian busboys gazed dazedly at the upended table, the blobs of food, and the piles of shattered crockery and glassware that lay strewn around the room. The other diners cleaned themselves off as best they could and applauded our group as we said our goodbyes. After a nod, a smile, and a "See you tomorrow" to Raymond, we returned to our office, refreshed.

—ALEXANDER WOOLCOTT GIBBS

"Uh, excuse me—you're in my light."

WALKING THE DUCK

(1957)

[*E. B. Quite was one of our very first staffers and one of our very best as well, so we were all sorry when he moved to a farm in Maine (all, that is, except our first editor, Ruts, who saw Quite's rural leanings as a ploy to win a raise and never forgave him). When, after some years of country life, Quite began unaccountably to write children's stories about animals, we at the magazine were nonplussed. I wrote him, suggesting he try something about animals that his friends—adults for the most part—could enjoy. His crisp response is suffused with what Sha, our second editor, called "Quite's enduring respect for the connections that all beings, human and otherwise, establish with their environment" and what Ruus called "flannel shirt disease."*]

TIME to put on our mittens! Waldo the duck waits at the wooden gate, a wee scarf wrapped around his throat. The moon, which last night hung in the sky as full and white as an antacid tablet (which reminds me, I'd better take my medication—my stomach's been rumbling like a calypso band), has been dissolved and digested by winter morn, replaced by a clouded sun. A cutting wind from the Canadian north is causing complaints from the barn (speaking of wind, speaking of complaints —where's that darn medication?), where Carlotta the cow is on a hunger strike. Carlotta hasn't "et" in four days, and the consensus among the chickens, that gossipy lot, is that no longer will she hear her most cherished calf say, "Move over, mudder, and give de udder udder to me brudder." True, Carlotta is lying flat on her back on a mattress of hay with her frozen legs stuck in the air, but I'm sure she'll come round. On the farm, what looks like death is often just a momentary paralysis. Take my wife. One rugged winter I came upon her as she sat in the bathroom with an empty revolver cocked at her head, wearing nothing but a flannel gown and fuzzy-wuzzy bunny slippers. She held that position for three weeks, until the spring catalogue arrived from Montgomery Ward.

Before she thawed, I had to do my business in the barn, which mighty annoyed the chickens.

Winter on a Maine farm makes for hard titties, if I may employ a country locution. Winter up here begins shortly before summer and ends long after spring, by which time you feel you can read the prophecies of Nostradamus in your breakfast porridge. Demands are many; indulgences, few. There are chores to be done, elk to be milked, nuggets of Yankee lore to be strained through the manure. We look upon a sky that may someday be a-whiz with guided missiles and think—

"Quack."

I'm coming, I'm coming. Waldo is always impatient to begin our morning constitutional. Mittens snug, earflaps down, I meet Waldo at the gate and lead him to the paved road that some call "progress" but I call pure foolishness. I left the city because the streets were crushed with smoking contraptions equipped with fins and radio antennas that my fellow citizens considered to be luxury automobiles. I prefer the sound of horses' hooves on stone and milk bottles rattling on the stoop, but even up here in Maine those sounds are fading into the Victorian past. Why, my neighbor Gus and his pillar-of-salt wife are

Barstool

"My wife is a putz."

• •

now tooling around town in a big chromed doohickey that looks like mass death on wheels. We wouldn't want to drive around in that big, ugly deerslayer, would we, Waldo?

"Quack."

Snowflakes begin to fall in loose asterisks.

```
*  *   *  *  *      **      **
*   *   *    *   *   ***    ***
```

HUDDLED together at the top of the hill is a group of children in a schoolbus shelter. The little sissies.

When I was your age, I—

"—I used to ride to school in a chariot," chimes in a wiseacre. He's wearing the pompadour and surly lip of that young Southern gentleman Elvis Presley, who so crazes today's impressionable teens.

"Quack," says Waldo.

"Quack to you, too, little duck," says this young dandy, whose hips begin to swivel to a secret beat all their own. Girls with red noses clutching schoolbooks poke their heads out of the shelter to regard the falling asterisks. Snowflakes alight on their eyelashes and lovingly expire. "See you later, little duck,"

says the high-school hepcat as Waldo and I head down to the hill toward the general store.

The general store is a fine American institution, a place to escape worry, woe, the screaming of jets overhead, and the wagging tongues of the womenfolk. Railroad ties burn in the mouth of the potbellied stove where Waldo is now warming his little webbed feet. Behind the counter are bottles of striped candy, boxes of birdseed, and discreetly hidden stacks of old girlie magazines that are brought out only for emergency thaw-outs.

"Quack."

"'Morning, Waldo." That's Ed Davis talking, a retired pig farmer whose chief form of exercise is moving a toothpick from one corner of his mouth to the other. Rumor has it that Ed was the man who taught Gary Cooper to say "Yup," but that was in his more talkative days, before his favorite pig died and he retreated into the tunnel of melancholy from which no light beams. Now he simply stares at his socks (his boots are drying near the stove) and stoically rotates his toothpick. As talkative as Ed is terse is the store's owner, Sam Drucker, who arrived from parts unknown with a white apron and a barrel of salted pickles. "Ebenezer, Waldo, I'm glad you're here. Me and Ed were just discussing the proper length of a hoe, with of course me doin' most of the talking. How big do you reckon a proper hoe to be?"

"W-e-l-l-l, I've got a big hoe myself," I say, "but I choke up a few inches from the top for short stroking in close corners."

"I never met a hoe too big for me," pipes a voice from the back room.

"Now, never you mind," snaps Sam, who doesn't like racy talk in his general store. "My cousin Wilbur," he explains. "Head as big as a Halloween pumpkin and just as vacant." He feeds another railroad tie into the stove and steers the conversation back to hoes. From there we touch upon related subjects: crop rotation, feeding costs, fence mending, birthing babies, bats in the hayloft, the best lotion for chapped hands, how long it takes spit to freeze in February—topics that won't make the hearts of the editorial writers at our leading organs of hoity-toity opinion skip a circadian rhythm, but that nevertheless enable this bony, noble nag called Democracy to proceed on all four hooves. Talk may be cheap, but tyranny requires uniforms and most of your spare time. Sparta is for crewcuts. Give me the Athens of bearded elders and mellifluous gab. Loosening the elastic band on my store-

bought underwear, I elaborate and elucidate for fifteen solid minutes on the fragile yet sturdy nature of Democracy, wishing I had a wad of tobacco in my mouth with which to punctuate a particularly salient point. But Sam hasn't stocked the place with a spittoon, and I can't bring myself to let fly with common homebrewed saliva. Best give my Adam's apple a rest.

FIGURING it's time to mosey on home, I stand up and notice for the first time that Waldo's webbed feet are sticking straight up in the air and his eyes are wearing a glazed expression. It's the sort of look the wife had before the Montgomery Ward catalogue hit the front porch with a jarring thud.

"Loosen the little fella's scarf," says Ed, stringing together the longest sentence of our acquaintanceship.

We carry Waldo out the door for fresh air, noting with relief the rise and soft subside of his downy chest. A loose snowflake strays from the deepening storm, only to be gulped into Waldo's open bill.

"Qu*ck."

"Very funny, Waldo," I say. "Waldo *wuvs* to eat snowfwakes," I explain in baby talk to Ed.

He sighs and releases a manly tear down his weathered cheek. "Edna ate snowflakes," he tells me. Edna was Ed's cherished pig, the only pig he ever hugged and called "momma."

I cradle Waldo in my arms as tenderly as the baby Jesus. The threatening sky is a rippling curtain of asterisks.

"Quack," says Waldo. "Quack, quack, quack."

"My, aren't we talkative?" Lowering my cap-visor, I bend toward the horizon and begin to tote the little feller home. By the time we make the turn at the gate, he's dozing in my arms, dreaming ducky dreams. —E. B. QUITE

Joe Leonardo

YOU CAN COUNT ME OUT

(1927)

[*Early in his career with us, Robert Densely covered the famous Dempsey-Tunney championship fight in 1927 that featured the historic "long count." In point of fact, Densely's assignment was to visit the Dempsey Tunnel Works, an Irish drilling company somewhere on Staten Island that specialized in making stanchion anchor-pockets for elevated subway lines. Densely, typically, had got confused. This was the last boxing story we were to consider for over fifty years. Some have attributed our magazine's neglect of the Sweet Science to Raws' prudishness; others have blamed it on Shum's abhorrence of the physical. The truth is, we have eschewed boxing pieces because of the precedent of this one, which, though delightful, did not appear because Densely did not bother to find out who won.*]

ONE of the many things (there are seventeen in all, but I seem to have left the others in my coat pocket) I never have quite understood about prizefighting—or, for that matter, bullfighting—is why the antagonists can't settle their grievances with a good heart-to-heart talk.

You probably should know that it wasn't my idea to write about this in the first place, although it does remind me of an amusing story about the two Italians who met at the Automat and—oh, never mind. They didn't really meet. They both just happened to be in this funny story I thought I might pass along, but come to think of it, it's not all that funny. In fact, the men weren't Italian, after all; they were Irish. What I mean is, they *looked* Irish, but then you know what they say: "When in Rome . . ."

The main reason I bring all this up (bring what up?) is that last week (maybe it was the week before; anyway, it was definitely June and after dinner) I found myself at Soldier Field in Chicago, watching the heavyweight title fight between Jack Dempsey and Gene Tunney, the two Irishmen I mentioned a minute ago.

I did think it odd that they should be holding a prizefight at a football stadium (and in "the Windy City," to boot),

but there you are; nothing's a sure thing in sports. It even seems a strange place to hold a football game (well, life is full of unexpected surprises that we can't do much about; I certainly can't, and I've studied the subject at some length—one hundred and thirty-seven feet, to be exact).

This particular match seemed to be of unusual significance to those in attendance, though I couldn't say just why. And even if I could've said just why, you wouldn't have been able to hear me above the noise of the crowd. When I inquired what everyone was so excited about, they just laughed and made smart remarks, which I thought rather rude of them, seeing as I was a member of the press and all. Chicagoans are not easily impressed.

After the two men had been batting each other about the head and shoulders for some time, the larger of the two men ("the Manassa Mauler" to most, but I just call him Jack) socked the other fellow a good one on the jaw (this would be

Tunney, according to my scorecard). Tunney fell over and struck the canvas—not a pretty sight, I can tell you.

As if that weren't commotion enough, at this very moment my pencil rolled onto the floor and fell between the seats, forcing me to spend the next five minutes down on my hands and knees burrowing through the legs of total strangers—to me, anyway. It was the three hundred and eighty-fourth pencil I've lost this year, and it's only June. What appears to happen is that the pencil leaps from my fingers of its own free will (I believe in free will, but there's a limit) and goes directly to the point farthest from where I'm seated—or, in some cases, sleeping. It isn't as if I've done anything to bring it on, for this even occurs with pencils I've just bought and personally sharpened, taking care to clean up all the shavings. No, they obviously have it in for me. "Look, it's good old Densely!" the pencil says (or perhaps only thinks) and, with that, wriggles free of my grip and falls to the floor, followed shortly thereafter by me.

When this happened at the Dempsey-Tunney fight, it was the fourth round (or "chukker," as they say in polo), though

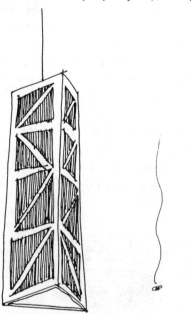

it might as well have been the sixth or even sixteenth. I wasn't paying much attention. Fortunately, they have people who are paid to keep track of the rounds and who wins and so on. I have other things to do, like lose my pencil. I can't be expected to do everything (loud chants of "You sure can't").

All I recall clearly is that the fight was still in progress when I located my pencil and that Dempsey was standing over Tunney, or maybe it was the other way around (it was hard to tell them apart, as both were wearing the same sort of clothes), and the crowd was on its feet screaming for Dempsey to return to a neutral corner (Fifty-seventh and Lex, I believe).

The referee seemed visibly distressed about something, and I wasn't in such a pleasant frame of mind myself; it seemed too much bother to call him over and ask for details. He began counting to ten, or possibly it was to five hundred by tens, the way we did when I was a boy in Worcester on long summer nights much like the one last week at Soldier Field, only that one was much longer and came to be known as the Night of the Long Count, or was it the Night of the Woeful Countenance?

IN any case (Marbury v. Madison), the man named Dempsey finally went to a corner of the ring (don't ask me how a ring has corners; geometry wasn't my subject), by which time Tunney had come to his senses (it was time somebody did) and appeared to wind up the winner—unless *he* was the man in the white trunks and Dempsey was the other one. I think it can safely be said that one of them came out the winner and that, whatever it was that got them so angry, they seemed to have settled it with no hard feelings. I'm sure, looking back in years to come, the boys will share a hearty laugh over the whole thing. —ROBERT DENSELY

HEARTY OF DARKIENESS

(1942)

[*S. J. Perlmutter wrote for the magazine for decades. In 1942, he could not resist involving himself in a controversy whirling around Riss, our editor, who had retreated before the city's rising tide of poor, huddled masses to the sylvan serenity of Stamford, Connecticut. Unfortunately, Rum's aversion to our newer Americans became widely known when a letter he'd written, expressing his opposition to the proposed construction of a public park near his home, was quoted in the New York* Times *of June 21, 1942: "Stamford is on the verge of becoming the playground of the Bronx and the dark, malodorous stretches of Harlem. . . . I do not mean to be undemocratic, but you couldn't choose a more alarming bunch of people in the world."*]

ANYBODY here mind if I preen? A recent adventure has left me buffing my nails rather conspicuously, and whoever thinks I shall forgo relating it may consider his name stricken from my list of perspicates. It began, as recent adventures so often do, with a phone call. I was puttering in the potting shed, having completed my matutinal calisthenic of pottering in the putting shed,

where it is my custom to knock Maxfli's into an Ehrlenmeyer flask while humming snatches of Moussorgsky. The eve previous, I had laid plans with regard to the chemical annihilation of a lustily thriving stand of sumac and was busy assembling the requisite ordnance when the woman to whom I had plighted my dog-eared troth summoned me to phone.

"It's one of your wretched friends

"Don't worry. She's a second child."

• •

from the magazine," she announced with diaphanously veiled contempt. "From the sound of it, he wants money or a favor."

"Damn you for an insolent baggage!" I might have checked the wench, but instead opted for the more housebroken "Thanks, hon" prior to traipsing into the kitchen. There, amid the inevitable tohubohu of Swiss chard and fenugreek with which Philomene, our dusky *gastronomeuse*, would inexorably decoct what I have grown accustomed, without laughing, to call dinner, I seized the receiver and gave greeting.

"Sid? Jim Thumper." My colleague was phoning to report that our mutual boss, editor of a magazine for which we performed eleemosynary literary services, was mysteriously unaccounted for. "He hasn't come in," my telephonister sighed. "And he won't answer the phone. I think there's no other choice but to go and find him."

"A grim journey upriver, into the teeth of mystery and adventure, eh?" I murmured.

"Hardly," replied the kill-joy. "Just take the train to Stamford and see what's going on."

"But why me?" I pointed out that I was in rural Pennsylvania, while Thumper himself, phoning from amid the topless towers and bottomless coffee cups of Manhattoes, could have assayed the journey in less time than it would take me to jink my haversack.

"Everybody here thinks it should be you," he ensuavated, ever the ingratiating celeritor. "We admire your powers of persuasion."

He knew his man. The remark stimulated my diplomatic fancy, and I was vouchsafed a vision of myself, khaki-clad and spiffed to the nines. In this somewhat surreal scenario (comprising equal parts Kipling, De Mille, and "Spicy Yarns for Boys and Their Pals"), I was toting a jute crop, my calf-length leather blagas gleaming, their passementerie trim aglow. Reed-slim, bowing at the waist, I greeted pooh-bah and panjandrum in the reception line at some fabulous palm-ringed colonial palace, His Majesty's viceroy to a tropical land of unlettered savages and compliant, tan-limbed wahines that was not, for once, Hollywood.

Then the cur pricked my ballooning fantasy. "Besides," he added. "We're busy here."

I retorted with pique: "Don't you suppose I'm busy, too?" A petulant whine was creeping into my voice. I beat it off with a stick, then added, "I mean to say, the garden wants changing, and some-one has to water the baby—"

"Suit yourself," came the reply. "But as long as he's unaccounted for, your check request can't get signed."

To seize the timetable of milk trains and consult the relevant listing was for me but the work of a moment. If the mem and bairns did not actually weep when I announced my departure, none-theless I could sense, amid the yawns, their pain. In our quaint local depot, renowned for its fine period mildew and skillfully concealed leaks, I mounted the iron horse for wildest Connecticut.

I did not know what to expect. My quarry was a man of legendary eccen-tricity; yet it was unlike him to neglect the turl and bel-tintoro of the office. Indeed, he was a man not so much dedi-cated to his dack as one unable to live without it. His absence augured cosh-tabula aplenty, a fact that prompted me, en route, to heave several agitated sighs. Most of them landed harmlessly on the floor, save for one, which struck a fellow-passenger several pews off—a dour bel-dame in flatteau and snood, off whom it glanced harmlessly and without incident.

It was thus fregulate that I arrived at the Stamford station, a pert little structure equal parts Tudor punnybox and prefab moderne. I seized my Gladstone to de-train, stood expectantly in the aisle, and was nearly trampled underfoot by a stampede of Moorish figures flocking past me from the rear.

"Yowza, we gwine hab us sum fun fo'

sho'!" cried one gink, resplendent in a shopworn white duck suit (Lord knew what the duck was left wearing), boatlike cordovan brautigans on his feet, a rakish straw skimmer on his poll. "Come awn, Rubeh! Le's go buy us sum o' dem con-vertible bonds at de stockbrokah!"

His paramour, an ebony matron with the girth of a Kungwah rhino, girt in a lurid floral muumuu, drawled, "Oh yeah, honeh. Ah can't wait to take de top down off one o' dem things!" The dyad joined hands and tripped off into the station.

"Odd," I mused aloud, peering out a window to confirm the stop. Stamford it was, and no doubt. "One would think we had held over at a Carolina beach resort."

DISMISSING the event as anomalous, I sallied forth once more, only to be run aground mid-sally by another on-slaught, this time from the opposite di-rection. Surging toward me down the aisle came a human tsunami, its collec-tive aspect suggestive of a crowd scene shot by Eisenstein of a bargain-hunting spree en masse down Orchard Street. "*Nu*, you're goink to vait until a writ-ten invitation already?" queried a big-boned *mameleh* of her dawdling son.

"Mama," piped the boy. "When we go to Abercrombie's, can I have a Martini?"

"Martini-schmini," she sneered to an invisible auditor. "Already he's a partner at Kravitz."

26

"Cravath," corrected the lad.

"Cravath-schmavath, keep *hocking* me and you'll get a *klop* on the *keppie*." The woman then directed toward me the scowl of a fishmonger sniffing putrescent herring. "So vhat are you starink?"

"This *pisher*'s calling for Martinis?" I blurted. I scrambled for my customary sang-froid, found it under the seat, and replied, "I meant to say, I merely find myself curious as to the reason for your visit to Stamford this day."

"*Vuh den*, it's closer than the Concord" was her shrugging reply. Then, collaring her slothful issue, she exited, and I followed.

I had not been to Connecticut since sitting as a judge, the previous May, for a children's playwriting contest at Stratford. (The winner, by unanimous vote, was a toddler's moody dramatization of the ecstasy and torment of breast-feeding, a memory play entitled "Waiting for Lefty." I still recall with pleasure its admirable curtain line: "So long, sucker!") My subsequent naïve tertimination—that most suburban Connecticut towns were alike as a litter of Indonesian binzies—collapsed at the *blik* of the odd and festive spectacle exfesticating before my spartulminizing peepers.

EVERYWHERE, as far as the bloodshot eye could discern, capered throngs of folk seemingly unlikely to claim Stamford as their native pueblo. As I staggered, mystified, out onto the street, a gaggle of Negro celebrants cakewalked past, dandily clad men and their racily decked-out *filles*, all hoisting small flagons of muscatel and giving three-times-three at whim. Across the avenue, numerous families of a distinctly Semitic cast—sobersided, scholarly Pa, skeptical sergeant-major Ma, saucer-eyed Son, and cup-chested Daughter—meandered along the storefronts, munching maxixe cherries from bags while blissfully window-shopping. (One happy clan had in fact just made purchase of a set of windows, which they bore down the street in triumph.)

THE town was riot with vacationists. Small children, of every race and creed, skittered underfoot and shouted with glee in a timeless masque of ball-tossing and purse-snatching. Quartets of chums dragooned genial pedestrians into levelling the Rolleiflex as they posed with self-conscious nonchalance before the picturesque bakery, the atmospheric notary, the unspoiled pharmacy, the cute little liquor shop where Tom found the most darling Médoc last summer. Here, in cosmopolitan mélange, disported representatives of the liveliest quarters of Lagos, Jerusalem, Addis Ababa, Smolensk, Charleston, and Prague. If, that day, there was a single ponytailed Protestant housewife abroad (or, for that matter, a ponytailed Protestant housebroad awifed), she escaped my ken.

But each second's rubbernecking meant additional delay in delivery of a lifesaving transfusion to my bank account. I dragged my ruck over to a cab parked at the station's stand. Its dozing driver cocked an indifferent eye. I expressed my desire to be taken forthwith to my editor's estate. "And a guinea if you get me there by dusk!" I added as mercenary inducement.

"Hey, watch it with the Guinea, pal," the hack snarled. "I'm Mick."

I apologized for the ethnic solecism, explicated, genuflected, and bade him drive as though demons of Hell were nipping his heels.

The house, when I arrived, looked outwardly placid: curtains drawn, front door shut. I rang the bell and awaited response, but heard nothing save the pounding of blood in my ears—a disturbing sensation, until I realized that

"Carruthers! Come in here!"

• •

the blood was my own. The door, for some reason, was unlocked.

A Stygian darkness greeted me, and I groped like a Malay blefula for the light switch. Attaining it, I discovered an unremarkable bourgeois living room— one not dissimilar to my own, in fact, save for the presence, here, of furniture capable of supporting an adult human body without skewering it with cushion springs or administering to it random subcutaneous injections of wood splinters.

"Hullo?" I called. No reply sounded to disturb the lunching termites surely carmigating in the wainscotting. Feeling a tad like a P.I. giving a digs the flanagan, I penetrated the manse.

The kitchen was deserted, as were the dining room and the study. Pristine silence swallowed my every bleated *cri*. All at once I was struck by the possibility that I had galloped off on a chase of the wild goose, that my *Zurchdrecht* had merely skipped town on impromptu

"What smell?"

•   •

holiday—in short, that no one was home. There remained only the bedroom to fastigate. Although I am but a modest rustic, who restricts his customary haunts to such rude barns and stables as those in which he shelters wife, children, and other livestock, nonetheless I knew my way around a suburban Colonial. Convinced that there had to be a light switch somewhere, I clawed at the wall like a lifer gone starkers in the clink.

A slight motion arrested my attention and hauled it downtown for questioning. I was conscious of the delicate susurration of a man panting, as though in the grip of ague, or in the ague of grippe.

I found the light and snapped home the stud.

"Goddamn it, Perlmutter, turn it off!"

THE voice was ragged, harsh, the impatient bark of a man who is used to being obeyed, if only by his dog. I found its owner spread-eagle on the bed, as though after a sweth induced by laudanum or pranda. He wore a dark Botany suit and a monogrammed Biochemistry necktie. The faint light of day crept round the drawn drapery and played upon his pug features; I bade it skedaddle and play in its room.

"They're out there, Perlmutter," the

man croaked. "The town is infested with 'em!"

"Uh," I replied, employing the scrupulously neutral opening with which I have always enjoyed great rhetorical success. "You mean—"

"I mean *them*, goddamn it!" He brandished an extended index finger like a chevalier his foil. "Negroes and Jews! You couldn't choose a more alarming bunch of people in the world!"

"How about Adolf Hitler?" I riposted. Thumper's motive for insisting I be the one to gallop to the rescue had become clear as a Waterford epergne.

"Who he?"

I explained the Fuehrer's more notable social and political views. During this lecture, my auditor snorted and scowled on his bunk, his recumbency unsavven. Finally I said, "So I'd say he's a fairly alarming slab of bacon, right?"

"You've got me there!" the fellow shouted.

I nodded, and gestured airily. "Then what say we hightail it down to the City, old sport—"

"Can't." The cul shook his bean. "Can't leave the house. There's one of 'em out there, and he's after me."

"One of—?"

"Negro fellow. Keeps trying to talk to me—goddamn it, Perlmutter, I don't want to be talked to by some Negro!" With an agility that took me aback, he suddenly leapt up and legged it into the walk-in voisère, slamming the louvered door behind him. "Just sit tight here till the whole thing blows over."

As it was manifestly unclear as to what constituted "the whole thing," and what would signal its expiration, I could respond with little more than well-meaning farlication. "Well, yes, but—" I had seen evidence of my employer's prejudices before, but this full-dress *son et lumière* left me flabbergasted and bollixado. Then the doorbell rang.

"Leave it!" snapped the closeted truant. "Just play possum and they'll scram!" He moaned. "Oh, God—it's horrible! Horrible!"

"Steady on, old son," I murmured. "It might·be the authorities, seeking to inform me I've won the Irish Sweepstakes." Despite his frantically whispered protestations, I left him there and made for the door. Opening it revealed a young black man in a natty, two-piece worsted suit, his expression a miraculous amalgam of boyish eagerness and guarded awe.

"Sir?" he asked, and, before I could shut the door, introduced himself and launched into an impetuous paean to the magazine for which my own unflagging labors, at wages that would elicit guffaws from a galley slave, had helped underwrite purchase of the very house in which its actual editor now so ignobly cowered. "I just want to say that I think it's quite the best periodical on the stands today," the man declared. "And I would be profoundly grateful if you might just look at a few articles and reportorial sketches I've written. I have them right here—"

H E reached into a slim leather McBain he had tucked under one arm and would have proffered the demorgant sheaves had I not stayed his hand and replied, with the genial twinkle of the born liar, "I'd love to look at them, young man. But not here. I dislike discussing work out of the City." After a moment's *fausse tristesse*, I brightened. "Say, here's a capital idea. I'm bound for town just now. Why don't you come to my office later today and we can have a corking good chin-wag about the whole thing."

"Oh, I know the address, sir—"

"Excellent. Nineteenth floor—and never you mind dillydallying with the receptionist, either. Simply inquire if

I'm at my desk, and then just barge right on in. Tell the girl I said so."

The fellow's reaction was warm, and after we parted with mutual expressions of gratitude I returned to the bedroom. Whether or not, en route, I actually rubbed my hands in satanic glee escapes recollection.

"Traveling salesman," I responded to mine host's unasked query. "Sought to demonstrate a high-octane vacuum cleaner—the sort of thing you drive through your living room like a car."

"High-octane?" he grunted suspiciously through the closet door, ever the precisionist where facts were concerned. "Who the hell proposes to run vacuum cleaners on gasoline? Don't they know there's a war on?"

"Er, it, uh . . . it runs on, ah, alcohol —gin, bourbon, other potables."

"A likely story."

"Granted. I conveyed your regrets."

"Good." The door opened and the prisoner emerged. "What am I going to do, Perlmutter? I can't hole up in here forever. My wife's with her mother— when she gets back, she'll give me hell. Oh, goddamn it all!"

"Why not go to the office?" came my disingenuous reply.

"Imposs—!" His obduracy gave way to sudden insight. "My God, I think you've hit it! Of course!" He smote his brow and chortled with relief. "The office! That's the last place you'd find one of those people! Perlmutter, you're a genius. But so am I, for hiring you."

I nodded with becoming modesty, the faint tint of a blush softening my manly aspect, but maintained a dignified silence.

His teeth were stained, his hair begreased, his hands and face ill-kempt as a vagrant's; he pronounced himself fit for immediate travel, and in a trice we were taxiing to the station. As we threaded through the undiminished carnival, he slunk down in the seat and found fasci-nation in the close study of his own knees. "It's not that I mean to be undemocratic, you understand," he mumbled. "But I can tell you one thing— coons are either funny, or dangerous. I mean to say . . . goddamn it, Perlmutter, for Christ's sake—this is Connecticut!"

I agreed, and remained likewise amiable until we had arrived. It was then that my companion succumbed to one of his periodic bouts of amnesia, forgetting utterly about the existence of his wallet. I paid the fare.

"Now, Jews aren't that bad, of course," he went on as we debouched. "But if you ask me—" And there he halted, and exoculated me with a ferocious squint. "Wait a minute. My God, Perlmutter, you're—" His face, at its ruddiest the hue of flour paste, blanched to an even snowier pallor. He fell silent for a moment, then asked hoarsely, "You, uh, you coming into town?"

I DECLINED, with murmurings of an intention to return to my Pennsylvania freehold. We bantered cursorily for a few minutes, deploring the latest shenanigans of the magazine's writers, artists, and other unemployables, before the train came soughing into the station. My companion stepped up into the car, then turned back to me and, with a snort employed by elephants on the Serengeti to indicate apology, stammered, "Listen, Perlmutter, about that remark about —you know. No offense intended."

"None taken."

He nodded, and I noted that his secret admirer had also boarded. I waved with a sprightliness that reflected my unfeigned inner state of heart's ease and spent a delightful half hour until my train came, luxuriating in the kef that military commanders know when they return to base and—wounded, tired, but withal intact—report their mission accomplished. —S. J. PERLMUTTER

Moveable Feasts

[Given the enormous backlog of manuscripts cluttering our offices, we are often surprised to find ourselves having to fill space. This Talk piece, comprising just a sliver of prose and a batch of doodles, is a superb demonstration of Jim Stevedore's ability to make a page look, as Calvin Pumpkins, who is at home in the art world, said, "delicate, open, intricate yet airy—just like a doily!"]

THE weather has been improving lately, and rumors are circulating around the office that winter may be over and spring beginning its annual run into summer. Usually we prefer not to break the rhythm of the day's work by lunching out, but one recent day looked so balmy that we decided to dine *al fresco*, purchasing our food from one of the local vendors whose carts, wagons, trucks, and (in the case of one Oriental gentleman selling steamed buns) rickshaw dot Fifth Avenue all the way up to the Plaza Fountain, around whose perimeter the largest selection of delicacies may be found and to which we made our way, mouth watering.

Our first stop was a very busy hot-dog cart. (We purposely picked the vendor with the longest line, as we thought those on it might have inside knowledge.) The vendor sold three configurations of hot dog: plain (*Illus. A*), with sauerkraut

Illus. A

(*Illus. B*), and with onions (*Illus. C*). The

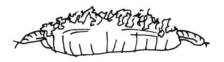

Illus. B

Illus. C

rolls were puffy, brown and white; the hot dogs, nude pink. When we at last stepped up to the cart to be served, we glanced down into the vat of steaming water in which the bobbing dogs awaited consumption (*Illus. D*). The water was murky,

Illus. D

and we could not see bottom. Stray flecks of onion and sauerkraut and red beads of fat floated on top. Suddenly we found it hard to swallow.

"How many?" barked the man.

"None, thanks, we've changed our mind," we replied, and ambled over to a bench to sit, take a few deep breaths, and allow our gorge to settle.

After a few minutes, we felt much better and, undaunted, approached an elaborately painted wagon called Devadip Deelites. The proprietor was a tall, muscular fellow whose head was shaved except for a little tuft right on the top and on whose forehead and down the bridge of whose nose ran a runny white mark (*Illus. E*). The Devadip Deelites include

Illus. E

buija (fried onion and dough balls) (*Illus. F*), herb tea (*Illus. G*), and vegetable

Illus. F

Illus. G

sandwiches on thick slices of very dense bread (*Illus. H*). We decided to order

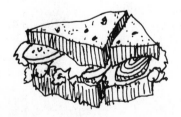

Illus. H

some freshly cooked buijas, but as we drew near the wagon, we could not help

noticing the topknotted fellow's hands as he shaped the little fritters from a big aluminum bowl of onion batter. They were very dirty hands (*Illus. I*), each nail-cov-

Illus. I

ering a thick black crescent. We strolled on, now following our nose (*Illus. J*)

Illus. J

instead of our eyes (*Illus. K*). Our nose

Illus. K

led us to a cart that seemed entirely ablaze

(*Illus. L*), hot flames roaring up out of a

Illus. L

grill to engulf skewered lamb that had been marinated in something luscious to smell. That's for us, we decided, and joined the small group waiting for their kebobs (*Illus. M*). As we waited, we saw a

Illus. M

young woman dig into one. Most of her lamb appeared to be nothing but fat and gristle, and the metal skewer was rusty. A little farther away, plastic glasses full of fresh fruit (*Illus. N*) were tempting but

Illus. N

on closer inspection looked tired and sweaty. Pancho's Tortilla Villa sold hearty

tacos (*Illus. O*), but they seemed impossi-

Illus. O

ble to eat without dribbling gunk on shirt or coat front.

Gabila's knishes (*Illus. P*) looked

Illus. P

leaden, and so did Big Philly's pretzels (*Illus. Q*).

Illus. Q

What will we have for lunch? Our hour was drawing to a close and we had not yet made our selection. In a flash, we knew what we wanted. On the way back to our office, we picked up our usual— egg salad on whole wheat, large Tab (*Illus. R*)—from the coffee shop next door and

Illus. R

returned to our desk to eat. Delicious! There's nothing like a brisk walk in the open air for working up an appetite!

34

[The staff of our magazine has always been close-knit. When one of our number dies, the loss is felt as keenly as that of a family member—in the case of Mr. DePinna, perhaps a second cousin.]

CHAUNCEY DE PINNA

CHAUNCEY DePinna, a staff member of this magazine for almost forty years, died at his desk here last month at the age of sixty-one. Sadly, the precise moment of Chauncey's demise will never be known. His habitual posture of repose, head slumped over folded arms, which in turn rested on the Sargasso Sea of papers covering his desk, was so familiar a sight to us that it was only after Chauncey had been dead for at least forty-eight hours (according to the coroner's report) that we noticed he had stopped breathing.

Chauncey appeared in our office for the first time in 1946, a hale young fellow just out of his army browns, scion of the family whose stylish midtown haberdashery bore their surname. Eager to establish himself as a writer, Chauncey offered to run errands and do odd jobs if we would consider his pieces for publication. He also offered to provide our staff a twenty-per-cent discount on all merchandise bought at his family's store. Many of us still wear DePinna shirts.

None of Chauncey's pieces ever found its way into our magazine. Still, his work was an unending source of hilarity in the halls and a first-rate target for japes around the water cooler. Put simply, Chauncey's writing was execrable, but reading it was a small price to pay for the convenience of having someone around who would do anything that needed doing, from cleaning the lavatories to running out to select a last-minute birthday present for some absent-minded staffer's spouse.

In 1951, Chauncey tried his hand at proofreading. He found the exacting work a challenge and became expert in matters of grammar and punctuation. It was Chauncey who maintained many of the archaic spellings ("focussing"), obscure notations ("coördinate"), and irrelevant, if, technically, justifiable, commas that have become familiar to our readers. Since he was frequently asked to step out for food when a deadline pressed, Chauncey became as knowledgeable of staff preferences in sandwiches and coffee as he was of concerns syntactical. He continued proofreading at the same desk in the same dimly lit corner until his death.

Chauncey DePinna had the eye of a hawk, the soul of a Health Department restaurant inspector, and the soaring aspiration of a great artist. When Chauncey was not proofreading, addressing envelopes, or emptying wastepaper baskets, he was writing. Hardly a week went by when he did not submit at least a brief Talk piece to one of the numerous editors whose tenures at our magazine he surpassed. His attempts were always rejected, always with enough encouraging criticism to send him back to the typewriter for another try just as soon as he'd finished the day's chores. While he was ever appreciative of editorial suggestions, Chauncey was incapable of incorporating them into his writing, and his later work was every bit as flat and jejune as his earliest efforts.

During the last five years or so that he was with us, Chauncey grew quieter and his hours grew longer. Reminiscing about him after the funeral, few of us could recall ever being in the office when Chauncey was not—except, of course, when he was off on an errand. Some believe he lived at his desk. As if to confirm this, examination of his effects showed that he used his bottom left-hand drawer as a laundry hamper. On top of his desk was a half-proofed set of galleys; he had just marked an egregious typo. The red pencil was still in his hand. In his battered briefcase was an unfinished short story of his own composition. We found it worthy and ambitious but, like so much of the material Chauncey submitted to us, utterly lifeless.

Now that he is as well, a loss will be felt by everyone at our magazine. Chauncey DePinna proofed our galleys and fetched our coffee; we will miss him.

•   •

[*As we grew, so did the listings that fill the front of the magazine. Both Rudge and Schwinn, the magazine's editors, insisted on listing places and events of the most idiosyncratic sort, all the while staunchly maintaining that we were providing information of real use to our readers. Rorfth justified the columns of society balls and philanthropic backgammon tourneys we diligently ran, hoping vainly that he would be invited to them. Shwiks, for his part, demanded a selection of recommended blood donation centers be placed between "Bacchanalias Around Town" and "Newsstands That Make Change." It never saw print; Shlag remembered that he does not allow the word "blood" in the magazine. Neither editor has permitted restaurants to be listed in our pages, owing to the conviction, held by both of them, that decency forbids comment upon public ingestion.*

I have been more honest than my bosses. Since my earliest days at the magazine, I have argued that listings should serve the people who read them more than those who write them, a posture bound to draw fire around here. Consequently, many of the listings in this book are appearing for the first time. Despite this, they are our finest, and they have one other feature in common as well: I wrote them.]

RAY'S PIZZA ESTABLISHMENTS

(An arbitrary listing . . . Pizza chefs lead complicated lives that are subject to heat prostration and immigration problems. It is therefore always advisable to call ahead.)

RAY'S PIZZA, 385 W. 37th St., at Ninth Ave. (009-9111)—The steam table is the center of activity here; sausages, slabs of eggplant, and meatballs stew in tubs of sauce that are stirred hourly. Cabdrivers hang out here, and outer-borough accents abound.

RAY'S LITE PIZZA, 51 Sixth Ave., near 12th St. (991-0911)—Tiny tables, a sleek black-and-chrome interior and a maître d' in black tie set the tone at this sociable place, whose specialties include Broccoli Pizza, Cold Fruit Pizza, and Pizza Lorraine. There is a small, thoughtful selection of canned sodas. Bring your own wine. The ratatouille hero is especially good.

RAY'S ORIGINAL PIZZA CLASSICO, 19 Mulberry St. (191–1919)—No chairs, no tables, and only the smallest of counter spaces. No additional toppings, no garlic powder, no oregano, no soda. Open Thursday afternoons in spring only. We hear it's wonderful.

RAY'S CAFÉ DU PIZZA, 45 Seventh Ave. South, near Commerce St. (991-9911)—Jazz on the juke is the main event here, and musicians like to hang out at this relaxing place. With luck, one may end up passing the red pepper to the likes of Chick Coregano, Chuck Mangiamo, and Bucky Pizzarelli.

RAY'S PIZZA 'N' BREW, 215 W. 51st St. (999-9190)—Basic après-theatre pizza house with a good, serviceable slice. Currently popular with the casts of several of the longer-running hits. Daytimes, you'll see a lot of messengers.

ROUYE'S PIZZA, 3 Coenties Slip (119-1909)—This establishment has been serving pizza to a devoted clientele for longer than anyone cares to remember. Its owner, Ray Rouye, is a descendant of Dutch settlers who ran an Italian restaurant in Rotterdam in the seventeenth century and were forced to seek new opportunities when the Gouda lobby cut off their Parmesan supply.

RAY'S ORIGINAL WORLD O' PIZZA, 2406-54 Ft. Tryon Park (919-1009)—A stately old bowling alley revitalized. Everything from Moo Goo Gai Pizza to Pizza Rellenos. We prefer the plain slice.

3 GUYS NAMED RAY PIZZA, Bergen Mall, Plainview, N.J. (201-109-0009)—We wouldn't have thought it possible that even one man existed with the actual name Ray Pizza, so the notion that there were three of them, that they met with one another and then started a business together, is a big bite to swallow. It's almost all true, though (one Ray's name was really Ray Calzone, but he had it changed legally). The pizza is worth the price but not the toll.

CHAPTER TWO

•   •

OUR

BEST

AND

VERSE

Fiction and Poetry

"*I*F *you can't be funny, be clever," said our first editor, Reen, and for the first few years our writers aimed for the quick laugh. I recall O'Samarra grousing bitterly that our magazine would buy nothing longer than a knock-knock joke. Rising to the challenge of our editor's minute attention span, O'Samarra and others fashioned a type of short story—brief, well-observed, brief, mordant, trenchant, brief—that even Rheum had to respect.*

After Shwee took over as editor, the scope of our fiction expanded mightily. Shoog's range of literary passion is astonishing: mysterious parables from South America, impenetrably technical science fiction from Czechoslovakia, even fiction that is not fiction, a distinction boasted by Truman Compote, whose "In Light Syrup" we commissioned. Shnee likes it all. At the same time, our poetry grew in complexity from the glacéed ditties Rint thought smart to the inscrutable verse of contemporary bards. Shooce likes that, too.

For thousands of our readers, the week's short stories are the centerpiece of the magazine. Far fewer feel that way about our poetry. For all, here is our best of both.

THE SWILLER

(1962)

[John Clever has staked out a portion of the landscape all his own, although some of it is in Westchester. Here, in suburbia, the mythic American Melting Pot is revealed for what it really is: a chafing dish. When this terse story came in, I called Clever to ask when we would receive the rest of the manuscript; only later did I realize it was complete and classic.]

I T WAS one of those glorious spring Saturdays when men sit around and think, *Today I'm going to get totally snockered on Gibsons.* Some think it as they glance over the tops of their skinny spectacles at their children haphazardly whacking a shuttlecock back and forth on the front lawn. Others think it while still lazing in bed, feigning sleep with just a sheet covering them and the muffled sounds of the house in orbit around them. Still others have already started.

Carlisle Ruiz wrapped his hand tightly around his empty glass as Cornell Wu refilled it from the pitcher of gin that had been icing on the Wus' flagstone back patio.

"Up yer wazoo," joked Cornell, winking, as their wives conspiratorially exchanged the secret details of their latest shopping excursions.

Carlisle slugged down half his drink and leaned back, gazing into the thin blue sky. "You got any Triscuits or anything?" he asked halfheartedly, wishing the girls would get drunk, too, so they couldn't criticize the men for getting sloshed. He thought of all the friends who shared his attitudes toward drinking and women, and it suddenly occurred to him that all their houses formed a zigzagging route between Cornell's house and his own—where two six-packs of malt liquor sat getting especially cold in the Amana freezing compartment. He thought he could stop at every friend's house on the route and have just one shot of gin. He'd still be standing by the time he got home and could drink the six-packs while watching "Dance Fever." There were the Amundsens, the O'Flahertys, the Grassis, the Schnitzels, the Kujiwaras, the Guptas, and the Little Running Foxes. Between the Grassis' and the Schnitzels' he could stop at Ataturk's Lounge on Main and Alewife, covering the section through town.

H E could do it, he thought; drink himself across Bellville. Feeling the little smugness that comes from the knowledge that one has had a good idea that nobody else as yet knows about, Carlisle tipped his glass up and drained the rest of his gin. After a moment of lightheadedness, he pitched forward onto the lawn, passed out cold. He didn't awaken until Monday morning, when, with a terrible hangover, he slowly got dressed and went to work. Of the weekend he remembered nothing.

—JOHN CLEVER

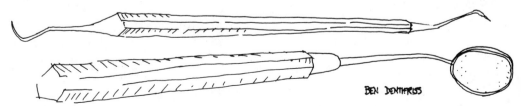

BEN DENTIFRISS

A PERFECT DAY FOR BANANA DAIQUIRIS
(1960)

[It is rare for a writer to achieve the legendary stature of D. J. Balinger, whose works still sell thousands of copies every year. Balinger is a very quiet and private man, and eavesdropping on his meetings with Shoob was said to be possible only with special aids. He moved to New Hampshire in 1966, exhausted by the endless infighting of what he called New York's "ratty litter of literati" and embittered by the failure of "Pal Zooey," a musical adaptation of the Glass family stories. Since the following was the basis for the musical's big production number, it's not hard to see why the show didn't catch on. As of this writing, Balinger is still inconsolable.]

ALTHOUGH it was a clear, sunny Tuesday morning, light easily penetrating the drapes drawn over the windows of the master bedroom, it was not the sunlight that stirred Bessie to wakefulness. Rather, it was the resonant swell and ebb of chanting from down the hall. Suddenly excited, Bessie very nearly shook her husband awake with the news that their firstborn was home. Then she remembered that their beloved Seymour had blown his brains out fourteen years ago while vacationing in Florida and that it was their youngest son, Zooey, who carried on the departed's passion for the Wisdom of the East. Les, sprawled big and comfortable over a good two-thirds of the bed, only stirred slightly at the chanting sound. Swatting the air around him as if at a taunting mosquito, he murmured, "Don't hand me any of that dharma crap, you little bastard," and then was still. Bessie shushed him anyway. She got out of bed and slipped on a rose-colored candle-wick bathrobe that had seen hard service since her daughters, Boo Boo and Franny, finally succeeded in disposing of her ancient midnight-blue kimono; she'd bought the robe at Orbach's, a store for which her well-bred children had nothing but contempt. She went first into the master bathroom to brush her teeth, then padded into the hallway, closing the door so as not to wake her snoring husband. She was ready for her coffee.

Bessie allowed herself to pause at the first door on her right. Putting her hand on the knob, she hesitated. She was standing at the door to the room in which her eldest sons, Seymour and Buddy, had grown up. The room was still full of their belongings, exactly as it was nine years ago when the word about Seymour came: books, papers, mounds of clothes, and, on the desk, a laughing Buddha, arms stretched overhead, face fixed in a rictus of enlightened good humor. Bessie entered the room very rarely, to dust or stand quietly, remembering. Buddy had grown away from the family and lived now in a small, unheated cabin near the upstate campus where he taught English literature and yoga. Once, Bessie thought Seymour would become a lawyer and Buddy a doctor. Buddy had fine, long fingers—surgeon's fingers, as she liked to call them whenever he visited. Buddy's last visit was eighteen months ago. She'd asked him if he ever intended to get a telephone put into the tumble-down shack he lived in. He left immediately. But after all, Bessie'd argued with the rest of the family at the time, Buddy was a grownup already, well into his thirties. (Bessie never remembers her children's ages precisely; in this way, she makes her own age vague as well.) Was it so wrong to want your oldest surviving heir to have a phone? What if something happened? Her tongue clucked as she removed her hand from the knob.

A T the next door, Bessie was bolder. She entered and stood gazing for a while at the twin beds pushed together for Zooey's comfort, the matching throw rugs, the identical chifforobes, and the pair of small desks. She thought of the twins, Walter and Waker, who'd shared this room. Poor Walter. She and Les named him after Walter Winchell, and then he went and got himself killed in Japan when the damn war was already over. Was it Waker who was killed? No, it was Walter. Bessie had a hard time keeping the twins straight, as she'd had when she was bringing them up. Giving them both names beginning with "W" made matters worse. Waker is still alive, she recalled clearly now, and lives in a seminary outside Indianapolis. He hardly ever writes (what a surprise to receive that first Christmas card from the seminary, depicting all the brothers in their cassocks and there, in the middle of the third row, fifth from the right, her boy, who had never, so far as she knew, had a religious thought in his life). Now Zooey

•   •

"Iron Butterfly or Led Zeppelin?"

had free run of the room and the twin furniture sets. The place was a mess. She turned and left, shutting the door behind her, and shuffled on.

THE door to the bathroom, from which the chanting issued, was closed. She did not knock, because she knew there would be no response. Instead, she turned the knob very gently. There, seated in the lotus position on the toilet-seat cover, wearing a makeshift dhoti fashioned from a bath towel, was Les and Bessie's youngest son and second-youngest child, Zooey. Although his eyes were wide open and he was facing the door, he did not seem to see Bessie standing there.

"OOOOOOOMMMMMMM . . . Good morning, Bessie! How are you?"

"You woke me up with this noise, you know. You almost woke up your father."

"My apologies, Mother dear. But I must say, if you can sleep through Les' snoring, you ought to be able to sleep through a little chanting. It's a mantra, you know. It's not just noise."

"Zooey, which is it who's in Indianapolis, Waker or Walter?"

"*Mother.*"

"Well, which?"

"How many times do we have to go through this, Bessie?"

"Until I get it straight, snot-nose. And don't call me Bessie, I'm your mother."

"Yes, Mommy."

"Don't mock me, Zooey. Have you spoken to her yet this morning?"

Zooey did not answer. Instead, he raised his right hand slowly to his face and with his thumb gently pressed one nostril shut while breathing vigorously through the other.* Bessie waited impatiently, tapping her foot noisily on the

---

*The sound this procedure makes is best described as vacuum-cleaner-like. The spray of particles the procedure produces is best described not at all.

tile floor (no mean trick in the soft, squishy pink mules she was wearing). As she waited, Zooey slowly lowered his right hand, then raised his left and repeated the exercise with his left nostril closed. Bessie sat on the edge of the tub and waited, "tsk"-ing loudly. She reached into a wicker tissue-box container that perched on the edge of the sink with two hairbrushes, a half-rolled tube of Ipana, and an Allenbury's Pastilles tin that contained dozens of bobby pins, pulled out two or three tissues, which she bunched unceremoniously in one hand, then leaned over to wipe her son's nose and face. Zooey ignored her. Eyes closed, he lowered his left hand and sat for several moments quite still, the only sound in the bathroom his deep, slow breathing and the distant whine of a garbage truck up the block.

The quiet made Bessie nervous. "Well?"

"You should never call me a snot-nose, Mother. It upsets me."

"God forbid."

"You'll make me late for my audition if you keep this up. Do you think you could leave so I can take a bath, please? Now?"

"My son the actor. Thirty years old and still living at home. Have you spoken to Franny yet today?"

"I know of no one by that name, sweetheart. Now, Walt and Waker—those are the ones you were wondering about, I believe—and Seymour and Buddy and that little girl of yours, you know, the one in Westchester—"

"Boo Boo."

"Bessie, why is it you gave us all such funny names? Zooey, Waker, Boo Boo—"

"I never wanted to call her that. Her name is Beatrice, damn it!"

"Now, Bessie, hold your water. No. I haven't seen Franny this morning. I imagine she's in her room. Isn't that where she's been most of the last three weeks?"

"What's the matter with her, Zooey? I know you know, she talks to you. They all did, still do, Zooey. Seymour always said you were the easiest to get along with. I wonder what he'd say if he could see you now, sitting on the toilet-seat lid, wearing a towel like Mahatma Gandhi or something."

"Thanks so much, dear, but I haven't the faintest what's troubling our Franny. Maybe she misses school. I mean, she's getting a little old to be taking semesters off to find herself. Maybe she misses her girlfriends, or dating, although those Princeton bozos she used to see never impressed me much. She's probably too old for undergraduates by now, anyway. It could be her job."

"Her ex-job, you mean, the third this year."

"Well, file-clerking isn't quite as much fun as majoring in art history, wouldn't you agree? Maybe she misses Bloomberg—"

"That smelly cat was a hundred years old! We did it a favor putting it to sleep."

"And who am I to disagree? Who knows, Mother? Bad karma is what it is, I suppose."

"What's karma?"

"Never mind."

"I don't think she's eating at all."

"When she's hungry enough, Bessie, she'll eat. Look, Bessie, you'd better accept the fact that your kids are just a little . . . odd."

"You're telling me? Two dead, one's in a seminary, one lives in a shack without a phone, another's way the hell up in Westchester and can't be bothered to call home and tell her parents she's alive,

you're out of work and on the pot chanting, and my baby girl sits in her room, crying and starving herself to death."

"Don't take it to heart, Mom. Happy families are all alike, right? Some families, such as our own, aren't so happy, but they have a real talent for—shall we say—peculiarity."

"Is that the kindest thing you could have said?"

"I suppose not, dear, but you did barge in on me right in the middle of my morning *asanas*, and now, if you'll excuse me, I'd like to take a quick shower since it looks like I won't have time for a bath, thanks. Or you can sit here and watch." Zooey unfolded his legs and, planting his feet on the tile floor, rose, offering his seat to Bessie with one hand, undoing his towel with the other.

"Spare me," said the mother wearily. She stood up. "I'll go and see how she's doing, as if I didn't know. You know, Zooey, with that smart, nasty mouth of yours, you'd make a wonderful lawyer. Think about it."

"*Maaa!*"

"I'm going, I'm going," Bessie said, slipping out the door, closing it behind her as Zooey dropped his towel and stepped into the tub. She heard him yank the curtain closed and his shout as he stepped into a shower that was as cold as he could stand. Zooey always took a cold shower when he was angry.

FRANNY'S room had also been Boo Boo's. Because of the difference in their ages they had only briefly shared it, so the room was layered with the effects of two childhoods lived at different times. Stuffed animals, scrapbooks, and Franny's dirty laundry were the principal decorative elements. Most of the wall space was occupied by some precariously mounted shelves, generously stocked with books: poems of Pound, the Aeneid, four high-school French grammar texts, "Adventures for Readers" (volumes one through three), the Upanishads, "Lessons in the Tao," and "Heidi," among others. Papers and more books littered the desk top.

Franny lay on her bed, fully dressed and rumpled, as if she'd slept with her clothes on. She gazed at, and from time to time softly poked at, a set of wind chimes hanging directly over her head. Her lips moved animatedly, but no sound issued.

Bessie spoke softly from the doorway.

"Franny . . . Franny, dear, how are you? Did you sleep all right? Would you like some breakfast? You should really eat something, you know, don't you think?"

"*Oh, Mom!*" Franny cried. Her eyes filled with tears. Her lips began to move silently again.

"Pardon me for asking. Pardon me for asking, but I just think a girl who sits around and cries all the time has got to keep her strength up. Of course, I could be wrong."

"Mother, you know what'll happen if I eat now, don't you? I'll just get sick. I'll either throw up or I'll *feel* like throwing up. I've never liked breakfast, you know that."

"You don't have to have breakfast now,

•   •

line

"Really. You just give them money and they do anything you want."

you can have whatever you'd like."

"Mom, I promise I'll go out this afternoon and have a cheeseburger, O.K.?"

"Yes, you'll do that and later on Lucy and Desi will drop by for tea. Franny, you haven't been out of the house in three weeks. Don't you think I notice? And in three weeks all you've had in the way of nourishment is cigarettes, which are not nourishment at all and make your room smell terrible. Cigarettes and pistachio nuts. And you read those damn books you get out of Buddy's and—the other one's—room. I'm sick of looking at those books, those what do you call them—those Rig-Vedas or whatever they are—and the other ones, the Upan—"

"Mother—"

"Your ashtrays are overflowing with pistachio shells, Franny!"

"I know—"

"I know what! Come into the kitchen and have some fruit. There's bananas and apples. Just have a little piece of something. It'll make you feel better."

There was no answer. Franny had gone back to playing with her wind chimes, her lips moving again. Bessie felt as if she had been dismissed. She stared bleakly at her daughter and, sighing, left the room and closed the door.

In the hallway, she bumped into Les, wearing his flannel robe over his pajamas, ambling barefoot toward the kitchen.

"Hi, sweetie, good morning," he mumbled sleepily, brushing his lips over her cheek in an absent kiss. "I'm ready for breakfast."

Bessie threw him a fish-eyed glance. "I'm ready for a drink," she muttered, then started off after him to the kitchen. "Les, you shouldn't walk around barefoot," she said.

In the kitchen she brewed coffee, toasted bread, poured corn flakes. As she peeled a banana to slice over her flakes, she noticed, crammed in with the cookbooks, which went largely unused in this largely noneating household, a Mr. Boston Home Bartending Guide. Setting down the banana, she leafed through it, surprised by how many drinks she'd never heard of. One in particular caught her attention. She scanned their liquor cabinet to see if there was any rum; there was.

Les, oblivious, sipped coffee and looked out the window. "Beautiful weather," he said. "Perfect."

Bessie got out the rum and the electric Mixmaster. She set them down by her half-peeled banana. She was already starting to feel better.

"Yes, it is, Les, perfect. A perfect day."

—D. J. BALINGER

• •

BOOKS NOT SO BRIEFLY NOTED
FICTION

BOG, by James Mushner (Beefy Books; $24.50). A history of four square inches of Georgia swampland. Mr. Mushner anthropomorphizes not only animals, but plants and inanimate objects as well. Over the course of some eight hundred and ninety-one pages, we get to know the deepest feelings of some ferns, a puddle of flaming lava, the big toe of a stegosaurus, a colonial horseshoe, and a piece of parking lot outside an Amway distributorship. While not the author's best work by a long shot, this is an excellent book to use as a paperweight.

NOTE: "Slingback Shoes and Dingbat Dates," by Rama Lamawitz (Upsy-Daisy; $14.95), a new short-story collection, contains many stories interchangeable with others that have appeared in this magazine.

CALL FOR FREDERICK BUTTERFIELD

(1946)

[*John O'Samarra was one of our best and most prolific writers (two hundred and twenty-five stories published in the magazine—an achievement which, when described to D. J. Balinger, reportedly caused Balinger's eyeballs to rotate in their sockets like ball bearings), as well as the first in our office to wear button-down shirts with a button in the back. One could have forgiven him much, the sissified excesses of his wardrobe and even the depressingly Paavo Nurmi-like velocity with which he wrote, if only he'd kept the door to his office closed while he typed. O'Samarra stopped speaking to me after I told him some of his novels were too dirty.*]

"HERE you go, Felix," said Butterfield, handing the doorman his Rogers Peet coat and plaid Brooks Brothers hunting cap as he stepped inside the door of the Metro Club. "Cold as a well-digger's knee out there today."

"Sure is, Mr. Butterfield," said Felix. "Not much doubt about that. Must be twenty degrees, easy."

"Makes a fellow feel terse as hell," he said, rubbing his palms together as he headed toward the bar. "Think I'll have a whiskey sour. See if I can't loosen up a bit." He glanced around and ordered a drink from Frank, the ruddy-cheeked barman, who had been at the club as long as he had, thirty-five years.

"The usual, Mr. B?"

"You know me by now, Frank," he said. "Secrets and all."

"Guess I do. If I don't, nobody does, and I've known a lot of men like you, too—most of 'em, in fact." He gave a short laugh.

"Well, we may talk alike, Frank, but don't be fooled by appearances. You know what they say."

"What would that be, Mr. B?"

"Can't tell a book by its cover." He smiled tightly.

"So they do, sir. So they do."

"What's new, Frank?"

"Been pretty quiet in here lately, Mr. Butterfield."

"That's what I like about these rich guys' clubs."

"You sure hit the old nail on the head there, Mr. B. Not much happens here, and yet, in a strange and meaningful way, everything happens."

"That's why I come in, Frank. Now, take yourself—you're a fine fellow, but just a little beneath me. Together, we form a kind of microcosm of American society."

"Even so, I *was* a member of Cap & Knickers at City College."

"Well, that's not the sort of club I'd want to be a member of, though it's all right for working-class Irish."

"So what did you belong to, Mr. B?"

"Never made it to college, Frank, but always wanted to join something. I applied to Hunt & Peck, Fruit & Loom, and Buck & Wing. How do you like them apples?"

"No kidding!"

"I always say, you can tell a man by the clubs he aspires to, where he sits in the steambath, and how he holds a salad fork."

"You said a mouthful there, sir."

"I try, Frank, I try."

Felix came into the bar and told Butterfield he had a call. "Believe it's your wife, sir."

"What makes you think so, Felix?"

"Lady said her name was Mrs. Butterfield. Didn't mean to pry into your personal affairs, sir—"

"Why, you stupid son of a bitch," said Butterfield. "Now look what you've gone and done." He hurled his drink at Felix, spilling liquor down his shirt front.

"Anything wrong, sir?" Frank asked as Felix busied himself elsewhere.

"Nah, it's awright," he said. "Everything's just fine and dandy, sugar candy, thanks to blabbermouth over there. How long has Felix been working here, anyway? He's an Arab of some kind, isn't he?"

"I believe so, sir. Lebanese, I think."

"When I joined, this was an all-white club."

"He's just an employee, sir."

"That's no excuse. Once you let the barriers down, Frank, it's Katy, bar the door... Jesus H. Christ, if my wife finds out I'm staying in town instead of going to Chicago for a meeting, I'll be ruined. My entire career and her fortune will be down the drain, all in the twinkling of an eye. Do you realize, Frank, that everything I am and have strived for turns on what happens in the next few moments?"

"I see that a lot here, Mr. B."

"Could I do something, sir?" said Felix, returning meekly, dabbing at his chin with a bar towel.

"Seems you've done plenty as it is, pal," he answered, striding out of the bar. He dialed the telephone. "'Lo, Myra? It's me, dear. Oh, sure, I'm O.K. Ah, the plane got delayed. Big snowstorm coming down from Buffalo, so I stopped in at the Club for a while. Look, I'll call you when I get into O'Hare so you don't have to worry. Yeah. S'long, hon."

Butterfield went back to the bar. "That was a close call, Frank... Say, if you see a tall woman around here later—slim, red hair, name of Vera—tell her I'll meet her around the corner at Chez Joey."

"Quick thinking there, Mr. Butterfield," said Frank, laughing.

"In an episode like this, you gotta be mighty fast on your feet, Frank."

"Ya sure do, Mr. B. I love the way you're able to twist these little slices of life around, slick as a whistle, year after year."

"Between you and me, Frank, I don't love my wife, but hell, she's a person, same as you and me, and she's got feelings, y'know?"

"'Course she does, Mr. B. Now then, sir, before you go, what'll it be? The same?"

"I feel like celebrating, Frank. It's not every day you pull one out of the fire like this. Pour me a Martini—very dry. Make it a double. Hell, I just saved my marriage!"

"If you can call it a marriage, sir."

"Yes, well, you've got a point there, all right."

"How 'bout an onion in that, sir?"

"No, Frank, I believe I'll skip the onion tonight. I won't be needing it where I'm going." He smiled tightly again.

"Sure thing, Mr. Butterfield. And where would that be?"

"Never you mind, Frank. If anyone asks, just tell them I had an appointment at O'Hare."   —JOHN O'SAMARRA

HOLY ACRIMONY

(1933)

[James Thumper's work possesses a childlike freshness and verve that were all too absent from the man's social behavior, which was unusually overbearing and testy. He was also fond of nasty practical jokes. Thumper and I got along exceedingly well, and if he were alive today I know exactly where I'd look for those missing crates of memorabilia.]

MR. GRAVLOX folded his arms and said that when he was a boy in Columbus, there was a dog he knew—a St. Bernard, actually —who would sit at the dinner table and drink like General Grant.

Mrs. Gravlox just scoffed and told him to stop making up stories when the children were present—and furthermore, to kindly refrain from using "who"

rather than "that" when speaking of beasts, especially dogs. "You said you knew a dog 'who' could sit at the dinner table," muttered Mrs. Gravlox. "Dogs are not human and thus not 'who's.'"

"Well, the dogs I know are as human as you or me—me, anyway," said Mr. Gravlox, "and if I want to call my old St. Bernard 'who,' that's my business. Ulysses was definitely a 'who' and not

• •

"All right, have it your way. I'll bark like a seal."

a 'that,' and you could look it up."

Mrs. Gravlox turned to her youngest child, pushed a bowl at her, and said, "Eat your turnips, Amanda, and don't pay any attention to your father. Obviously, the man has gone crackers again."

"Have not!" said Mr. Gravlox, pouting and sliding down in his chair under the table, his customary position during domestic squabbles. "Anyway, nobody goes crackers nowadays. They go bananas, or perhaps bonkers."

"People do *so* go crackers," insisted Mrs. Gravlox, rising up to her full height and spreading out to her full width, "or my name is not Elsie Gravlox."

"In Columbus, nobody went crackers," argued Mr. Gravlox.

"In your case, Edwin, if you are not stewed, you're crackers. I should know. Now, please leave the dinner table and go to your room."

"Ha!" chortled Mr. Gravlox. "*Now* I've got you, Elsie. My name is not Edwin. It is Erwin. Edwin, you may recall, was your old doormat. My name is Erwin and always has been."

"I've certainly known my share of has-beens," snorted Mrs. Gravlox, snapping him with her dishtowel. "Erwin, Edwin—what does it matter? Anyway, you never knew my first husband."

"No, but I'm sorry he died so young," grumbled Mr. G.

"Don't quibble, dear," said his wife. "It doesn't become you."

"Nor moonlight you," he mumbled under his breath. "And I'll quibble all I damn please. If you're going to carp, I'm going to quibble. It's only fair."

"All's fair in love and war," piped Mrs. Gravlox, "and this looks like war."

"Doesn't that just sound like something you'd say," snarled Mr. Gravlox, edging over to the sink, "and I've about had my fill of it, not to mention you." With that, he seized a meat cleaver from the sideboard and brandished it under Mrs.

Gravlox's nose as the children scattered. "I guess we'll see who's crackers!" he cried, specks of spittle foaming on his lower lip.

"Now, now, Erwin, I don't mean anything by my constant badgering. It's just a way to get your attention in a society where women earn only twenty-three cents to every dollar earned by men. We have no voice in the workplace and are forced to make ourselves heard in the home, where we still have the greatest influence and are responsible for all the major decisions, especially in the area of child-rearing."

"I'm afraid it's too late for manifestoes," sneered Mr. Gravlox, grabbing his wife by an apron string and pushing her against the stove.

"Don't you think maybe you're taking this whole battle-of-the-sexes thing too seriously?" his wife asked as demurely as possible. "Up until now, it was all so whimsical."

"All milk over the dam, my dear," said Mr. Gravlox, wielding the butcher knife.

"Don't mix your metaphors, dear. It's *water* over the dam," corrected his wife. "You're thinking of 'spilt milk.'"

"As for whimsy, forget it," he snapped. "I'm up to here with drollery. We've seen the last of wry raillery around this house. Where has it gotten me? A man can stand only so much fey whimsy until he cracks."

"I knew an actress named Faye Wimsey," snickered Mrs. Gravlox.

Her husband glowered.

"My, my, aren't we in a foul mood this evening," she added, attempting a light, bantering tone.

"I am not," he growled. "You know I abhor poultry in any form."

"That's very clever, dear," said Mrs. Gravlox, smiling sweetly and eyeing the knife in his hand.

"No need to patronize me," he cried.

"Merely because you are a large, ungainly woman, hideous to behold, with an urge to smother any male in your path, does not mean that I am forced to remain pussy-whipped forever."

With that, he raised the cleaver over his head, one hand resting on the dropleaf kitchen table, and was about to take a Ruthian swing at his wife when she kicked the table leaf out from under him, causing Mr. Gravlox to collapse on the floor at her feet as the cleaver clattered to the ground.

"That's one for you, Elsie," he said, his eyes narrowing. "You may have won the battle of the sexes, but you haven't won the war." The two of them scuffled on the cold linoleum, but it was Mr. Gravlox who finally grabbed the gleaming meat cleaver and, in one swipe, neatly lopped off his wife's head as their daughter yelled "Touché!"

Later, he had her stuffed and mounted over the bookcase, alongside his favorite stuffed seal trophy. For years afterward, whenever guests came to his home for cocktails, Mr. Gravlox would proudly point to the menacing creature hanging on the wall and explain, "That's the last Mrs. Gravlox over there."

—JAMES THUMPER

• •

"Miss Klopperman, I want you."

ROTS OF RUCK

(1977)

[Ann Weedie shot to literary prominence in 1977 when this story won a Ladies of the Canyon Award for short fiction. Miss Weedie's work is controversial, judging by the mail we receive. Some readers think her characters are depressed; others say they are not depressed, only sad; a small faction maintains that they are neither depressed nor sad, but alienated. Miss Weedie shrugs off these speculations with a toss of her well-maintained hair and a pealing laugh, then goes about her business, which includes, in addition to writing, a thriving real-estate agency that she operates, she says, as "a change of pace from my ceaseless wrestling match with the Word—that's with a cap."]

RUTH sleeps late, not bothering to call in sick to the real-estate agency where she answers the phone and types letters. She does not want to face the morning. The first man she lived with, Ray, called her "Earthworm" because, he said, earthworms go to sleep when they are faced with an obstacle they cannot dig their way around. Ruth did not see herself as an earthworm and assured herself that when she came across an obstacle, she knew how to get around it. One day, Ray came home from the RC Cola plant, where he worked on the bottling line to support his woodcarving, to find all his belongings sitting by the door in neat bundles. Taped to Ray's box of chisels was a note which read, "Dear Ray—Dug my way around it. Rots of ruck, Ruth."

That was three years ago in Cambridge. Since then, Ruth lived with Rob, broke up with him, met Russ, went with him briefly without moving in, broke up, married Rupert, divorced Rupert, met Roy and moved to Arlington, Virginia, with him two months ago. Last night at dinner, Roy announced quietly that he was taking off for a while to travel with his friend Rudolph and that he'd stay in touch. Then Rudolph appeared, and the two of them packed up all of Roy's clothes, books, and records, placed them in the back of Rudolph's station wagon, and drove off, chatting animatedly. Ruth said nothing because she could not think of anything to say. Only later that evening, when she realized that Roy had taken both of her Laura Nyro albums, did she cry.

Shambling into the kitchen, Ruth rinses out a dirty mug with a rainbow on its side. She wonders why Roy forgot or neglected to take his mug. On the kitchen counter next to the sink is a pile of unopened mail from the past week. She thumbs through it, looking for something to read while she waits for the mail. Before the tea kettle whistles, she pours, then mixes Coffeemate into the Taster's Choice. Granules of undissolved coffee float and swirl on the surface. Ruth usually makes her coffee too soon and often reminds herself to wait until the water boils before pouring it over the instant coffee. Otherwise, the granules may lodge between her teeth. She will have to floss later. She runs her tongue over her teeth and ponders her gums.

AT the bottom of the stack of mail is the magazine in its plain brown wrapper. On the stepstool in the corner are the past five weeks' issues, still in their wrappers. Ruth takes her coffee and the pack of cigarettes lying on top of the stove and sits at the table by the kitchen window. She decides to browse through the magazine while she waits for the mail. She looks for a long moment at the cover, a pastel sketch of a man walking his dog along a beach. She tries to remember the last time she was on a beach and yawns. She riffles the pages, enjoying the discreet breeze and the darkling smells of ink and paper. A card offering subscriptions falls out of the magazine and alights for a moment on her lap. She reaches, but it slips off her lap and onto the floor, where three identical cards lie under the kitchen table from past issues similarly riffled. They will stay there until Ruth sweeps, three weeks from now. Ruth sips her coffee, puffs her cigarette, and begins to read a brief piece describing a man's reflections on trimming his hedge and finding his clippers need oil. The man is reminded of the need for renewal both in nature and in the man-made world. Ruth yawns again, thinks about making herself another cup of coffee and then thinks better of it. Enough caffeine for today, she decides decisively. Draining her cup and stubbing out her cigarette, she rises and slouches into the living room. Her cat, Robbie Robertson, snoozes in a small square of sunlight on the mottled sofa Roy called the Green Slime. Ruth pushes Robbie Robertson aside and lies down with the magazine. In a few minutes she is snoring lightly, the magazine forming a little tent of pages against her face, embracing her with its smoothness.

R UTH starts, wonders where she is, sighs and relaxes. The thud of the mail falling to the floor from the mail slot in the front door wakes her with the same sound Rupert's keys made when they hit the floor after he'd pushed them, stuffed into a pair of socks, through the mail slot of their front door the night he left. With the keys was a brief note listing his reasons for returning to the seminary and a business card from his lawyer, Roy. Thuds disquiet Ruth. She gets up quietly to get the mail and takes it to the kitchen table to examine.

There is a bill from the power company, a postcard from Ruth's friend Rod, who is visiting Rome, a bill from her gynecologist, and a fund-raising letter from some charity. Ruth puts the last on the bottom of the pile so quickly she does not know for sure the letter is from a charity; but she believes so. Finally, there is the magazine. She makes herself a cup of Mellow Mint tea and spikes it with a shot of Cherry Kijafa. She regards the new cover, an elegant, simple ink drawing of a vase of flowers, done on what appears to be nubby canvas. Very pretty. She lights a cigarette and scans the table of contents. There are several stories, an article about a psychologist she's never heard of, and a report on herb farming that is the first of a series. She riffles the pages and the subscription card flutters to the floor with the others. She admires a gorgeous swimsuit by Perry Ellis, or Calvin Klein, or Ralph Lauren, but cannot remember which after she turns the page. How did those men get those names, she wonders. Well, Ralph's O.K., she supposes. She thumbs on, stopping to smile at a cartoon depicting an irate, paunchy businessman dressing down a skinny hotel desk clerk. On the next page, a series of skewed drawings of buildings puzzles her. She wonders if there's a joke she is missing. Opposite it is the first page of an article about rosemary that is sixty-seven pages long. She starts to read. As she nears the end of the first paragraph, which consists of a quotation from an agricultural journal published in 1889, she begins to feel logy. Before she is ready to turn the page, Ruth lays her head down on the kitchen table squarely on top of the densely lined drawing of a sprig of rosemary that decorates the page she was reading. She drifts off, her right earring touching one of the magazine's staples.

WHEN she awakes, she looks at her watch, still blinking sleep from her eyes. The little hand is at five and the big hand is between the eight and the nine; not quite a quarter to five. Time to water the plants. She has been talking to the plants for over a year. In that time, her Swedish ivy has improved, but a coleus and two spider plants have died. When she brought the second dead spider plant back to the plant shop, the clerk joked with her.

"You should talk to these babies," he said.

"I do."

"What do you say to them, rots of ruck? Here, try this ranunculus. They're tough."

She was silent as she waited for her change. That night she watered the new plant, then sat down and tried to draw it out. She asked the plant where it was from, what its favorite minerals were, and where it would like to be placed in the room. The plant did not answer but thrives. This afternoon she doesn't say much, just moves methodically from room to room with a tea kettle filled with cold water, watering.

Almost seven, time to think about dinner. She recalls meals she's made for other people. Ray's favorite dish was pizza, of course. Rob's was macaroni and cheese. Russ liked Popeye's Fried Chicken with cole slaw and gravy. Rupert liked steamed vegetables. Roy liked steak. Ruth wonders what Rudolph likes. She likes raspberry yogurt with raisins and Reese's Pieces in it. That's not enough for dinner, Ray, Rob, Russ, Rupert, Roy, and even her old high-school beau, Ross, each in his time, told her. She looks in the refrigerator and finds a Dannon yogurt that should be good until tomorrow. No raisins, no Reese's. No matter. Ruth goes into the living room and puts on a record that Rupert (or could it have been Randy?) liked to play when he was shaving. "Uno, dos—Uno, dos, tres, quatro," the beat-up KLH says. Ruth smiles slightly as she sits on the Green Slime with her magazine and her yogurt. The yogurt makes her lips purse. The stereo blares.

"Woolly Bully . . . Woolly Bully . . . Woolly Bully . . ."

Ruth cries quietly to herself, manages to stop by forcing herself to leaf furiously through the tiny ads at the back of the magazine. Gradually, she calms down. An ad for speed reading catches her attention. She makes a mental note to write for their literature before she rests the magazine on her chest and closes her puffy eyes, Sam the Sham and the Pharaohs singing her a lullaby, and the late afternoon turning into the early evening, sort of.

—ANN WEEDIE

OF THE BREEZEWAY

(1968)

[*"Dike Upjohn," observed a jealous young Talk reporter back in 1967, "looks like someone went to central casting, said, 'Give me a writer,' and suddenly there was Dike. He wears the right kind of corduroy pants and the right kind of tweedy sweater. Good sneakers, too." I couldn't agree more with this assessment and bear Dike no ill will for the hard times he's been able to avoid because of his looks—although I do feel it was very small of him not to give me the name of his barber, especially after all I've done for him. His work has kept pace with his appearance, growing fuller, more commanding, and longer-haired with the years. This story, one of his first to appear in our pages, is strangely easy to follow.*]

THE kitchen reeked of Mr. Clean, its authoritarian aroma erupting from the whimsically polka-dotted vinyl. The smell produced in Porter an exhilarating vertigo as he slouched to the sink for a glass of water.

From the sill of the window, he took the plastic tumbler, at once translucent and blue, and let the water run to chill, the aerated downward-plunging cascade disappearing into the perforated sink strainer in a swirling Charybdis of swirling.

His mother lifted the brown A & P grocery bag that served as an enclosure for the day's accumulation of garbage. She offered it up to him, and he received it gladly. She made a frantic wave of her hands that expressed, while acknowledging his manhood, all her subservience, dominance, and fear of winged insects, encapsulated in an aggressive nonchalance that left him confused.

He stepped down, into the breezeway. Compressed against the concrete was a pinkish object, bulbous as some tropical fruit, possessed of nodular protrusions of incrementally varied size, each with its own pale eye: his foot. The naked concrete was cool to his bare sole. Here the floor was slab-on-grade, with direct thermal continuity to the tempered mass of the earth. In the kitchen, the flooring had been warmer, hinting of plywood subfloor over wooden joist: testaments to the builder's art, of temporal human endeavor, all suspended over hidden recesses of basement.

It struck him that a garage at dusk is a beshrouded airplane hangar, except that it is smaller and can be used to house a Camaro. As Porter stood there, a rupturing occurred: the haphazard beginnings of a voiding that he sensed initially with an affront to his nose and then a wetness of his hands. The grocery bag, in this too stressful role, was failing.

Porter limboed tenuously to the near barrel. As he deposited and secured his burden, he espied topmost the crumbled white angularity of the odd, flat carton from Ray's Drive-Thru Pizza. He toyed with the arc-segments of unconsumed crust, as if playing tiddlywinks with urinal cakes, the smudges of red sauce pilose with anchovy shards. Gazing guiltily over his shoulder, he popped one onto his eager tongue.

Porter suddenly stood erect, the negligée of pubescence dropping from him. And with a cloying, queasy sensation along his innards, he was drenched in the certainty that though life was a satisfying series of simple gestures like the one he had just completed, there would come a time when he could tell someone else to take out the garbage.

—DIKE UPJOHN

A CHANCE MEETING WITH ROSSANO BRAZZI
(1963)

[*A roué in the old-world manner, Arturo Spumante never failed to show up at our office parties with flowers for the young women in Accounting, who returned the favor by sending out his checks promptly. Roger Devill swears he once saw Spumante wearing a pinkie ring, but no one believes him. Arturo, when asked if this story was based on real life, smiled and said nothing. That sort of thing does a lot for a writer at our magazine.*]

HE knew that he was very sensitive. He used it—this sensitivity—like a bullfighter's cape to attract women. With graceful veronicas, he worked closer and closer to his prey, thinking, *I am doing this for the sport of it*, and when he was just to the point of victory, he would pull back and say to himself, *No. She is not sensitive enough for me.* But then he would perform the deed with them anyway, because in the end it did not matter that *they* were not sensitive enough. What mattered was that *he* was so sensitive—perhaps the most sensitive person ever—that he needed to have them even if they were fat and gross and stank of roll-on deodorant.

Once, when he had lived in New York, he was walking uptown on Broadway in the theatre district and he saw Rossano Brazzi standing on a corner in animated conversation with two glamorous women. Rossano Brazzi was wearing a seersucker sports jacket and smugly swinging an attaché case while he spoke to these women, and he thought, *What does Rossano Brazzi need with an attaché case?* It was at the time in his life when he was a stockbroker, though stockbrokering had never given him pleasure. Even the money he made in such huge amounts left him keenly disinterested. As he watched Rossano Brazzi in his seersucker jacket, he thought, *Bah. He is not so sensitive.* And so thinking, he approached Brazzi and pushed hard on his shoulder, saying, "You are not so sensitive. I am more sensitive than you." He said this angrily, in a way calculated to gain a response. He saw that it worked.

"Whatever you say, pal," Brazzi responded with only the merest trace of accent, and the actor shepherded the two glamorous women away from him. He watched them walking west, into the sun, savoring the sensitivity of his vision and thinking, *There. Perhaps now I will become a photographer.*

AND so it had been. He had taken many, many pictures by now, and he had long since quit being a stockbroker. In the town where he now lived there was a square on which there was a motel. Often he would tell his wife he was going to the Fotomat to see if his film was ready and spend the afternoon sitting in the square, watching the young girls. In the nice weather, he would purchase a *fiasco* of sweet wine and sip it in its coarse brown bag. If he was lucky, he would spend some time at the motel with one of the young girls, paying his friend the owner the day rate. The owner would often sit opposite him in the square and leer at him. He had a wide range of expressive hand gestures and noises that he used in order to divert the attention of the young girls away from him. His favorite was the sign of the *gnocchi*. He considered it his most expressive gesture, as he had once been arrested for making it at a parade.

If no young girls consented to go with him to the motel, he would pass the time talking with the motel owner about all the young girls that had consented to go with him in the past. Their favorite story was of the time he had been with one young girl in one room and had come out to purchase another *fiasco* of sweet wine. During the trip, things had gone his way and he had convinced another young girl to come with him to a different room in the motel. He spent the afternoon running between the two rooms, much to the amusement of the motel owner. The motel owner laughed at him and employed every gesture and noise he knew, occasionally asking to join them in one room or the other. But he had rebuked the motel owner, telling him that of course he was not nearly sensitive enough.

AND so the days passed, sometimes with luck and sometimes without luck. It made him feel like he had made a moderate success of himself, and he thought perhaps this was all one could expect from the world—young girls, *fiaschi* of sweet wine, and an occasional dividend from the stock portfolio built up so many years before.

—ARTURO SPUMANTE

"Heimlich!"

DEW DROP DEAD

(1979)

[*Few of our current writers have enjoyed the acclaim accorded Dion Barmelthe, of whose boldly experimental creations critic Anatole Boyardee has written: "Once in a decade there is a writer who can put whatever he wants on the page and a magazine will buy it. Today, that man is Dion Barmelthe. Who knows what the hell he's talking about?" Dion was followed in our pages by younger brother Frankie, whose cool, gamy explorations of anomie among the K-Mart crowd prompted Marvin Mudcake's enthusiastic tribute in* Esquire's *1982 "Writers Younger than We Are" issue: "Frankie Barmelthe's stories track psychic tremors so minute, they might as well be about nothing at all. The cartographer of a region littered with fast-food wrappers and big, fuzzy dice, Barmelthe puts the Henry James in Jamesway."*

It is not widely known, but the brothers began their literary careers as "The Battling Barmelthes, Tag-Team Fictionalists," working the grueling crucible of writers' workshops and literary conferences across the Southwest. The Barmelthes, who hail from the extremely large state of Texas, evolved their unique method of joint authorship as a means of passing long nights on the prairie. At first, each would write a passage and pass it to the other for embellishment or continuation. By the time the following story was created, live onstage at the University of Iowa Writers' Cow Palace, the Barmelthes were working at separate tables, Frankie on an IBM Sweet Potato 400X, Dion on his battered Smith-Corona electric portable, Lucille. Changes of authorship were made voluntarily, by judges' fiat, or simply when Dion or Frankie slammed his keyboard too loudly to be ignored. The Barmelthes went their separate ways some years ago but remain "relatives, absolutely," as Dion playfully remarks. What follows is a superb example of the brothers' uncanny ability to mesh two wildly divergent sensibilities, creating an emotional impact that more than one reader has likened to vertigo.]

D.B.

We were swabbing the deck, Queequeg, Mr. Smee, and I, when the attack began. Up in the crow's nest, a quiescent man named Crowhurst sighted the ship when it was a mere speck on the horizon. How all hands flew into action when he called out that the frigate flew the Jolly Roger! No observer would have suspected we were enfeebled from three weeks' subsistence on half-rations, punishment for one of our number stealing the ship's precious cache of frozen strawberries. But this was no time for recriminations. This was what we'd signed on for, not the idiotic routine of high-seas boating. We wanted blood!

In the galley the pantry squad, ably led by Mrs. Davis (the Scrapper's wife), struggled to finish tidying so they could join the fracas. Several long, teetering stacks of individual-portion-size breakfast cereal boxes fell from the uppermost shelves, hindering the men who were trying to polish the cutting board with club soda.

F.B.

Cleaning up as you go is part of the fun, I always—

D.B.

We fired our cannons as quickly as we could load and aim them through the little holes (not unlike the Cruiserline Ventiports on an old Buick) made for the purpose in the side of the boat. It was no use. Their firepower was great, their will to conquer irrefutable. As they drew close, we managed a terrific last salvo. "Blam!" we cried as bits of buccaneers spattered over their sails, their decks, and into the sea. Still, the pirate hoards kept coming.

We fought them hand to hand. Most of our number were killed. The boat fell to the brigands. I shimmied up the mainmast, hugging it closely as Crowhurst zipped past me and crashed on the deck, a victim of lost footing. From above I could see clearly now (although the rain had not fallen); the ship was full of dead bodies and individual-portion-size cereal boxes, which our pitiful, remaining few had taken to hurling at the invaders, insubstantial responses to their sabers, bullets, and torches. I became depressed.

F.B.

And then I see her, a tall, blond woman wearing a snug angora V-necked sweater that really shows off her full bosom nicely. She—

D.B.

She was a prisoner on their ship. The man who works the fish counter at the Jefferson Market tied her to a row of belaying pins with stout twine that he carried in his Danish school bag. I crept down the mast stealthily, so as to escape notice, and tiptoed through the carnage to where I could easily board the pirate vessel with a small leap, which I executed with considerable grace, given my numerous flesh wounds and bad mood. Reaching her just as the fishmonger left, I untied her wrists and slapped them several times to restore circulation. After some moments, she regained consciousness. Then, thanking me from the bottom of her heart, she—

F.B.

She asks me what kind of beer we have on tap and orders a Stroh's Light. No one is watching the Pirates game on the tube anyway, so I turn it off.

Lunchtime is seldom very busy at the Dew Drop, since all we offer is sandwiches and bar snacks: nuts, pretzels, and pickled eggs, which sit on the bar in a big jar labelled "E-Z Peels." They are, too, but they smell awful and are rarely ordered.

The two women linger over their grilled cheeses and Stroh's Lights. The one who spoke to me keeps stealing glances. I stand behind the bar, turning the pages of my *New York Review of Books*. Duane, my boss, would make me put it away if he were here, but he's not. He's home working on his motorcycle.

Eventually, the women get up to pay. As they approach, I lift the beverage gun and, pressing the lower right-hand button, squirt club soda on the bar.

"How come you're pouring soda on the bar?" the big blonde's smaller, darker friend asks.

I take my time answering, rubbing the soda into the wood with a lot of elbow grease. The flexion makes my arm look good. "Club soda conditions the old mahogany strip. Soaks in, draws up the natural oils and things in the wood itself." Perhaps this is true.

"It does? Should I try it on my furniture at home?" the blonde asks.

"Couldn't say." I finish wiping down the bar, pour myself a glass of Tab from the beverage gun, and return to my *New York Review*, flipping the pages to a lengthy essay about Joseph Conrad.

D.B.

"No hope for it at all," said Chief

Petty Officer Kurtz as we watched our boat sink. Then we scurried belowdecks of the pirate ship and hid in a storage locker that should have contained salt pork but did not. We pooled our weapons: a harness-maker's leather awl, a badly nicked sabre, and several dozen rubber bands. Billy Carl Black, the mystic of our group, attempted to project a psychic wall of invisibility that would conceal us until we made a landfall. Unfortunately, his poor brain was not up to the effort and he dropped dead of an aneurism, *tant pis*.

I found a porthole right by the storage locker, low and close to the water line. I remembered, too, that I had an inflatable dinghy hidden in my rucksack. As we struggled to inflate it in the tiny locker, we were discovered, *faute de mieux*. All hell broke loose, *laissez-moi te dire*.

Luckily, we were standing on a trap door. When we opened it, we found, much to our surprise, that we had pulled out the ship's plug. Water rushed into the hold with such force that our group was hurled up onto the poop as the craft listed, suddenly sinking. For the second time in less than an hour, the sounds of dying rang in our ears.

No one noticed that our little rubber dinghy had drifted off. Without it, our group was too weak to do much but cling to the flotsam and wish upon a star until the clouds rolled by.

F.B.

"A man who gets that wrapped up in his reading can forget a lot—if you know what I mean," drawls the blonde, who is still standing by the bar, waiting to pay.

I'm wary now, so I close the paper and casually grunt, "Um—huh?"

"You can't just stare at my friend and me the way you did all during lunch and expect no one to say anything."

"Was I really staring? Whillikers," I say in a light tone tinged with irony.

"Here's my number," she says, scribbling on a card and flipping it to me. It lands on the freshly wiped bar. "Call me when you get off work. My name is Dede. And this is Sharon." She points at the little one, who is waiting in the doorway, shifting her weight from foot to foot.

"Pleased to meet you, Dede—and Sharon, you too."

When the door closes behind them, I pick up Dede's card. She works at Sears. I need a new oil filter and some socks. Maybe I'll drop by there later.

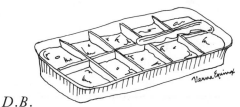

D.B.

André, our *sous-chef*, whose warm, barely seared lamb salad was one of the joys of sea travel in the halcyon days of the great cruise ships ("floating kitchens," as they were known), found our dinghy and paddled about, calling each of us by name. What an extraordinary memory! Even I did not know all our crew members' names, and I carried a Filofax with me at all times for jotting down such things as names, appointments, and those little *aperçus* that pop into one's mind at the strangest times. After a search of many hours, André plucked three of us from the water: four survivors out of a party of one hundred and eighty-five. We lay exhausted, slumped over each other, salty water sloshing over the *zaftig* gunwales of our badly overloaded rubber boat. André puttered with the emergency rations with which the dinghy was equipped and pulled together a charming light supper of hardtack brioches and Kendall Mint Block. Night fell; we slumbered.

I think I'm dreaming,—

F.B.

Pinch yourself.

D.B.

I think I'm dreaming,—

F.B.

Pinch yourself.

D.B.

I said, I think I'm dreaming,—

F.B.

Do you really? Here, let me.

D.B.

Ouch! All right! I'm awake!

F.B.

I'm tired and antsy as hell by the time the night waitress, Sue-Ann, comes tearing in out of breath at six-thirty, forty-five minutes late. She takes off her short denim jacket and puts on an apron, concealing her pert little chest over which she seldom wears a brassiere. She smiles at me as we squeeze by each other behind the bar.

"Sorry I'm late," she says, "but it was the kids. They go to their father's for the weekend, and I had to get them ready. The bar looks good. Been shining it up with soda?"

"Um—yeah," I mumble. I think she noticed me staring at her chest.

"You have great potential as a home-maker."

"Do I?"

"Sure. Ever been on a laundry date?"

"No."

"You have plans for later?"

"Um—no, nothing special. I'll just eat something and then hang out at home, I guess. Why?"

"I'll call you when I get off, O.K.? We can have a laundry date. I'll bring my All, you supply the Bounce."

Sue-Ann is taking stemmed glasses from the drying rack and placing them into the racks overhead. She looks good, stretching up in her tight, faded jeans, especially when she goes up on tiptoe with her back to me, sliding a Martini glass into place. I can see the line of her panties through her jeans. She turns around and smiles when she sees I'm looking at her behind. I back across the room to the door, telling her to call after work, we'll see. I'm tired. I think I'll take a nap when I get home.

D.B.

I've always been a light sleeper, especially in open rubber boats, so I was the first to realize we were no longer floating free. We had drifted ashore on a small island—an atoll, I believe it's called.

I assessed our condition. One of the limp bodies in the dinghy was dead. How considerate of him to have made no fuss; adversity brings out the best in men. I woke André. We took the corpse to the edge of a rocky outcropping along the shore line, and there we laid it out. It would eventually wash out to sea. I could not muster a prayer, so I turned to André. He spoke in French, too quickly for me to understand. I assumed he had plopped some sort of benediction upon the deceased, but when I asked him what he had said, the doughty little Wog said in his broken English:

"I have maked the apology for not providing—how you say—the showy funeral. He was *mon ami*. He was the pastry chef. We shall not have pastry while we are here. *Je suis desolé.*"

"That goes double for me," I said, for I felt I might not last without at least the hope of a kiwi tartlet to brighten my day.

"Even the salad spinner went down with the ship," André said. "There is nothing left. Nothing," he added, and sat over the dead man, crying.

I set out to explore. It didn't take long; you could walk the circumference of the island in fifteen minutes. All along the shoreline lay the carcasses of dead fish and bottles containing messages. One was from a third-grade class in North Carolina. One was from a sailor aboard the U.S.S. Nimitz. Another was signed "Lovies from Margueritaville, Marguerite Duras, Marguerite Young and Marguerite Yourcenar." Inside a Yoo-Hoo bottle was a subscription offer from *The Village Voice*, which made me homesick. Ah, for a slice from Ray's with mushrooms and extra cheese! Instead we lived off what we could find on land or pull from the sea. Limpets loomed large in our diet.

We patched our little rubber boat as best we could and decided to head north, navigating by the stars. Our last night on the atoll, we built a campfire and sat around it singing "Michael, Row Your Boat Ashore." Then we closed our eyes and tried to get an early start on our reminiscences of this island paradise where we had barely survived. We didn't want to forget anything we might want

to pine for in later years down the road, down the road, down the road apiece.

F.B.
The apartment complex I live in is called Down the Road Apiece, but residents call it Down the Interstate because it's so close to I-55 you can actually smell the traffic. The buildings are made of concrete block, but they're textured and painted to look like adobe, so the place has a southwestern air.

When I get home, I remove my sneakers and put on thongs before pouring five or six fingers of gin in a tall glass with ice and enough Sprite to cloud the gin. I pull a Celantano's Pizza out—

D.B.
Ray's, I think—

F.B.
—CELANTANO'S PIZZA out of the freezer and put it in the microwave.

"Lip, lip, lip, lip, lip, lip, lip, lip,
Mum, mum, mum, mum, mum, mum, mum, mum,
Shoo ba doo wap, shoo ba doobee wap,
Ba dooo."

[How this got into the magazine, I'll never know.—E.T.]

"You mean to say that up here commas after introductory adverbial phrases are optional? No shit!"

• •

While I'm waiting, I read the mail: a few bills, a lot of junk circulars, and the new *Ploughshares*. When the pizza is ready, I pull it out of the oven and, with my drink, my Old Golds, and my "Duino Elegies," head out to the courtyard and the pool.

It's quiet around the pool at night. Television sounds and talk drift out from the surrounding apartments. Flying insects immolate themselves on the purple bug light by the manager's office. The sun has not yet set, but the floodlights in the pool go on automatically at 6:30. Soon it's dusk and I'm squinting at my Rilke. A squiggle of congealed cheese falls from a slice of pizza and lands in the crease of the book. I scrape at it but can't get it out, even though I haven't bitten my fingernails for weeks.

A car pulls into the parking lot. From the sound of the engine I know it's a little Toyota or Datsun, underpowered but scrappy. Wooden clogs scrape across the gravel; it's Virginia from apartment 23N. She calls herself Gigi. How Gigi can drive a car with clogs on her feet astounds me. She hums to herself as she closes and locks the driver's door and walks, crunching gravel, to the trunk. The tune she hums slides between "Up, Up and Away" and something by the

Eagles that I recognize but can't name. Gigi, a few years older than I am, is divorced and has a four-year-old son. She sees me on her way to 23N.

"Oh God, what a day! My feet are killing me," she says.

"Um—yeah . . . Punishment for wearing wooden shoes," I josh.

"Christ, help me with one of these, will you?"

It is an order, not a question. I take a bag of groceries from the trunk and walk alongside her, barefoot. She steps on my big toe with a clog. I wince. At the door we hear gunshots and pounding music from the TV, the high-pitched voice of a little boy, and the babysitter's voice telling the child to shut up. There is a crash. Now Gigi winces.

"Out of the frying pan. Here, I can take that now," she says incorrectly, because I have to hold both her bags and the one I was already carrying so she can get her keys out of her large shoulder bag. "You're a sweetie. Want to come over for a nightcap later, after the kid's asleep? Or I'll come over to your place. How about it?"

"Uh—yeah, maybe, I suppose," I mumble as Gigi opens the door. I hand her the packages. Stepping backward to leave, I tread on a sharp stone and hop away, cursing. Gigi laughs as she slams the door. A quarter of an hour later, in my apartment, I hear the sitter leave. I refill my drink and chuck the empty bottle.

D.B.

In the end, it was a message in a bottle that saved us, an old five-and-a-half-ounce Coke bottle, with the curves and fluting that make it so unmistakable, so classic. We found it in the belly of a big fish that we caught with an improvised hook and line fashioned from my belt. The fish had swallowed the bottle whole, assuming, no doubt, that it was some gigantic plankton. We, smarter than the fish, knew not to eat it but to open it. The message inside, though soggy with sea water and fish juices, was legible and provided directions to an island paradise. There was an X on the map and next to the X these words: "You are here." How did the author of these words know where we were? Astonishing, but who were we to argue? And what did we have to lose? We kept paddling. The one who was not André died. Soon, I passed out.

I AWOKE alone in a room whose high walls were plain white. No windows, the only light source a porcelain fixture overhead. With a twist of the knob, the door opened onto a blank white corridor, evenly lit and continuing as far as the eye could see. How very, very Beckett, I thought when, way down the corridor, André appeared. "*Zut alors!*" he cried joyously when he saw me. "I prefer Zoot Sims, but what the hey," I replied. We embraced and undertook reconnaissance together.

We came into a great hall decorated with hanging flags of unknown origin and the stuffed heads of many animals: stags, antelopes, vicuña, musk ox, and, in serried ranks of ten or twelve per decorative plaque, voles. No people anywhere. We felt like prisoners. Fortunately, we were prepared for that. Coping with imprisonment was precisely what we had been trained to do. Both of us had seen "The Colditz Story" many times in the event of just this sort of eventuality.

Imagine our surprise to find that leaving the building was no problem. In fact, a doorman held the door open for us. Within two blocks we came upon a *bodega*, where we stocked up on supplies: powdered milk, sun-dried tomatoes, and a small Wedgwood candy dish. Wedgwood always brings me good luck; it's my lucky ceramic.

F.B.

At 10 P.M., I drive over to the all-night 7-Eleven to buy some things: tongue, soda, frozen dinners, chips and dip. I get back just in time for the evening news. Just as the sports segment begins, the phone rings.

"Hi. It's Dede. You're a hard man to track down."

"Dede?"

"This afternoon. At the bar. I was with my friend. You poured soda on the bar. Cute."

"Dede! Um—yeah. What a surprise!"

"I agree. You're the one who's supposed to be calling me."

"I apologize. Truly."

"Forget it. So—you busy now?"

"Um—well, I don't know."

"My address is on the card. You still have the card, don't you?"

"Of course I do." Do I?

"See you soon," Dede says, and hangs up. I'm brushing my teeth when the doorbell rings. My mouth full of toothpaste, I go to the front door and ask who it is, speaking as clearly as I can: "'Ooo iz i'?"

"Who do you think it is? It's Gigi."

The phone rings again. "'Ol' on a mini'." I run to the phone, spitting in the kitchen sink as I pass. "Hello?"

"It's Sue-Ann. The place is so quiet, it looks like we'll close early. You want to come over and pick me up or what?"

"Sue-Ann! Um—well . . . I'm really bushed, you know. I think—" A blast of the doorbell sounds. "Hold your water! Uh, Sue-Ann, that's a neighbor, dropping by to borrow some hand tools."

"Great, you'll be up for a while, I'll head on over. We'll have a drink or some coffee or whatever. See ya!" Click. Sue-Ann's on her way over, Dede's waiting for me, and Gigi's at the door. I tiptoe into the bedroom, draw back the curtains, and slip out the window to my car. At the twenty-four-hour drugstore at the shopping mall, I drink coffee and browse *The Kenyon Review* for several hours. By the time I get home, it's almost four A.M. I turn in right away, ignoring the notes that have been slipped under the door.

D.B.

We never found out how we came to be in the huge place with the immense dining hall, but we live there still. André and I each have our own apartments, a suite of rooms apiece. I own the *bodega* and import a full line of Wedgwood products. They don't sell well, but I don't care. I keep them around for myself. For now, I am content to hang around the Sixth Avenue newsstand, leafing through the rare-porcelain magazines, timing my trips to Balducci's to avoid the crowds. There will, I am sure, be more unexpected events, mutinies and uprisings, as well as moments of serenity and deep calm: grist, all grist. The pen, as they say at the P.E.N. Club, is mightier than the sword.

F.B.

"I guess I'll have the swordfish steak," she says, her voice wafting clearly over the evening din. My boss decided I have to work a couple of nights a week. I don't mind, better tips. Dede is here tonight with a date, a clean-cut guy in a blue blazer with a pink polo shirt open at the collar. Dede wears a very sheer black silk blouse. The double thickness of the pockets over her breasts makes the garment more provocative but less revealing. We look over at each other a couple of times when they first sit down, but soon give it up. Too complicated.

D.B.

The aroma of double-thick swordfish steaks is wafting over the Wedgwood shed. Our neighbors suspect André and me of obscure violations of local custom. Why, only the other day the First Selectman said—

F.B.

"Hey, schmuck, something the matter with your ears? I need three lights, a pitcher of Busch, a Seven-and-Seven rocks, and a shot of Black Jack up."

Sue-Ann's really angry at me, has been since last week. Gigi was very angry, too. Now, when she comes home late from work, I hear her clogs as she walks all the way around the back of her building to enter her apartment without passing me. I rang her doorbell one night to apologize, but when I told her who was at the door she wouldn't open it. I must have stood there for a good five minutes.

I work at the Dew Drop three nights a week now: Tuesday, Wednesday, and Thursday. That leaves two afternoons free. I usually spend them hanging out at the high-school playing field. I like to watch the cheerleaders practice.

—DION AND FRANKIE BARMELTHE

Suicide Note

BOOKS NOT SO BRIEFLY NOTED
FICTION

THE TRAFALGAR EXCHANGE, by Robert Bedlam (Behemoth Sons; $20.01). The latest lump of prose by this durable yarnspinner concerns the efforts of a Manhattan real-estate developer with one foot in the C.I.A. to evict a rent-controlled tenant who may have been a Nazi. The plot, more complicated than a bank-loan application, involves several murders, the theft of a secret recipe for fudge-chunk cookies, the raising of the Andrea Doria, the women's pro golf tour, several more murders, and the Pope. Unfortunately, it all rings too familiar: the story is identical to Bedlam's previous best seller, "The Runnymede Recital," which itself was a crude reworking of "The Skibinfinch Affidavit," Ludlam's earlier success, which by his own admission was an adaptation of his 1972 thriller, "The Linzertorte Legacy." Although this weighty tome will doubtless anchor thousands of readers firmly to their beach chairs this summer, others may find a cool drink and a light snooze a more relaxing way to await the film version. The title refers to the suspected Nazi's telephone number.

THE PEPPERMAKERS, by E. Grant Vendicott III (Pemmican; $6.95). A lavish, sweeping historical melodrama that spans twenty-six generations of the Van Beaver family, North Carolina's legendary manufacturers of pepper. Vendicott can be forgiven for describing a baseball game in sixteenth-century Europe and for making no mention of the Civil War even though much of the action takes place during the years 1860–1865; factual errors aside, he presents a rich tapestry of ill-conceived fiction. We're not sure why, but Charlton Heston is among those pictured on the dust jacket.

I'M SO TERRIBLY HAPPY

(1932)

[*I carried a torch for Dorothy Perky, as did most of the men at the magazine in her day. Who wouldn't have been taken with her wit, her spirit? That she drank and cursed like a sailor only enhanced her charm. I frequently accosted her at the office water cooler, hoping to trade quips. She usually pretended not to hear me. One day I complimented her, in acerbic fashion, on some wide bracelets she was wearing over heavily gauze-swathed wrists. "What's the matter, Dot?" I asked. "Your bangles giving you blisters?" She slapped me and stormed off. Ah, women! One can't live with them, one can't live without them, or so I'm told.*]

"I'M so terribly happy," she said. "I'm really just so terribly happy, Mother."

"Sure you are, dear," said Cynthia's mother. "It's always like this before the wedding. You're only twenty-two and you've still got your looks, but you'll change."

"Oh, Mother, must you be such an old cynic about love? We shall always be happy, Ethan and I. So what if he's not as clever as all the witty women in your circle? We're both just incredibly in love, and you're all divorced and middle-aged."

"Don't forget jaded and down on our luck."

"Oh, pooh!" said Cynthia. "Why do older people have to be such wet blankets?"

"Don't pout, dear, it's not attractive," her mother scolded. "Oh, you'll be a wet blanket yourself someday, my darling. It takes time. I was in love once, plenty of times. Everybody was. We got over it." She smiled and looked up from her book, a slim volume by Strindberg.

"Mother, you give me the creeps, you really do," said Cynthia. "I thought you'd be happy for me."

"Well, dear, I am happy, if you're happy."

"I was," said her daughter, "until you went and ruined it all for me. Just because you're a dried-up, bitter ex-chorus girl is no reason to make my life miserable."

"May I ask you just one question, Cynthia?"

"Certainly, Mother."

"Why Ethan?"

"Well, because . . . I love him . . . and he loves me, he said . . . and we want to be together forever as husband and wife. For heaven's sake, Mother, why does *anyone* get married?"

"I'm not sure, dear. That's why I was asking."

"I hope you're not implying that we *have* to get married," said Cynthia, dabbing her nails with pink polish.

"Of course not, dear. Of course not."

"Oh, now I'm all mixed up and disillusioned and sardonic," said Cynthia. "Darn you, anyway."

"Better now than later, I always say," her mother said, smirking ever so gently. "And better late than never."

"But I love Ethan. He's going to be head of the firm someday and make just scads of money, and we're going to move to the country and have children and live in a swell little house with shutters and a hammock in the backyard and . . ."

"Good for Ethan and you, dear," said her mother, yawning and laying down her book. "Excuse me, I'm going up to my lonely bed now. Would you turn off the light?"

"Of course, Mother. G'night."

Cynthia slumped in her chair, frowning, and thought to herself, *Maybe I'll call Ethan and explain that I need time to think things over... Maybe he's not the man for me, after all. He is kind of short and dumpy and he doesn't say much or read any books, just the* Evening Graphic, *and actually we don't really have very much to talk about...* She got up, went to the telephone, and dialed Ethan's number. A drowsy voice answered.

"Hello, Ethan? It's me, and I have to say something. I...I...don't think we should get married just yet. I think maybe it's a little too soon. I want to wait awhile...Yes, I know...I'm sure you're disappointed, Ethan, but try to understand. Sleep on it and we can talk tomorrow, O.K.?...Good night, Ethan."

E THAN hung up the phone and rolled over on his side. "Guess who that was," he said to the slim, blond Copa girl next to him. "She wants to call it off."

"Well, I'll be a son of a gun," the girl said. "Are you sad?"

Ethan shook his head and laughed. "I'm so terribly happy," he sighed.

—DOROTHY PERKY

SALON DE NEW YORK
(1929)

Oh, how I love the literary
Parties of the season.
The tone is high, the talk is gay—
It flows with wit and reason.
"How do you like the new O'Neill?"
They'll ask me for a starter.
They'll speak of Shaw and Proust and such,
Not "Getting Gertie's Garter."
The metaphors will flash and fly,
The insights pierce and thrill me.
I'll be too rapt to taste the drink
With which the host will fill me.

(God, did you see that tramp he's with?
Who made her dress, Earl Carroll?
This *is* nice stuff—it must have aged
Within an oaken barrel.)

I'll meet the brainy boys and girls
Who'll tell me what the *nous* is:
Scott, Willie, Edna, Ernest too,
And all their friends and spouses.
They'll speak of heroes, foes, and fads
In language rich and fiery.
Bon mots will fall like April rain.
I'll press each in my diary.

(The second door, just on the right.
Whoops. Steady! Yes, that's so.

Perhaps you shouldn't have mixed Scotch
With rye, gin, and Pernod.
Oh, Zelda, what a jazzy dance—
Hey, watch the bric-a-brac!
My, my, what pretty underpants—
You wouldn't like them back?)

And maybe there will be Someone,
A fair but strangely shy one
Who'll pay me fervent compliments
Straight out of Keats and Byron.
He'll understand, as others can't,
My passions rare and tender.
He'll be more fine, more sensitive,
Than others of his gender.

(Is that your wife? Of course, you can't
Be seen to carry on here.
We'll be discreet—I'll see you in
Five minutes in the john, dear.)

L'ENVOI
And as the guests grow randy,
    unintelligible, and tighter,
I think how much worse they'd behave if
    no one were a writer.

—DOROTHY PERKY

"Herb here just moved to Greenwich and was wondering if you would sponsor him at the club."

THE NAFKEH OF BOCA RATON

(1983)

[Irving Bathsheba Single is probably the most overtly Jewish writer ever to appear in our pages. Certainly, he is the only one who drinks tea from a glass.

Mr. Single's work addresses the Jewish experience in Europe and America. A youthful novel, "This Is My Gut," describes the agonies of maintaining a kosher diet in steerage. Two collections of short stories—"I Can Get It for You for Bupkes" and "For Two Cents What Did You Expect?"—deal with his years as a philosophical fruit peddler and kibitzer on Manhattan's lower East Side.

As his literary reputation grew, Mr. Single left Manhattan for the bosky precincts of Long Island, where the spiritual crises of a rapidly expanding, affluent Jewish community provided the inspiration for works like "The Momzer of Manhasset" and "Third Synagogue on the Right." In 1970, Mr. Single moved to Key West, Florida, where he lives today. Single spends his time deep-sea fishing (marlin are his favorite sport fish), supervising his state-wide string of wine bars called Single's, and writing.

SEVERAL days a week, the wives would feed them, dress them, and drive them to the Maimonides Mall. There, as the women shopped, the three old men whiled away the blazing-hot afternoons in the air-conditioned comfort of Sugarman's Semi-Kosher Delicatessen, to the left of the waterfall and right across the atrium from Ray's Pizza Volare. Sugarman's was seldom busy during the week. Wives would stop in to stock up on rugelach, Hebrew National Salami, or, for their husbands, dietetic cookies; a few widows, past caring about calories, would lunch, between purchases, on Sugarman's "Genuine Turf Cheesecake." The men were left to themselves to nurse their coffees, read the papers, play casino, or argue. They argued about ancient baseball games, dead friends and enemies, Catskill resorts, and the best way to reach obscure corners of New York City, Westchester, and the Island. Once, they'd led busy lives *schlepping* from one obscure corner to another. Now the three lived in huge, appliance-packed homes within walking distance of each other in the same retirement community, Shtetl-in-the-Sun. Their days were filled with shuffleboard, visits to specialists, and waiting to hear from their children. Their nights were filled with ghosts from the past and nightmares of the future.

Sugarman's was a place they understood; Sugarman's reminded them of New York. Flies buzzed around the open bowls of pickles, sour tomatoes, and sauerkraut that graced each table, scenting the chill breeze of the air conditioning with acrid aromas of brine and pickling spices, mouth-watering reminders of the days when they could eat real food. Today, the cards were shuffled and dealt by Feivel, at sixty-nine the baby of the group, formerly a blouse manufacturer and now the group's principal advocate of gambling for small sums "just to keep it interesting." The sums for which they played were very small; it was rare for one of them to win or lose more than a few dollars. This afternoon, Reuben had lost $2.80, which was a lot of money for a retired sewer-and-drain contractor to lose, so it was with relief that he noticed Baruch, whom no one had seen since his wife became ill. He was strolling through the mall dressed in black from head to toe, including an arm band. A two weeks' growth of beard blurred his features.

"Baruch, what's happened, why are you dressed in black here in the Florida sunshine?" said Reuben, dropping his cards on the table face up so the hand could not continue.

"I'm in mourning for my wife," Baruch replied brightly, jauntily seating himself in the table's remaining chair. He reached into the pickle bowl, selected a small, deep-green, very sour pickle and ate it in two bites, smiling as he chewed. Then he called out, "Hey, boychick! Manolo! Pedro! Juan! Whatever your name is! Waiter!"

A dark young man sitting at the end of the counter put down his copy of *Nugget*, meticulously stubbed out his cigarette, and approached the table. He acknowledged Baruch with the slightest of nods.

"Waiter," Baruch said, "you'll get me a cup of Sanka and some dry toast with sugar-free jelly on the side, please. No, wait! On second thought, get me instead real coffee and a slice of that delicious-looking babka I saw on my way in here. The hell with my diet. Mourning is tough."

"You lost weight," said Mo carefully.

"Thanks. Watch, I'll gain it right back after a couple slices babka."

WHY in the world was Baruch so jolly?

"You know," said Feivel, who had gathered up the cards with some annoyance and now shuffled them quietly, hoping to lure Baruch into the game, "the wife and I haven't seen you since the Purim dance at the clubhouse. You both looked great. What happened, if you don't mind my asking?"

"Nah, why should I mind? I remember that party. Funny hats and noise-makers and dancing. Activities and entertainment all the time, like a cruise ship where you never dock. I'm selling and leaving by fall, knock wood."

"Bad memories, sure. Now is a good time to sell," said Mo. A retired C.P.A. and lifelong hypochondriac, Mo was comfortable listening to other people's misery and proffering solemn advice. But Baruch's obvious good humor upset Mo, who secretly hoped he would survive his own wife, and soon. A recently bereaved widower shouldn't be so cheerful. "Losing a wife is a terrible thing," he said sympathetically to Baruch, who smiled broadly as he stirred milk and sugar into his coffee and wolfed a great bite of babka.

"Are you kidding? I'm lucky to be alive. One of us had to go. Thank God it was her, the *nafkeh*," Baruch declared.

Feivel stopped shuffling. "He calls his own wife a *nafkeh*?" he asked incredulously.

"*Nafkeh*, *curveh*, hooker, whore—what do you call a woman who puts a price on her favors? And then doesn't even deliver?" Baruch cried.

"He's gone tutti-frutti," Reuben muttered.

"What do you think, I'm crazy from grief? Relief maybe, but not grief," Baruch said. "*Gottenyu*, it's two weeks since the funeral and I'm still tired. With her, who had time to rest? Every night a party, people over for drinks, every day shopping, by her the national sport of Florida. For twenty-three years before we came here, my first wife—she should rest in peace—and I lived in an apartment the size of a shoe box. This one, from the day she moves in, she's asking me if I really need my den. She wants to turn it into a walk-in closet. And cosmetics! I think she kept two Avon ladies in business with the junk she piled up in the medicine chest. Her cooking? The worst. Small portions, too."

"So, *schnook*, why in the world did

you marry her?" asked Mo, who often asked himself the same question.

Baruch slowly withdrew his coffee-filled saucer from beneath his cup, lifted and tipped it, pouring the coffee into the cup. He mumbled, "She persuaded me."

"How? How in the world?" Even taciturn Feivel was curious.

Baruch returned the saucer to the table and raised his cup. "Reasons of passion," he said dramatically, then popped the last of the babka in his mouth and sipped coffee. "You're all looking at each other, not knowing what to say," he joked, lightly spattering Reuben, Feivel, and Mo with wet babka crumbs. "You're all wondering what I could have seen in her, right? After all, she was no great beauty, and—"

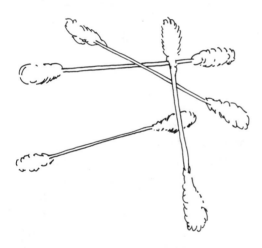

"What are you saying, she looked fine, very... very... My wife used to say that your wife looked very *smart*!" Mo said.

"That's already a different thing, isn't it? 'Smart' is what beauticians say. 'Smart' you can buy with a credit card. Just between you and me and the pickle bowl, I had trouble kissing her at first. But I was so damned lonely, I kept trying anyway. When I moved down here with the first one—she should rest in peace—it was all right. But after she died, I'm in that big house all alone, watching the tele-

vision, clipping coupons to redeem at the Family Mart, staying out of the sun I shouldn't get skin cancer. Some weeks, the only person I talked to was the cleaning lady.

"One day, I'm sitting under an umbrella by the pool, thumbing through the papers, and a woman I've never seen before asks me to rub sunscreen on her back and shoulders. Never seen her before in my life! Maybe I should have known what was up then, but I enjoyed myself. *Oi*, such writhing! Never mind. We idly chat. She's visiting her sister at Casa Anatevka, over on Rokeach Road. You know, I think she told me that so she wouldn't sound like the gold digger she was, because after we were married she never mentioned her sister again. I found out later she rented by the week at a Travel Lodge in Pompano and trolled for husbands at all the condo communities in the area: Farbissen Farms, Meshuggeneh Mansions, Château Geshrei, all of them.

"Pretty soon I was going around with her to social functions, to the dollar-fifty movie matinées, to the dog track, where the both of us gambled, but with my money only. She acted very flirty, very sexy, but that first day with the sunscreen was as far as I got. She says she can't 'give herself' to me unless she's sure I love her. I'm wondering why a grown man should listen to this. But I did. At least with her, I thought, I get out of the house, I even feel young again—you know, in the pants. Good enough for me. But for her, not good enough. She tells me that ever since the loss of her first husband—he should rest in peace —she's gone downhill. Miserable. A familiar story. But a new marriage, someone to *do* for, and she'll pick herself right up again. 'You know who my husband always said I looked just like, don't you?' she says. I says, 'No, who?' She says, 'Morgan Fairchild.'"

"Morgan Fairchild?" Reuben asked.

"Morgan Fairchild. How did she know Morgan Fairchild is my favorite? Was she guessing? Could it have been true? She says, 'The love of a man made me look like Morgan Fairchild once, and it can happen again.' I says, 'I love you, I love you.' But no, it's got to be a wedding or nothing. And no funny business until after the ceremony. So I agree.

"Our wedding night I'll never forget. I was ready to go, but she makes me sleep on the Castro in the den, which was full of her *chozzerai*: clothes, wigs, jewelry, boxes and suitcases. In the morning, she promises, she'll be a new woman. Then she goes into the master bathroom and locks the door.

"I WISH I could tell you I slept like a top and awoke to find a bombshell making my Postum and bran muffin. But when I got up and rushed into the kitchen, there was only her, sitting there at the table looking at some papers—the same one I'd married the night before, only I'd never seen her without her makeup. Jesus H. Christ."

Baruch looked around the table. Three open mouths gaped back at him. Only Feivel could speak.

"No Morgan Fairchild?"

"You should live so long. And as shocked as I must have looked, she looked even more shocked. 'Baruch,' she says, standing up like she hasn't laid eyes on me in a hundred years, 'how are you?' I says, 'Fine, I'm fine.' She looks at me very oddly for a minute, then says very brusquely, 'Sit down, I'll make you breakfast. We have a busy day.'

"'What busy day?' I say. 'This is our honeymoon.'

"'Baruch, darling, we don't want to waste our honeymoon lying around. Eat, we'll get dressed, we'll go to the driving range to hit some golf balls, and on the way there I want to stop at the discount

mall on Federal Highway; Reuben's wife found a place there that's got designer seconds as cheap as Loehmann's in the Bronx. That I've got to see. Here, drink your coffee.'

"'In the morning I take Postum,' I said.

"'Don't be so picky, Baruch. It's decaffeinated. Just drink it. I made myself a bialy with a smear. Take half. I want to get to the mall when it opens.'

"'I like a bran muffin, toasted very dark and dry,' I told her sadly.

"'What's the difference? Honestly, Baruch, is this what you're going to be like? Maybe I made a mistake.'

"'Forgive me, darling, for mentioning this, but I thought—remember—you said—'

"'Spit it out, Baruch, what's troubling you?'

"'You don't look the slightest bit like Morgan Fairchild.'

"'I don't? *Oi vey.*' She ran and looked at herself in the mirror hanging over the wet bar. 'Well, Baruch, what can I tell you? It's going to take a little time. Within the next day or two—'

"'The next day or two?' I ask. I stole a glance at the papers she'd been examining: the deed to the house, a life-insurance policy I'd had for years, and my will.

"'So it'll take a few weeks, Baruch, what are you going to do, sue? Besides, haven't I started to change? Admit it, darlin', I'm already halfway to gorgeous, no?'

"Truthfully, she wasn't. In fact, without her fall in place and her makeup on, she looked like a *golem* with a face-lift. But I continued to hope. I decided to give her a chance.

"The next two weeks were the most exhausting of my life. As if to prove to me she was getting younger and more energetic, every day she woke me up a little earlier than the day before. Every day we *schlepped* around shopping, hit-

"Bellville! Bellville! Next station is Bellville! Bellville! Bellville! Bellville! Next stop: Bellville! Bellville! Next: Bellville! Bellville! Bellville!"

•   •

ting golf balls, sightseeing—what she called 'doing the town.' Then we'd come home. I'd need a nap. She'd try on her newest clothes and discuss with herself in the mirror where we'd go for dinner. Lift a pot to cook a meal? Forget it. Every night was the same story. She would apologize that her transformation wasn't happening fast enough to suit me. Very snotty she was. Then she'd say there'd be no moofky-poofky until I stopped complaining. Who was complaining? So I slept in the den amidst her stuff."

"Why did she never unpack, I wonder," murmured Mo.

"She'd have less closet space if she unpacked," said Feivel. "The blouse industry lives on women like her."

"One night I was lying there on the sofa bed, sure it was the last night of my life. There was no mistaking my wife for Morgan Fairchild; I'd been hoodwinked. I lay there, counting my pulse. The thumping of my heart got louder and louder, deafening. Was I having palpitations? Was I dropping dead? Suddenly, the heartbeats didn't sound like heartbeats anymore. They sounded like laughter, like my first wife's laughter: high, ringing, the kind of laughter that makes you think your fly is open even when it's not. I sat up in bed. Standing there in a little pool of light in the pitch-dark room was my first wife."

"*Gevalt*," Reuben whispered.

"She looked just as I remembered her, in her flannel housecoat, old slippers, curlers, hairnet, and cold cream. She was laughing so loud I thought she would wake the neighbors. With the greatest effort, she calmed down enough to say, 'Don't worry, *bubeleh*, no one can hear me except you; no one can see me except you. Anyway, it's not likely your latest dependent is in a hurry to rush in here. Then the whole thing would look like murder.'

"'Murder?'

"'You don't realize the position you're in, do you? You've lived longer than any of the others. You've almost got her beat. She hasn't had such a victim since the lascivious furrier she snared in Odessa caught onto her right before the marriage. Him she shot, I think.'

"'Even on the other side you're looking out for me.'

"'You always laughed at me, Baruch, because I was such a worrier. I checked on where our doctors went to school; I wouldn't even use a dry cleaner without a reference. Why should I be different now? When you remarried, I snooped around, you shouldn't end up with a harpie. This woman has been widowed three times in the last four years alone. Each time the grabby old chippie got the domicile and a good chunk of the estate. Honestly, Baruch, you should have been more careful.'

"I didn't want to believe her, but I knew she was telling the truth. I asked, 'How did the other three die?'

"'Each one she promised that once they were married she'd turn overnight into the spitting image of his sexual ideal—usually a *shiksa*, what else? When the husbands figured out it was a lie, they dropped dead. The first, a retired pharmacist from Del Ray, thought she'd become Debra Paget; the second, a Boca dentist, thought she'd be like the young Betty Grable, and the plastic surgeon from West Palm was expecting Diana Ross. He did your wife's breast implants and tummy tucks for free, too. You know what those cost?'

"'Where was she before coming to Boca?'

"'First of all, she's been in Florida for at least twenty years. People get suspicious about all her marriages, and she has to move on. You know, she doesn't look bad when you consider she's two hundred-something years old.'

"'Two hundred—'

"'At least. She matches descriptions of the *Nafkeh* of Lvov, who was widowed twenty-six times between 1768 and 1791, the *Nafkeh* of Lisbon, who broke Sephardic hearts in the 1870s and '80s, and the *Nafkeh* of Cedarhurst, who disappeared in the late fifties after being widowed twice in each of the Five Towns.'

"'What do I have to do to survive?'

"'You must outlast her. She is trying to kill you with recreation, but it's wearing her out as well. Keep it up! It's a duel to the finish now. Good luck, Baruch, you sweet *nudnik*. Get some rest.' And with a great snort of laughter, my first wife disappeared and I was sitting in the dark with the cartons.

"I MUST have found new strength through fear. Instead of dropping dead as I thought I would that night, I ran around. I took my bride to bingo games, mambo lessons, a full day's excursion on a fishing boat. I threw away her Dramamine before we got on board the fishing boat. Boy, did she puke! Six weeks after my first wife appeared to me, the second one and I went to Epcot Center. I insisted on driving there and back the same day to save the price of a motel room. When we got home, I turned on the light and took a good look at her. Crow's-feet. Wrinkles. Veins. Her fancy hairdo had collapsed on top of itself, and dark roots mixed with gray showed through the yellow floss. With all the conviction I could muster, I forced a smile and a hearty '*Nu?* How's about a nightcap?'

"She looked at me with eyes widening in amazement. She shook her head and lurched away. I heard her stumble into the master bedroom and slam the door. She was on the brink of exhaustion. Unfortunately, so was I.

"The end came one morning on Collins Avenue. I told her I'd heard about a little discount shop that sold generic perfumes at cost. Cost! In her heart she must have known she lacked the strength to make the trip, but she couldn't say no to the bargain. So off we went. I'm feeling a little faint, but even so I keep *noodging* her about the early-bird aerobics classes that were starting up by the pool at six A.M. Just what she needs. The weather was in the eighties but breezy, so she was wearing her mink bolero jacket. We're crossing the street when suddenly her legs start to wobble; she can't balance on her high-heeled espadrilles. She keels over. I get her across the street and sit her down on the pavement in the shadow of a shopwindow awning. There's a sharp noise like a window shade snapping up. Her face-lift had collapsed. Under her chin, there appears a wattle as big as a turkey's. Her whole face seems to melt down into her neck, chin spilling into her bosom, arms and legs going limp and shrivelling to nothing. 'Two hundred years old,' I said. 'Two hundred years. You're no Morgan Fairchild, but you're not doing bad for two hundred years.'

"'More than two hundred,' she managed to say hoarsely. 'Much more. And I'll be back.'

"Her head disappeared along with the rest of her. Except for a wisp of smoke and the smell of hairspray, she was gone. I was crouched over a pile of clothes without a person inside them. The *Nafkeh* of Boca Raton was no more. Are you going to drink your water, Mo?" Without waiting for an answer,

Baruch took the glass and drained it.

Reuben had forgotten his $2.80 loss. Mo's coffee was cold. Feivel remembered to take his insulin tablets.

"What did you do with her things?" Mo said.

"I returned some to the stores. She'd never even taken some of it out of the boxes. The tags were still on. In the den I found deeds to her other houses, a couple passports under different names, and wedding photographs with the three other husbands, all done by the same photographer, Lipschitz of Lauderdale. She probably got a special rate. I also found a crumbling Portuguese marriage license from 1888 and what I think is a Ukrainian caterer's bill from 1763."

"That old, and she pops up right here in Boca Raton. *Oi gevalt*," said Mo.

"You said it," said Feivel.

"*Oi gevalt* is right," said Baruch, wondering if he'd ever feel the same about Morgan Fairchild.

"You can say that again," said Reuben.

"*Oi gevalt*," said Baruch.

—IRVING BATHSHEBA SINGLE
(Translated, from the Yinglish, by Elie Ailey.)

•

BOOKS NOT SO BRIEFLY NOTED
FICTION

VALLEY OF THE VALPACKS, by Samsonette Lark (Shockin' Books; $19.84). In the first chapter of this new work by the author of "Hollywood Swine," a young Brooklyn street tough named Danny Vuitton is accidentally zipped into a garment bag by his parents and plopped onto the freight car of a train heading west. Although he nearly dies from exposure, the boy survives to become the softside-luggage king of Los Angeles. Along the way, there are some vividly etched scenes of life among the rich and glamorous denizens of the suitcase industry.

WITHIN THE CONTEXT OF NOT HARVARD

(1975)

[George H.M.S. Twee came to us in the mid-seventies, at roughly the same time as droll Ian Brassière, saucy Victoria Gnu, and exotic Jemima Kinflick. Once, while working with George on one of his pieces, I asked, "Now, George, is your protagonist on the boat or is he only dreaming he's on the boat? Which is it, man?" The same question, more or less, can be asked of much of George's work. This rather formal casual introduces Mr. Twee's most enduring character and, as usual, fills us with the sense that, no matter how befogged we may be, the author knows what he is doing and is almost certainly extremely bright.]

The Pitch

YOU better not pout. You better not cry. You better not fight. I am telling you why:

Billy Beefalo is coming to town.

Billy Beefalo is coming to your neighborhood, in fact. Driving down your local streets. Passing by your favorite shops. Perhaps, for a lark, stopping at a sweet shoppe in your neighborhood to buy a small York Peppermint Pattie, for Billy *loves* a York Peppermint Pattie, unwrapping its glossy, silver-foil wrapping and placing it on his tongue and letting it sit there, tasting cooler as it melts, a sensory paradox—that is, the Pattie tasting cooler while it is actually getting warmer—that has fascinated Billy to the point of amusing him. But I digress. Billy Beefalo may even drop by your living room for a personal, and I mean *really up close and personal*, visit. If you're lucky. Of course, he is coming to visit with the understanding that you did not attend Harvard. Billy would feel better, to tell the truth, if you were not acquainted with Cambridge, Massachusetts. What would please Billy the most? Funny I should ask. Billy Beefalo would be most pleased if, when he arrives, you were to drop to your knees and confess your utter spiritual vacuity, your profound stupidity, your surprisingly blissless ignorance. Then he would like it if you were to beseech him piteously, yet courteously, for his explications of, and advice on, not only your petty life and its petty problems, but also those that arise out of mere consciousness in a world so much of which is neither Cambridge, Massachusetts, nor Manhattan. There is no need to be afraid. Billy Beefalo wants to help. Tell him your honest feelings. Really.

The Warm-up

Here is the joke Billy Beefalo uses to warm up new participants in his self-reorientation, enhanced self-knowledge, self-fashion-shakeout, and self-makeover sessions: Two men are seated next to each other on the commuter train from Grand Central to Dobbs Ferry. They chat over too meeny Martoonis, then one of them asks rhetorically, "You went to Harvard, didn't you?" His companion replies, with swiftly summoned languor, "Well, actually, I did. How did you know?" The first man says, "Simple. You've mentioned the place eight times in the last half hour." The Harvard man, not to be outdone by some yahoo wearing, he quickly notices, a *tie bar* (can you *imag-

ine?), says, "Well, since you mention schools, I'll wager you went to _____ (Billy changes the name of the institution depending on his audience in order to maximize his bon-mot impact)!" The other fellow says, "Say, that's true. How did you know?" The Harvard man says, "Simple. I saw your class ring when you were picking your nose." The jollity produced by this story ensures that everything runs smoothly. The participants in the session are soon ready to reveal themselves to Billy. Of course, by this time the session is usually over and Billy must be off.

The Complication

The Subterraneos, Lucinda and Ramon, are planning a party that they want to be *the* party, the standard against which all other gatherings this season will be judged. Billy Beefalo has been hired as a consultant. He insisted, as usual, that he be paid in custom-made shirts, his embroidered initials hidden in a place he will *never* reveal. The Subterraneos have been planning their fête for much longer than Billy has been around them. Naturally, the guest list is what takes the most time and is probably the least trivial aspect of what many people, all of whom would be *wrong*, consider a trivial enterprise, the throwing of a party.

Does one *throw* a party or does one *give* a party? If thrown, at what or whom? If given, to what or whom? When the Subterraneos plan a party, they conceive of it as something *thrown*: hurled, heaved, chucked, pegged, flung, tossed, lobbed, catapulted, cast. This is how they wish and expect their parties to feel, like an explosive, transitive act, not a passive entity, a *gift*—feh! To whom is this putative gift being given? The guests? For

"This is my husband, Harley. He's an unspeakable pig."

what? For showing up to eat your food, drink your liquor, grind stains and fallen canapés and bits of grime and soot that come from the bottoms of their shoes into your carpet? A party is a *gift* to your guests? *Don't make me laugh!*

But I digress.

What does a party feel like to you? Does it feel like something you throw or something you give? Don't be shy.

Good.

The Subterraneos are going to a good deal of trouble to assemble the best people for their party. In this way, what might otherwise be thought of as a casual get-together of friends for their mutual enjoyment will take on the importance of an *event*. The assemblage of correct people, in the sense of their being the correct people *for this assemblage*, will become a shared myth of great power. In this sense, the trivial is not merely raised to the level of myth but, in the raising, becomes even more trivial. Thus the party takes on the symmetry of paradox, but I digress again.

Billy Beefalo looks over the Subterraneos' guest list and approves. The Wainscottings, Winty and Minty, are on it. The Walpurgisnachts are on it. I. P. Free and I. P. Daily are on it, as are Dolores de Lovely, Seth and Kitty Mofongo-O'Hara, and the Belle-Tacos, Lupe and Gaylord, who have already agreed to come provided they can bring Lee Taco-Belle, their cousin, who is visiting from out of town. What guests! What panache! What chic! What a lot of cocktail wieners you'll need, Billy Beefalo does not forget to remind the expectant hosts.

The Party and Conclusion

That the party was a success was attested to by all who attended. There was plenty to eat, plenty to drink, and plenty of Good and Plenty for dessert. Guests circulated freely within the sparsely furnished rotunda area of the Subterraneos' loft. The talk was scintillating and everybody looked great, especially Dolores de Lovely, who looked, as one wag put it, delightful to hold, and Gaylord Belle-Taco, who had refurbished his pompadour just for the occasion. So far as the Subterraneos' neighborhood (or context) was concerned, they had touched all the bases.

Except one. They had not invited the Aspire sisters, Emily and Anomaly, who live all alone in the big Aspire mansion, Toast Points, which sits grandly, all thirty-six rooms of it, including six bathrooms, sauna, wbf, and carport, on a sloping lawn that sweeps back and up

J. Nagy

from the main street of the neighborhood (or context), Old Money Street. The Aspire sisters are the remnants of the grandest family for miles around, and they both have enjoyed the educational opportunities and orthodontia that are two of the birthrights of aristocracy. It was rumored that they had passed through or, in any case, been pretty close to Cambridge, Massachusetts, many years before when as teen-agers they hijacked the family Bentley and chauffeur, forcing the latter to drive the former, with them in it, to a fried-clam place in Ipswich of which the sisters had heard. They might even have driven right by you-and-I-and-Billy-Beefalo-know-what Yard. And Billy Beefalo *would* not, *could* not, have stood for that.

—GEORGE H.M.S. TWEE

BOOKS NOT SO BRIEFLY NOTED

FICTION

THE OX-BRIDGE INCIDENT, by Evelyn Wow (Viking Funeral Press; $18.95). A balanced, gracious novel of English aristocracy between the wars, this is a companion piece to "Chariots for Hire," the author's comic lark about London cabdrivers during the same period. Here, Wow transports us to a world of nice lawns, nubby tweeds, and buffed young men grabbing each other beneath their subfusk, while on the Continent the hourglass begins to run out, or something like that.

BETH, YOU ARE MY WOMAN NOW, by Melva Toast (Fjord and Peckerwood; $19). Yet another sweeping novel of the Babylonian captivity, this one with a romantic twist. Kalifa, wealthy "even beyond dreams of avarice," falls in love with Beth, a young maiden with "lips so red they were as berries." He pursues her relentlessly and finally purchases her, only to find that he cannot really possess her unless he is nice. Desperate to win her soul, he sells all his other females (except his cook and cleaning women) and, in a somewhat less than unexpected role reversal, pledges himself in service to her. She laughs at him, and he cuts out her heart, cooks it in a casserole, and serves it to company. Nothing new here. There are several effective descriptions of what it must have been like to walk up all those steps on the ziggurats, but someone should tell Miss Toast that they didn't have designer jeans then.

GENERAL

ANOTHER WORD MEANING GLORY, by Zutto Premangé (Interlingus; $11.95).

This history of the Roget family and the Thesaurus that bears their name is an inspiring tale of superhuman determination in the face of long years of cross-indexing. It is also a searing indictment of the netherworld that is reference-text publishing. A portion of this book appeared, translated into synonyms, in this magazine.

THE SEMIOTIC COOKBOOK, by Rosie Name (Cleanth Books; $35.40). The recipes in this handsome and elaborate book are as tantalizing to decipher as the results are to eat. No lists of ingredients or preparatory steps are provided. Instead, the pseudonymous author gives us riddles, parables, maps, and anecdotes about fictitious chefs. The diligent reader will learn how to prepare such delicacies as Madeleines Maybe Baby, Wracked Lamb, Positively Short Bread, Word Salad, Trout Quintet, and Seven Types of Yakitori.

BLOOMSBURY KIND OF GUY, by Guy Fusspot (Dipsy Doodle Books; $12.95). Guy Fusspot is a distant cousin of Lytton Strachey and a nephew of Vanessa Bell, lived two blocks away from Leonard and Virginia Woolf, and met E. M. Forster once at a jumble sale. An inveterate stroller, the young Fusspot liked to take the air in all weathers, and the routes he favored are described here in more detail than one might wish. What makes these dimly recalled memoirs of more than passing interest is the fact that Fusspot did not know that many of the people he glimpsed through the windows of their homes were writers, even though whenever he saw them they were hunched over desks.

ANNALS OF SCANSION

GIVING GOOD FOOT—1

(1962)

[In the fall of 1962, a young man from Princeton ("the University as well as the town," he painstakingly pointed out), New Jersey, joined our magazine. His name was John Mc-Phumpher, and he began as a staff writer without portfolio, which is to say he was placed under my supervision with the understanding that I'd keep him out of trouble and teach him our ways at leisure. I suggested he do a piece about poetry, a form of interest at our magazine chiefly because poems are, for the most part, larger than drawings but smaller than articles and so fill odd spaces well. McPhumpher produced a four-part work on the subject of metrics, which, though superbly written, was so obsessively detailed that one of our fact checkers suffered an emotional episode. After the first part of the article appeared, from which this excerpt is drawn, the general consensus around the office was that John was a writer who'd not yet found his voice. The following week, sadly, I lost the final proofs of the next three installments in a mishap involving the office hot plate and some lighter fluid.]

THE man at the head of the large lecture hall seems completely at home, striding back and forth behind the lectern, gesturing with his pointer at a couplet scrawled with the flattened side of a short piece of chalk on the large green board. His full beard, tousled hair, and beefy, wool-knit Rooster tie closely match his baggy tweed suit in both color and texture. All exude the bituminous aroma of the man's well-used pipe, the stem of which, chewed and pocked with years of caked spittle, perches in his breast pocket, awaiting the end of the lecture. The students in the first four rows of the hall, seven in number, take notes attentively. Occasionally, one of them holds up an arm to ask a question or answer one of the lecturer's. In the rearmost six rows, some hundred and forty-three students who must pass this course to graduate wait for the lecture to end. A few talk softly. One reads the campus newspaper, which he keeps in his lap, discreetly out of the lecturer's sight. Eight shade their eyes with their hands and doze lightly.

The lecturer lectures on. "Fascinatingly, the variety of verse forms that we have come to take for granted in English poetry is a recent development. Now, in Old English there was only one verse form, a single line containing four equally stressed syllables with a pause in the middle, which we call a medial caesura. All these restrictions put a heck of a crimp in the style of a lot of our early poets, and there's no telling what they could've done if they'd been able to use, say, sprung rhythms or free verse. Of course, that couldn't have happened in a million years back then, since the principal linking element in poetry wasn't rhyme at all, but alliteration. How about that? Pretty wild, huh? The number of unstressed syllables in a line varied according to a set of rules so complicated that it is not yet fully understood, even by me. We'll be dealing with that mystery next week. So finish 'Beowulf.' If you really want to have some fun, try reading it aloud. Don't worry about the pronunciation; just take a shot and have fun with it. And remember: Breathe! Render unto the caesura that which is the caesura's!" Groans, a paper airplane, and a smattering of diffident applause greet the joke as class ends.

THE lecturer's name is Ronald Footling, and he teaches poetry appreciation at a number of night schools in and around Indianapolis, Indiana. I met him at a symposium on the future of the sonnet held at Princeton University, which is near my home in Princeton, New Jersey. Footling has taught and done research at the University of Texas in Austin, Alfred University in Hornell, New York, the University of the Redlands in the state of Washington, and Balliol College, Oxford. The work on which his reputation rests, a series of monographs about the metric tendencies of poets as dissimilar as Robert W. Service, Gerard Malanga, and Ezra Pound, has been done over the last eight years, since he settled in Indianapolis with his wife, Elizabeth Barrett Footling, and their son, e. e.

A big, seamed, fuzzy man, Footling has a consuming enthusiasm for scansion that infrequently overpowers the indifference and downright torpor the subject usually inspires in others. "I knew what I wanted to do when I was a teenager and read 'The Raven' for the first time," he says as we walk to his car. "Poe really got to me. Not only the dank atmosphere, but the sheer feat—no pun intended—of sustaining trochaic octameter over a narrative of that length. Whew! Just thinking about it makes me feel all goose-bumpy inside. Anyway, that opened the door for me. Pretty soon, I was scanning everything from Richard Crashaw—my dad had a big volume of Crashaw's stuff, and I used to sneak it up to my bedroom to read by flashlight when I was only eight or nine—to the Burma Shave rhyming signs you'd see on the bigger roads around here. You'd be amazed at how many different metric patterns there are, just in English verse alone, let alone foreign forms, where they do some really wild things—like

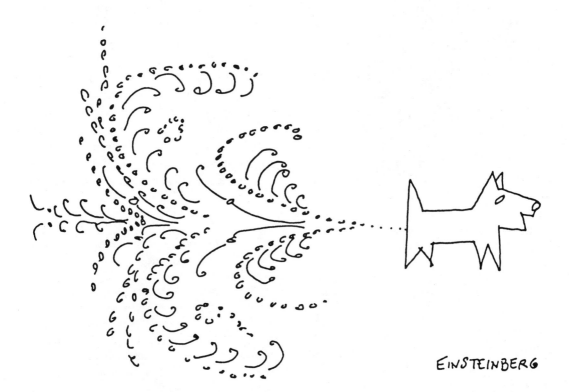

EINSTEINBERG

the French with their wacky Alexandrines all the time! Even in our own mother tongue, you've got the dactyl, the anapest, the trochee, your iamb—everybody knows the iamb, Shakespeare used it—and, of course, the spondee. And that's just for openers. Here's my car. It's a Honda Prelude. I got it in honor of Wordsworth. It's the only car on the market named after a poem."

THE roads around Indianapolis cut through Cretaceous shale beds, pre-Ordovician sedimentation, and many planned housing communities. In these parts, prehistoric beasts of immense size and variety gave up their mineral components to the intertongued strata of mud, old car parts, and Mesozoic gook upon which the modern city and its suburbs are built. Ronald Footling pays the landscape no attention at all.

As we drive, he explains the diversification of English verse forms from 1400 (the Great Vowel Shift) to the present day ("Papa Oom Mow Mow"). His own theory, which has caused two departments to deny him tenure and one irate colleague to call him "a dumb, stupid moron" in public, is that the sestina and not, as most scholars believe, Edmund

Spenser is the logical ancestor of the Spenserian stanza. "All Spenser did was copy an Alexandrine and add a little more to the end of the stanza," Footling opines truculently. "Would you credit a painting to the guy who frames it? Jeez!"

Forty-five minutes later, the shuddering halt of the car shatters the glassy-eyed trance into which I've fallen, having listened to Footling trace the development of the Petrarchan sonnet from its invention in Italy to its wide adaptation by the sixteenth-century English poets, pointing out as he went that the influence of the octave-sestet line scheme held sway far longer than had been previously assumed.

We have arrived at the Footling home. Footling threatens, or rather promises, to show me the documentation for his controversial views after lunch. Still exhausted by the arduous flight to Indianapolis from Princeton, New Jersey, where my home is, I ask if we might continue our discussions at a later time. Ronald Footling cheerfully agrees to take me back to my hotel before lunch, though his wife, a wiry, fair-haired woman with a tendency to wear earplugs when in the same room as her husband, is not pleased to see me leave so soon. I promise to be back with a fresher mind. "It won't be fresher for long," she remarks as Footling heads out to the garage, talking about something I can't hear. Catching up with him, I realize that he is explaining once again his reason for buying a Honda Prelude.

—JOHN MCPHUMPHER

[*This is the first part of the first part of a four-part article. In this part's remaining sixteen thousand words, Footling explains why he bought a Prelude to a tollbooth attendant, the driver of a truck waiting next to him at a traffic light, and the server at Indy Ray's Pizza Pit Stop. Later, he delights his graduate seminar in American poetry when he recites "The Cremation of Sam Magee" standing on one foot.*]

TRYST AND SHOUT
(1967)

[*At my behest, John Beebleberry agreed to speak with McPhumpher during the latter's researches for the metrics series. For five years after the interview, Beebleberry wrote nothing but art criticism. This is the first poem he completed after his unwilling hiatus.*]

Moments passed, undeniably, and with more of that old hurry-
    up-and-wait.
The takeout menu on the table between us, our mood growing
    more fractious.
Sharp, this change, as a hunger pang—or, of course, the bev-
    eled edge of melancholy.
One thing led to another, so it almost seemed, the doors tum-
    bling sequentially open,
As in that Cocteau film we saw last week in Millerton.
And then, I was remembering, we went to Friendly's.

Don't be upset, you joke, there will still be time.
There always was, time, that is, for, or on the side of, us, and,
    finally,
Time to bring the cake in from the rain.
Still in this circumstance the very room soars so vaulted and
    granular
That I'm sprawling, also tangled, in gummy weeds and scented
    fondants
That you once might have banished with your particular yawn.
O but the way you look when you read that magazine!

Our day had been so mossied, there by the pond.
Then the peonies' brief flaring curtsey at dusk.
Now in some sad room upstairs a guest long-forgotten darns
    his drawers
and listens, trembling, for the dinner-gong.
Or am I that guest?

For God's sake calm down, you scream, prettily enough.
I tell you about the guest and the frenzied wings in the attic.
You say, but this is a ranch house
And your clean logic
          slices
                through my soliloquies.
I'm healed, convinced, intellectual again,
Realizing, as if for the first time, that Bucci's closes late on
    Saturdays.
We'll open the door together, quietly note the clotted moon,
You and I, on our way to dinner.
Or else we'll boil up basmati rice with lentils
And all night we'll dream of India, the silvered continent,
And its stately embassies, processional, on East Sixth Street.
                          —JOHN BEEBLEBERRY

GREETINGS, NAMES

(1986)

[*In 1976, Roger Devill took over the authorship of the Christmas poem from Franklin Stove Sullivan, who had written it for over forty years. When Roger offered, with his usual vehemence, what he called his "humble potlatch of rhyme" for this collection, I leapt both at his offer and out of harm's way.*]

Once again the season lowers,
Slushy streets and snowball throwers;
Carols where you least expect 'em,
Halls that pall 'cause you ain't decked 'em.
Christmas specials spawned in summer,
One more time, "The Little Drummer."
Obligations pounding at you,
Screaming kids demanding that you
Name eight reindeer, plus or minus.
Dasher? Let's see. Snoopy? Linus?
Partridges once more in pear trees,
Skaters, hope their derrières freeze.
Blaring trumpets, crashing cymbals,
Joy to Bloomie's, Macy's, Gimbels.
Frantic shoppers, cards at ready,
Make believe they're J. Paul Getty,
Out of sorts and out of cash . . .
Now's the time to have a bash;
A good old blowout, nothing arty,
Everyone can join this party.
Before you drop, before you wear down,
Come on over, let your hair down!
Friends and neighbors, glad to see you!
Barbara Jordan, Nick Fotiu
Bon soir, Bergens! Edgar, Polly,
Hi, Picasso, Hello, Dali,
Put your coats down by Madonna
(Uh-oh, hope that's Sean Penn on her),
Thrilled to have you here, we mean it,
Mr. Mister, Mister Peanut,

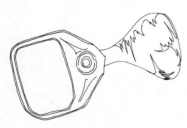

Dragon, Carmen; Dragon, Ollie,
Steinberg, Saul and Goldberg, Molly.
Arthur Prysock, Arthur Frommer,
Curt LeMay, our favorite bomber.
Yuppies, yahoos, Yurts and *yentas*,
Mingle with the de la Rentas.
Richard Simmons, fey *aerobiste*,
Euell Gibbons, who eats no beast.
Charo's pregnant; who beguiled her?
Cornell's Wilde but Thornton's Wilder.
Dance the samba, do the hustle,
Helga Testorf, Bertrand Russell.
Richards, Mss. Renée and Mary,
One so straight, one quite contrary.
Major Deegan, General Tire,
Bernie Goetz, *please* hold your fire.
Rajneesh Baghwhan, exiled swami,
Milton Berle, *beaucoup* salami.
Arthur Treacher in a bowler,
Sydney Greenstreet, Sidney Toler,
Sylvia Sidney, Sylvia Fine,
Arlene Francis, what's *her* line?
Beauteous women, men of parts,
All our fave non-martial Arts:
Farmer, Shamsky, Carney, Deco,
Say hello to José Greco.
Solzhenitsin and Yvonne,
Gulag-guy, meet Goolagong.
Come in from the snow and hailstorm,
Charlie Farrell, Margie (Gale Storm).
Shecky Greene, a born-to-clown guy,
Caryl Chessman, "*Don't sit down*, guy!"
Brothers Grimm and brothers Mayo,
Hail the Wolfe boys, Nero, Beo.
Channing, Carol; Channing, Stockard,
One and all are getting snockered.
Horton Foote, who wears no socks,
Timothy Bottoms, Wally Cox.

Fill the glass, this night shows promise,
Someone wake up Dylan Thomas.
Tallulah says it's too, too thrilling,
Dancing slow with Lionel Trilling.
Beer for Beattys Clyde and Zelmo,
Grog for Admiral Zumwalt (Elmo),
Toast the Dons (Ameche? Fagen?),
And the Rons (McDonald? Reagan?).
Emile Verban, Stanley Hack,
Zooey, Franny, Mabel, Mack,
Charlie Chaplin and his Oona,
Charlie Weaver, Charlie Tuna.
That reminds me, check the pantry,
Food for Elmers Fudd and Gantry,
Snacks for Max and Marlin Perkins,
Holding out on slaw and gherkins,
Goose and turkey, stuffing, sauce.
Eat like Kate Smith, eat like Hoss;
The less that's left, the less to clean up.
Eat the pâté and terrine up,
'Til you're stuffed up to the gills, son,
'Til you look like old Don Wilson.
Bring the Cheddar, slice the Stilton
(Taylor-made for Nicky Hilton),
Crackers with the Camembert
(Ginger Snaps for Fred Astaire),
Goat and Gouda, head, Havarti,
For Rachel Carson, Rico Carty.
Fill your plate with curd and rennet,
Benny Bengough, Constance Bennett.
Noël Coward's a mozzarell' man,
Laughing Cow for Lillian Hellman.
What's the matter, feel *facochte*?
Not to worry, pick a doctor:
Gooden, Mengele, or Schweitzer.
One's no fun, the others nicer.
Idi Amin, how they hanging?
No, don't answer. Who's that banging
On the roof, is it Kriss Kringle,
Sack a-bulge and bells a-jingle?
Give the old roué a toddy,
One more round for everybody!
One more time, a little drink-o;
Hemingway is good and stinko.
He did *what* into the punchbowl?!?
Pardon me, here comes my lunch, whole.
What's the ruckus? Who's the red-ass?
Just benign but crusty Ed As-
Ner, but trouble could be starting;

Time for friends to be departing.
Alfred Gingold's nurse is coming,
Johnny Buskin's hugging plumbing.
Rambo's shooting all the Asians
(Really, some guests try one's patience).
Hope you wake up home and thriving
(Monty Clift should not be driving).

Morning comes, *amis* and *paisans*,
Heads pikestaffed and breath like bisons.
Gone the raconteur, the funster;
Mirror's showing Herman Munster.
Whom did I insult, let's think now;
What I need's a little drink now.
Somewhere Dottie P. is smiling,
S.J., E.B., A.J. filing
Copy that I wish I'd written,
Funny stuff galore befittin'
Days of dash, panache, and élan,
Of Lefty Grove and Grover Whelan.
What the hell, this Yule is finished,
Mon odeur un peu diminished.
Light the fire, hope this log'll
Clear the air of suspect dogg'rel.
What's the chance of one more pun?
Pickens? Trevor? (Slim to Nunn).
                              —ROGER DEVILL

BOOKS NOT SO BRIEFLY NOTED
MYSTERY

TROUBLE IS MY GLISCHKII by Stumo "Pete" Palloukha (Barnstable & Kvass New Sleuth Series; $9.95). Novice mystery writers have maintained an energetic search for new handicaps with which to make their detectives stand out from the crowd. There have been blind sleuths, those confined to bed or wheelchair, and those forced to operate in any number of hostile *milieux*—framed and on the run, female in a male environment, disguised as a zebra—that hampered their effectiveness and therefore made their ultimate triumph that much more satisfying. Now comes Favvyes Plyetkin, a Latvian private eye who lives in Darien, Connecticut, and speaks no English. This may be carrying a good thing too far. It strains our credulity beyond breaking to ask us to accept a detective who can interrogate suspects only with the aid of a dictionary. Plyetkin, stoical, plodding, and meticulous, spends the better part of thirty pages on a wild-goose chase generated entirely by his having confused the English words "provenance" and "sinkhole." The climactic trial scene, with its Latvian answers and footnoted English translations, can be mighty slow going. One would like to see the author try something a little less freighted with novelty for its own sake, or, as his detective might say, *"Zhdoob na kveliotn, ha-ha!"*

RULES OF THE GAME

Effective immediately, three copies of form 277-B *must* be submitted with every proposed change of venue in advance.
—*Memo from the N.Y.C. Board of Education.*

If it's just proposed, it *has* to be in advance, retardo.

• •

ELEMENTARY SCHOOL EVENTS

(Unless otherwise noted, elementary schools are open Mondays through Fridays from around 9 to between 3 and 3:15.)

ASSEMBLY PLAY—Mrs. Esposito's kindergarten students present "The Importance of Eating Breakfast," a one-act play with original music about nutrition, with students appearing as toast, eggs, and corn flakes. The Dance of the Muffins is the tastiest part of this show; the rest is rather half-baked. June 10, 8:45 A.M. (P.S. 234, 335 Greenwich Ave.).

CAKE SALE—Miss Merritt's second-graders, Mrs. Blum's third-graders, and Mr. Spinnoli's special students are selling brownies, sheet cake, toll-house cookies, gingerbread men, M & M's, and tropical fruit punch to raise money for their end-of-year picnic. At 4 P.M., several door prizes will be raffled off, including a Muppet lunch box and a Duncan Pro Model Yo-Yo. June 7, 2:30–4:30 P.M. (P.S. 166, 132 W. 89th St.).

FINGER-PAINTING EXHIBIT—Jennifer Foster and Jimmy Fuchs and Barbara Korn and Dorothy McConkey and Benjamin Rosenwald and Sidney Washington and Hank and Bobby Winters all get their paintings on the bulletin boards in Miss Cavallo's social-studies room, and lots of other kids don't get theirs put up at all. June 3–21 (P.S. 6, 45 E. 81st St.).

PENMANSHIP CONTEST RESULTS—Works ranging from descriptions of summer vacations to lists of barnyard animals demonstrate third- and fourth-grade classes' writing skills. Blue-ribbon winner Jesus Ortiz's "Alphabet" in Bic Pen on white lined paper includes both capital and small letters and demonstrates unusual control for a left-handed nine-year-old. June 19–21. (P.S. 208, 21 W. 111th St.).

OUR

STRANGE

BEDFELLOWS

Politics

*O*UR *first editor, Ramp, was uninterested in politics. He was curious about a number of particularly vivid personalities—Jimmy Walker, whose wardrobe and flair he admired, Fiorello LaGuardia, whose mixed ethnic ancestry and close identification with the working class embodied so much of what Roontz feared, and Winston Churchill, who everyone at the magazine thought spoke beautifully —but for the most part he viewed politicians with equal measures of suspicion and contempt, surely appropriate predispositions to hold toward a group composed largely of lawyers.*

In the early seventies, our second editor, Shpot, became aware of this country's war in Asia. A little later, he began to brood about nuclear weaponry, a subject about which he'd thought little since 1946, when he edited a long piece about Nagasaki. Soon his agitated conscience, not to mention that of my esteemed (or at least very serious) colleague, John-Boy Shill, had transformed our Notes and Comment feature from a gentle meditation on topics of the moment into a weekly sermonette whose moral energy was such that many of our readers began turning directly to the reviews (after skimming the drawings).

Old current events seem older than just about anything, so the selections in this chapter are of recent vintage (I have avoided our more apocalyptic pronouncements, which seemed to me more appropriate in the mouths of sandaled prophets than in the glistening pages of our magazine).

After poetry, McPhumpher's next assignment was politics. He produced a first-rate, six-part article on voting booths that was to have been excerpted in this book. Unfortunately, final proofs of the excerpt were destroyed during a misadventure involving a larcenous youth (disguised as a Ray's Pizza Express delivery boy) and his miniature water cannon.

DOWNWARD AND BACKWARD WITH THE ARTS
TERRIBLE, SWIFT BLUE PENCIL
(1979)

[Nothing gets our libertarian dander up like the issue of censorship. While our pages never carry an oath stronger than "Phooey!" or a noun more explicit than "thigh," we see no reason for our readers to be deprived of other venues in which to waste their eyesight.]

FRED Neachy has the biggest desk at Neachy Toyota in Shoe Trees, Long Island. Virtually covered with executive statuary, the desk at first glance reminds one of a serious model railroader's layout. Among the eye-grabbers is an Iwo Jima inkwell with a tri-colored ball-point firmly in the grasp of the flag-raising leathernecks, a soldered nut-and-bolt sculpture of a batter entitled "Yaz," and a pink ceramic elephant balancing on one foot and waving a top hat. Set apart from these objects is a triangular length of finished pine bearing a legend in white type on a black plastic plate. Mr. Neachy is an alderman on the Shoe Trees Board of Estimate, a notary public, and the coach of the local Pee Wee Full-Contact Karate Club, but the job most important to him is that of president of the Shoe Trees School Board and it is this high office to which the sign on his desk refers. It says: "THE BOOK STOPS HERE."

WE FIRST became aware of Mr. Neachy's good offices when he was quoted in connection with the controversy over the Shoe Trees School Board ban of the Clement C. Moore classic, "'Twas the Night Before Christmas." In speaking for the board, Mr. Neachy explained that the reason for its decision was the poet's use of the words *courser, flash, breast, Vixen,* and *Blitzen.*

We don't often find ourselves on Long Island, but we thought Mr. Neachy's judgments called for some *mano-a-mano* elucidation, especially after what he called us over the phone. It was to this end that we finally got around to visiting Neachy Toyota, some months later, on the way home from the beach. After some preliminary chat about a Corolla floor demonstrator with factory air, AM/FM, and radials all around, we drew our chairs up to the aforementioned large and bustling desk. Mr. Neachy, in a pastel suit, open-necked guayabera shirt, and barely tinted aviator sunglasses, leaned back and announced, "I am a doer." He then offered us a stick of Juicy Fruit and, when we declined, unwrapped it and folded it into his mouth. After a manic carnival of initial cudlike exercise, he asked, "What can I do for you?"

We told him we had come to discuss the banning of "'Twas the Night Before Christmas." The chewing slowed to a reflective pace, and Mr. Neachy turned to regard a Cressida revolving inexorably on a turntable in the window while we silently observed that a hot pilot could land an AWACS on his haircut. He then deliberately said, "Believe half words obscene." In response, we asked if he felt the obscene words in question were all pronouns, articles, and verbs, to which he replied, "You." Guessing that this involved another omitted verb, we riposted with "Yours," citing the deletion of an obscene preposition. Apparently less than pleased with our attempt at empathic parsing, Mr. Neachy then said, "Go in hat," which we pointed out was just another excision of verb form and pronoun, adding "Our." We then asked Mr. Neachy to elucidate his views regarding *courser, flash, breast, Vixen,* and *Blitzen.*

After more chewing, a sigh, and a reminder about the Supreme Court's validation of "local standards," Mr. Neachy extended a hand, palm up, and said, "You got to approach these things in context. What do we got here? We got a guy and his 'mama' going to bed dressed up in a 'cap' and 'kerchief.' Then the guy runs to the window to 'flash' at the 'breast.' He even yanks on his 'sash.' I think that's pretty clear. As far as 'Vixen' is concerned, what would you think of a guy in a bright-red suit with a pet named Vixen? Or Dasher, Dancer, or Prancer, for that matter. I wouldn't want my kids near him."

"Granted," we said, acknowledging his unassailable logic. He still hadn't answered our thorniest poser, however, so we asked, "What about 'Blitzen'?"

"That's Kraut hooker talk for 'around the world,'" we were told.

At this point, we asked Mr. Neachy to define several other words for us. He graciously acquiesced, and we began at the top of the alphabet with a random sampling. *Akimbo*, in Mr. Neachy's lexicon, meant "dog-style"; *blend*, "interracial marriage"; *castanet*, "lowborn Hindu prostitute"; *degustation*, "just generally going to the bathroom"; and *etiquette*, "G-string and pasties."

After the letter "*f*" (*frontage*, "what you see on a nude pinup"), Mr. Neachy stopped us to say he intended to ban all words starting with "*q*," which he referred to as the "fairy letter" responsible for *quasi*, *queen*, and *quadruped* ("a type of gay orgy"). When we said with a laugh that banning the letter "*q*" cer-

tainly was a "queer" idea, he told us that we were finally catching on.

We asked if there were any more titles currently targeted by members of the school board. Mr. Neachy informed us that they had a whole fall lineup that included, among others: "Black Beauty" ("Conceptually incites racial strife"); "Yogi Berra's Secrets of Hitting" ("They didn't work for me"); "Gray's Anatomy" ("Or anyone else's!"); Lublin's "The Uses of Quantum Theory in Quark Location as a Proof to the Existence of Black Holes" ("We got a large '*q*' problem here"); and "The Zubin Mehta" ("I don't see any reason for a kid to read an Asiatic sex manual"). When we raised the objection that Zubin Mehta was a human being and not, to our knowledge, a sex manual, we were told that the board members would not be limited by the restriction of obscenity in book form only and that they were foursquare against the newspaper feature "The Enquiring Photographer" as well as highway "yield" signs and the area of mathematics that deals with "units."

WE NODDED thoughtfully, which Mr. Neachy seemed to accept as theoretical agreement. Looking furtively in several directions, he took a large, round hatbox from his bottom drawer and placed it carefully on the blotter. Then, pulling the drawstring that secured the top, he whispered that inside rested Ernst Roehm's ceremonial *Sturmabteilung* cap and would we like to try it on, just for a minute. We politely declined, even after the added information that the cap had been worn by General Roehm on the infamous "Night of the Long Knives." Mumbling something about the traffic on the Long Island Expressway, we beat a hasty retreat, thinking that perhaps we'd get a desk sign of our own that says: "BETTER READ THAN DEAD."

—SUSAN STOOPTAG

RING AROUND CITY HALL

THE MAYOR STEPS IN IT

(1981)

[Before our magazine's messianic leanings were manifest, our principal political interest was, of course, our city. The stalwart Andy Logy has for years followed the complicated goings on downtown with a diligence that confounds those of us who can't wade through the newspaper.]

Monday. 7:30 A.M. "MOYDE," says New York's Mayor, and three of New York's Finest slam him to the ground as they pull out their weapons. Just returned from a "sister city" trip to Paris, the Mayor is not seeing the humor in his protectors' mistake as he wipes his face clean of the unscooped poop at which he has been pointing. Thus begins the process every schoolchild learns in what was once called civics class—how a powerful person's obsession becomes a law. The week that follows this untoward incident

• •

"Yes, I agree. The juxtaposition of unthreatening primitives in conflict with the cutting edge of socio-linguistic currency is a tired laugh."

tells us more about how the city's legislative process really works than a rerun of "Mr. Smith Goes to Washington."

> To: Commissioner Irving Stetson
> From: Mayor
> Re: Canine Waste
>
> I want to prohibit dogs from defecating on the streets, and I want a proposal for such legislation by c.o.b. Wednesday. As the Department of the Interior is responsible for wildlife affairs, the Federal government should be responsible for all funding. If the Feds won't pay for our expenses, develop a plan for shipping collected dog-doo to locations throughout the Sunbelt. I'd like you also to investigate how we can convert said doo into energy in our planned resource-recovery plants and then offer the energy at reduced costs to businesses relocating from Manhattan to the ghetto of their choice in Brooklyn or the South Bronx. See if Dr. Haluva can declare a health emergency this week.
>
> Also, you know my feelings about repeat offenders. I believe public sentiment would support the death penalty for pet owners who are caught three times letting their dog drop some in the street; needless to say, so would I. Please work with Norm Flagman on this. Kate Muldoon will get the law through the Council. Steve Wronski will make sure that anyone you need in this administration will help in this urgent and very important mattter.
>
> By the way, nice work on the Horse Diaper Bill.
>
> cc: Wronski
> Muldoon
> Flagman
> Haluva

Monday. 11:30 A.M. Messrs. Wronski, Stetson, Muldoon, Flagman, and Haluva receive their respective copies of the memo. Commissioners and mayoral aides in our fair city are a rather diverse lot, united only by belief in the literalness of the printed sign on the Mayor's desk. This sign, which faces out from the desk to all who enter, sets the demanding tone that some see as the key to this administration. For several years, the sign read: "If you say it can't be done, you won't be doing anything for anyone in the tri-state area as long as I'm alive." For a while, it read: "Do it, or your children will suffer." It currently says: "I can ruin you."

Willingness to please is not always a blessing for city officials. Stetson, a known tough guy who was engaged in some of the city's most important projects of real merit, reads the memo and says, "Holy s––t—dog s––t—bull s––t." He then calls a meeting of his staff, one of whom disagrees with the idea. Stetson says, "Tough s––t" and goes to work in earnest to fulfill the Mayor's request.

Muldoon reads the Mayor's memo and wonders how she is going to get this law passed in a week when the Rebuild the South Bronx, House the Homeless, and Save the Subway Fare bills are scheduled. She knows that failing on the as yet unnamed bill on canine-waste disposal will put her into serious disfavor with her boss even if she succeeds on the three other bills. She calls in her assistant, Joseph Sooty, an excellent worker but the butt of a lot of jocularity inspired by a 1950s television sit-com called "Car 54, Where Are You?" wherein the two main characters, both police officers, were named Toody and Muldoon. City government administrators frequently take pride in hiring the best person for the job despite physical grotesqueries, speech defects, bizarre cultural or religious garb, or other immediately identifiable problems. Muldoon's source of pride had been hiring Sooty, knowing full well she was going to face numerous bad Sooty and Muldoon jokes. Undaunted, they went to work.

Besides a lack of concern about physical abnormalities, government employment offers a haven for enormously competent people with other sorts of eccentricities. Steve Wronski is known for his volatile temper, something he's been trying to curb for over fourteen months. Strangely, Wronski decided that the first step to self-control was to avoid the foul language for which he has achieved great renown around City Hall. Equating the avoidance of profanity with control of one's temper, he has taken to making up words, sometimes failing at that and shouting English-language words of no relevance to his situation. His temper remains totally unimproved. On receiving his copy of the Mayor's memo, his office erupts in what sounds to people down the hall in the press office like "What a rebulsherating idea—that flartsome angjam is pushing me too parkstein far—BRUCE RAMBERG!" Some of the visitors in City Hall pity Bruce Ramberg, but the cognoscenti only wonder what's bothering Wronski this time.

Norm Flagman once managed what was known as the Quality of Life Portfolio, a curious mix of ethnic politics (excluding American blacks and Puerto Ricans, but including Asians, Indians, and West Indians), street vendors, landmark preservation, street fairs and festivals, and a mélange of minor amenities like preserving the remaining marble sidewalks of the city and keeping the American Dental Museum from leaving

Manhattan for a less costly location in Los Angeles. His role this time is to see that the streets become elegantly free of the brown substance without people on the East Side of Manhattan feeling that the quality of life has been lowered by being compelled to clean up after their dog. Norm is the only recipient to see nothing strange in the Mayor's memo; he reads it between one meeting with a group seeking landmark status for a transvestite dress shop in Greenwich Village and another to follow up on disposal mechanisms for the newly signed Horse Diaper Bill.

Dr. Harold Haluva is known as a cold, charmless man of impeccable professional credentials. His tenure as Commissioner of Health has been noted for its utter lack of initiative and creativity. He is a workaholic who has never missed a day of work due to illness, and his response to every potential health problem is to deny its existence. Once Wronski missed three consecutive days, suffering from what his personal physician called the flu; in a meeting with Haluva upon returning to work, he described his symptoms, to which Haluva responded, "Not only didn't you have the flu, you weren't even sick."

Haluva's other quality of note is the certainty with which he will resist the involvement of his department in any city policy or program. The Mayor and Wronski let Haluva survive in his job because he was a world-famous public health authority whose reputation was enhanced by his calm, his gray hair, and his sobriety of tone—that of an even-tempered, unapproachable, but benign family doctor. As long as the Mayor continued to avoid public scorn for his health policy, Haluva could continue privately to infuriate all around him. Occupants of City Hall are known to wait around for the moment, thirty seconds after a Haluva-Wronski meeting, when such sounds may emanate from Wronski's office as "That zeflouncitous pudvah, he deserves factatious grapples, MACHAH, MACHAH, MACHAH, MACHAHA!" Post-Haluva outbursts are the likeliest to contain real words in various verb or modifying forms, e.g., "that blimping fnorn." A sound that seems like a long-drawn-out rendering of "facial" ("FAAACIAAALLL") is a post-Haluva favorite. "Snack" in staccato form—"SNACK SNACK SNACK SNACK SNACK"—follows almost every Wronski-Haluva encounter. The mysterious "GRUMSKI" is heard only following meetings with Haluva and was the source of the City Hall rumor that Wronski's mother's maiden name was Grumski.

Wednesday. 9:00 A.M. Implementation. The city's street-cleanliness inspectors (who refer to themselves on this day as the Turd Herd) are accompanied by new forms that include multiple-choice questions regarding the amount, color, quantity, consistency, and location of canine waste. Samples are brought to the Health Department labs. Muldoon and Sooty begin to soften up key members of the City Council by subjecting themselves to jokes on the level of "ca-ca under Sooty's footy." Flagman has spent the night dining with

friends and seeking their thoughts on the topic, then rereading two articles from back issues of *New York* magazine: "Elegant Excrement: The Best Pedigrees," which named the ten smallest breeds, and the self-explanatory "Free-Stepping: Ten Neighborhoods Where You Don't Have to Look Down." Haluva devotes an hour to sharpening his tactics. Wronski's office calls a meeting for Thursday morning. A flurry of preparatory meetings must now take place.

Wednesday. 5:00 P.M. The paper starts flying. Each of the principals receives a copy of the proposed legislation, the Turd Herd report, and Haluva's statement on health hazards. The reports have a familiar tone. The report of the Turd Herd includes references such as "New York has less dog excrement per capita than other comparable cities," accompanied by a chart showing Philadelphia as the unchallenged watch-your-step capital of the nation; "Dog dropping on the street has decreased steadily for the last five years," a fact inscrutably tied in the memo to the end of the fiscal crisis and better management practices; "The quality of the excrement on our streets is superior to that in other cities and is the best since animal-feces testing began in 1969"; and "Nevertheless, we can and we must do better, for the sake of all our citizens." Buried later in the report are references to superior excrement in Manhattan and poor-quality feces in large parts of the Bronx and Brooklyn.

Haluva's report cites research that questions the existence of excretory systems in canines, thereby disputing the possibility of dog-doo on the streets. It does not dispute the existence of dogs, but does note that "In the absence of a reported case of dog rabies in NYC in 30 years, the Department of Health cannot verify the current existence of dogs within the boundaries of the city."

Stetson's report includes a plan to test for dioxin created by burning dog-doo in large quantities and describes a plan to sell low-cost energy created by burning the stuff to businesses in the South Bronx by 1993. It also describes a *pro bono* advertising campaign enlisting the city's schoolchildren as "Poop Troopers," deputized to turn in violators to the police. A prototype lapel button with a smiling dog defecating into a plastic bag held by a smiling master is attached to Stetson's report. The report also defines federal government policy: "The philosophy of the new federalism is that cities should take care of their own s––t."

Thursday. 8:20 A.M.
Haluva is the first to arrive for the meeting. Wronski's secretary lets him know that Haluva is present. Five minutes of SCHNITZ, FRITZ, SCHLITZ, HNRITZ, etc., follow, marking the first time a pattern of sustained rhyming monosyllabic words is heard from Wronski's office. By 10:30, Stetson, Flagman, Muldoon, and Haluva, joined by representatives of the Office of Management and Budget (OMB) and the Office of Operations, have arrived and the meeting begins. Stetson defines Sanitation's operational role as disposing of the "additional refuse volume due wholly to public canine defecation." "You mean dog s––t on the streets," Wronski inserts, a clear signal to all that his patience has been overextended in the first ten minutes of the meeting.

Stetson's estimate of the cost of "resource recovery on-site fecal source separation equipment" ("You mean s––t separators," says Wronski) is $37 million per plant in capital costs and an additional $18 million per plant in annual operating costs, allowing the city to offer a two-hundredths-per-cent reduction in energy costs if Chase Manhattan

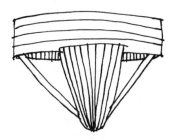

agrees to move its international headquarters to Bedford-Stuyvesant.

Muldoon lists the sources of funding at the federal and state levels for the proposed legislation. This takes fourteen seconds. Rural communities, she notes, do not perceive prohibition of dog waste on urban streets to be among the highest federal or state budget priorities. She has lined up four sponsors for the bill, all of whom represent districts where major NIMBY (Not in My Back Yard) projects are planned. They will act as sponsors in return for scrapping three shelters for the homeless, two jails, and three sewage-treatment plants. No other sponsors in the City Council are remotely possible.

Flagman says he can get the Women's Art Society, Mothers for Clean Shoes, and the Save Our Streets Coalition (SOSC). Haluva argues the no-dogs, no-excretory-systems, no-health-problems line, conceding that a 150-pound man who ingests dog feces exclusively for twenty-three consecutive days might die.

OMB points out that by freezing all Sanitation raises, using only the schoolchildren's Poop Troop as enforcement agents, offering the resource-recovery-produced energy at premium rates, and sentencing convicted offenders of this law to work as unpaid city employees, the city could turn the law into a profit maker.

The Office of Operations presents its plan: Assign half the police homicide squad to three eight-hour shifts as twenty-four-hour dog watchers; assign one-quarter of all street cleaners exclusively to collecting the unscooped droppings into hand-held sacks, a variation on the successful one-man, one-truck productivity program; establish a Feces Control Board to adjudicate and assign convicted offenders to city jobs; have Sanitation bring one per cent of its street samples to Health's labs; burn the rest of the stuff in the resource-recovery plants when they're built in four years; in the interim, store the doo in warehouses in abandoned sections of the South Bronx while offering it to community groups turning vacant lots into gardens; and authorize every city employee to write summonses.

They agree to have the law written, incorporating each of these ideas, and to submit it for the next day's City Council vote. On leaving, Haluva compliments Wronski on the meeting. Wronski closes his door, and one sustained word-sound is heard for a full seventeen minutes. Observers later report that the word-sound contained no vowels.

Friday. 1:00 P.M.
The legislation is passed by the City Council and dubbed the Pooper Scooper Law. The plans for the shelters, jails, and sewage-treatment plants are abandoned. To Wronski goes the job of informing the commissioners of Human Resources, Correction, and Environmental Protection. The Rebuild the South Bronx and Save the Subway Fare bills are held over for the second consecutive time (last time to pass the Horse Diaper Law) and have lost four prospective votes: one Council member who breeds bulldogs, another who owns an Irish wolfhound (the largest dog and therefore producer of the largest doo on earth), a third Council member who has simply vowed "never to vote for anything this putz of a Mayor wants again," and Councilman Zuckerman from the Bronx, who told me: "What's New York without dog s——t? This law will kill the tourist

industry. What's next—no fat in the pastrami?"

Friday. 3:30 P.M.
At a City Hall press conference, the Mayor proudly announces the passage of the Pooper Scooper Law. Stetson, Muldoon, Flagman, and Haluva are present, flashing appropriate smiles. As the conference proceeds, a sound can be faintly heard from Wronski's office: "Fat crackling strami the sparking blimping end, MOOOOOOOOOOOWEEEE-EEEEEEEENNNNNN . . ."

—ANDY LOGY

•   •

BOOKS NOT SO BRIEFLY NOTED
GENERAL

GOD AND ME AT YALE, by William F. Shuckley, Jr. (Jay Press; $17.76). This revised edition of the well-known conservative's precocious autobiography shows us its young author learning how to look down his nose, cock his eyebrow, and dart his tongue. In a buoyant epilogue covering recent years, we see him practicing Sousa marches on the harpsichord, discussing United States policy in Central America with his Guatemalan servants, and preparing for the annual masked ball at Bohemian Grove (Shuckley apparently makes a fetching Scarlett O'Hara). Far too much of this book was excerpted in the pages of our magazine.

•

Nixon was his own worst enemy in that respect. One week there was a joke going around that he was a terrible poker player because he couldn't stand pat. He heard it and started telling it on himself, but he'd screw up the punch line, saying, "Because I always take more cards." It was all grist for the mill.
—From "The Good Fight" by Joe Klein.

Or water under the gate.

HAMMURABIC ANNALS

KING OF ARTS

(1986)

[*Renata Addled's superb writing transcends the need for research. Here she expertly limns the consequences of putting a lot of actors into political office: they all want to direct.*]

ONE of the oft-stated goals of the Reagan Administration has been the evisceration and dismantling of the business regulatory infrastructure. This is, of course, an outgrowth of the President's conservative view of the limited role the federal government should play in the nation's marketplace. One by one, regulation of the environment, banking, transportation, occupational safety, and the like has been weakened or eliminated, heralding a return to Mr. Reagan's cherished principles of *laissez-faire* capitalism.

Contrary to his commitment to commercial deregulation, the President has long had a secret agenda for regulating the arts through a series of government-imposed minimum aesthetic standards.

News of this startling plan began leaking earlier this year when John Gavin, a Reagan intimate and one time co-star, hastily resigned his post as ambassador to Mexico, returned to Washington, and dropped out of sight. Sources at the Ambassador's residence in Mexico City reported that, for months prior to his resignation, Gavin held secret telephone conferences thrice weekly with the White House, often in the wee hours of the morning. Given Mexico's strategic importance, news of these conversations would not have raised eyebrows but for the report that Gavin, flushed with excitement after one of these nocturnal dialogues, told his staff that in his new post "it will be payback time for 'Fear Takes a Picnic.'"

THE media's curiosity was piqued and the White House besieged with inquiries about the Ambassador's mysterious new assignment. After weeks of stonewalling, sprinkled with craven denials that Gavin had been tapped for a new post, Presidential Press Secretary Larry Speakes stunned the Press Corps with the news that the President had surreptitiously established a new agency of the Executive Branch—the President's Panel on Minimum Esthetic Standards (PPMES). PPMES, Speakes announced, is to be chaired by Gavin and will supervise the rigorous aesthetic testing of all artists before they are permitted to perform or display their work in public.

As might be expected, the press's first question concerned the President's ability to establish such a powerful and controversial panel without making the news public until now. Speakes explained that Mr. Reagan had anticipated an initial hue and cry from "the unenlightened among you" and had asked Attorney General Meese to find a method of keeping the panel under wraps until its members had been selected and a draft report prepared. As a result of the Attorney

"*Yes, as a matter of fact, I have been drunk since the last census.*"

General's research, Mr. Reagan issued his Executive Enabling Order *in quartus privatato* (a Latin colloquialism originally meaning "in the small room where the potatoes dry"). Under this obscure executive procedure, last invoked by President Adams in 1797 during the Haymen's Embargo for reasons of national security, the Chief Executive is permitted to withhold news of executive action for the length of a harvest.

Speakes declined further comment but announced that new arts czar Gavin would hold a press conference the following morning at PPMES' temporary headquarters above the Frusen Glädjé on "I" Street.

THE next morning, the Presidential Press Corps and concerned luminaries such as Army Archerd and John Simon squeezed into Gavin's office. After first apologizing for the disarray (PPMES is moving to permanent headquarters at the Bureau of Weights and Measures), Gavin introduced the three other members of his panel—Vanna White, Barry White, and Jesse White. Ms. White and the first Mr. White are, of course, the famed quiz-show hostess and singer/composer, respectively. The latter Mr. White portrays television's lonely Maytag repairman who, Gavin explained, was a personal inspiration to the President during the difficult days between the 1976 and 1980 Presidential campaigns.

Gavin then made the following statement: "Since his tenure as President of the Screen Actors Guild and spokesman for 20 Mule Team Borax, the President has felt strongly that the American people should be protected from inferior and morally objectionable art. In those halcyon days, the public could savor Perry Como, learn from Bishop Sheen, or enjoy the good clean fun of 'Masquerade Party.' Now our people are confronted with choices like bat-biter Ozzy Osbourne, sex endorser Dr. Ruth Westheimer, and the sordid 'Love Connection.'

"Accordingly, inspired by recent efforts to eliminate offensive song lyrics, the President has authorized this panel to establish minimum esthetic standards for all artists as a first step to reducing provocative confusion and artistic bankruptcy. Mr. Reagan knows that all right-thinking citizens will support the establishment of these standards whatever the negative reaction from so-called civil libertarians and free thinkers."

At the conclusion of this statement, Gavin reported that the panel had, indeed, completed a draft report for the President. ("It's sort of a white paper," he quipped.) As he gave his closing remarks, the room erupted into a predictable pandemonium of questioning.

Over the next hour we learned that:

1. The President views PPMES as a logical extension of the function of the Food and Drug Administration. ("If we control what the American people put into their stomachs, it stands to reason we should control what they put into their minds.")

2. The President chose to take action now, not because, as rumored, he had just finished "Home Front," but because he had received reports that Colonel Muammar Qaddafi was a heavy investor in the Rupert Murdoch media empire.

3. PPMES would consider a "grandfather" exemption from testing based on a formula of years of experience, apparent popularity, and geographical proximity to Rancho Mirage, California.

4. The leading candidate for executive director is Dr. Leo Buscaglia. Gavin has offered the position of test administration director to Wayland and Madame. ("The embracive versus the abrasive," commented one wag in the crowd.)

5. The initial target of PPMES testing will be street mimes because of their unregulated proliferation. The President also believes that this is one pilot project that will galvanize public opinion in favor of PPMES.

Finally, after repeated requests to preview the proposed art guidelines, Gavin explained that Attorney General Meese had proposed Miranda-like warnings for artists. PPMES has established the Ono/Bono standard for singers, the Cimino standard for filmmakers, the Christo standard for visual artists, and the Dano standard for television detective sidekicks. Gavin further explained that the following are preliminary standards subject to adjustment as PPMES gains experience:

The Ono/Bono standard. All singers must have a vocal range greater than Yoko Ono's and the ability to read music better than Sonny Bono, who, as of this writing, cannot distinguish a treble clef from the international restaurant symbol for "No Bare Feet Allowed." The "twitch-and-twirl" clause of this ruling stipulates that Caucasian singers who attempt Motown-like microphone histrionics shall promptly have their work permits revoked.

The Cimino standard. All motion pictures for theatrical release must be no more than ninety-seven minutes in length (not coincidentally the maximum period Reagan can sit in one position without dozing off). The number of extras employed must be less than 10 per cent of the population of the municipality in which the film is made. Gavin announced that Mr. Cimino, who has violated these standards in every one of his films, has been ordered by the panel to direct a training film for chaplains entitled "Parables for the Bivouac."

The Christo standard. So-called works of art that utilize in their construction or execution lucite, sisal fibers, microprocessors, textured vegetable protein, or plush toys shall be immediately confiscated and remanded to the custody of the Repository for Sub-Standard Artistic Endeavor located in Quantico, Virginia. These works will be considered for export to the museums of developing third-world nations. Gavin noted that, in deference to the First Amendment, artifacts constructed of these materials and employed during religious festivals, rites, or rituals shall be exempt from this rule.

The Dano standard. Named for Jack Lord's sidekick on "Hawaii Five-0," this standard merely codifies the longstanding unwritten rule that sidekicks of video crime fighters be ethnic *in extremis.* Gavin cited the Shadow and Cato, Paladin and Heyboy, the Cisco Kid and Pancho. Oddly, the character of Dano was portrayed by James MacArthur, son of Helen Hayes and, clearly, a Caucasian. Gavin pointed out that this was an exception to the rule: offspring of famous performers are free to portray sidekicks in any medium—good news for the likes of Lorenzo Lamas, Lorna Luft, and Dean Martin, Jr.

There will probably be constitutional challenges to the President's daring master stroke, but many applaud the efforts of this administration to rein in artistic indulgence and obscurantism. "No one wants to tell America's artists what they can and cannot do," Gavin concluded, "but for the United States to realize its creative potential and all that sort of what-have-you, it's going to take a really concerted effort, and so on."

At the end of the proceedings, aides walked up the aisles to distribute camera-ready articles covering the event, accompanied by profile shots of Mr. Gavin's good side.

—Renata Addled

TOMES

(1958)

To Err Is British

[*Occasionally, a reviewer's enthusiasm for a book cannot be contained within the Not-So-Briefly-Noted format and our readers are left to face a full-tilt evaluation.*]

IN his introduction to "The Legacy of the Green Thrush" (Pachyderm & Tweeter; $24.95), what must surely be the definitive work on public servants with feet of clay in twentieth-century Britain, Professor Hugh Constant-Reamer paraphrases Montesquieu: "History is written by slugs with their spectacles on about toffs with their knickers off." Nowhere is this truer than in England, where a mere whiff of misdemeanor in high places is sufficient to keep headline writers busy for months. The British climate succors scandal like none other on earth, even when the consequences to the native soil are demonstrably disastrous; consider, for example, *l'affaire* Philby, Burgess, Meredith, Wilson, Pickett *et al.* (in which it was only recently discovered that *al*, the notorious sixth man, was the KGB mastermind of the entire operation). The amount of pleasure taken by the reading public in such scandals seems at times directly proportionate to the amount of damage done to national security.

"The Legacy of the Green Thrush" was undoubtedly a difficult book to research. Death and illness have claimed many of the chief participants in that series of events known as the Green Thrush Scandal, which rocked England (and the rest of Europe) in the twenties; time (it is now thirty-four years since the first meeting of the Dear Friends undergraduate society at High Dudgeon College, Oxford) has coagulated the memories of most of the rest; and, naturally enough, very little was written down.

Nonetheless, Professor Constant-Reamer has succeeded in telling as much of the story as will probably ever be told, and in telling it vividly and compellingly.

He had, of course, a fascinating cast to work with: at the vortex, the pathetic young Earl of Languedoc and his sybaritic retinue; the egoless Virginia Gwaltney, a widow at seventeen, whose alcoholic jottings on a dining-room tablecloth caused a half-million pounds to change hands six times; the insufferable opportunist Arnheim, who arrived from the streets of Berlin with Spartacist blood on his hands and a charter to raise money for the *Small-Freikorps*, an insidious new boys' organization; a glad-handing Australian film star, Eugene Hawtrey, "the Singing Sheepherder"; not to mention spear carriers of all persuasions from four continents.

There are still, however, too many loose ends:

> Didn't the minister realize that, after he appeared at the Landsdowne Committee's meeting at the India House all tarted up like a drinks waitress, thoroughly pissed, alternately nodding off and singing at the top of his voice the maiden's lament from "Wid the Fishmonger," *questions would be asked?*

A good question, and one of many. In the end, the author's research, exhaustive as it may have been, could not quite penetrate the cloak of belatedly acquired discretion under which the remaining principals live out their days; yet it is hard to imagine some future slug with spectacles coming closer to the truth.

—EDWARD HEATHBAR

GIANT POSTCARD FROM WASHINGTON

(1982)

[Nowhere is the exquisite symbiosis between writer and editor more evident than in this preliminary draft of one of Elizabeth Drone's pieces, complete with Mr. Shash's observations and queries. Notice how his remarks gently coax her down uncharted avenues of exploration and away from her tendency to drop the occasional name squarely on her foot. Miss Drone's stature as Washington's most fastidious reporter is not maintained easily, as her bleary-eyed admirers will agree.]

March 10

AT APPROXIMATELY 7:31 A.M. Senator Owen Applecheeks, the ranking minority member of the Senate Ways and Means Committee, strides into the Senate dining room for a breakfast meeting on grants for research into the plausibility of multi-source, ground-based irrigation systems, an issue that I have been told by thoughtful observers is of incalculable importance to this country in that it will affect our ability to feed our children, remain energy-independent, and, most important, maintain our technological edge in soil-conservation techniques.

Applecheeks is a tall, genial, ruddy-faced man with a handsome cleft chin and a mole on his left cheek. He went to Yale (class of '64, Davenport), where he graduated *summa cum laude* with distinction in his major, comparative geography. He grew up on a pig farm just off Highway 50 east of Worthington, Minnesota (population 10,789). His parents were Methodists who instilled in him, from an early age, the idea of public service as a higher calling.

[Miss Drone: If I might add a minor point here, I would propose that you ascertain a few more of his attributes, at least enough to justify another lengthy article about a junior Senator from the Midwest. Could I trouble you for his height and weight, the address of the pig farm, the name of his teachers, grades one through twelve, and his SAT scores (verbal and math)? Please do not regard it as an imposition when I ask you to contact his freshman-year roommates and the genial black lady who worked in the dining room and remembers him fondly—there must be one. Also, where is Minnesota? Thank you./W.S.]

Applecheeks sits down with his legislative assistant, Diane L. Alexander, and his assistant legislative assistant, Ferris Harvey. Miss Alexander briefs him on the salient points of the morning's news.

[Miss Drone: I think we need a bit more here on Miss Alexander and Mr. Harvey, to wit: their opinion of Applecheeks as a person, the names of their law schools and colleges, years of graduation, GPAs, SATs, their respective collar sizes, their brand of wristwatch, and their favorite ice-cream flavor. Thank you./W.S.]

Applecheeks' good cheer is evident. He attacks his bowl of Grape-Nuts and drinks his grapefruit juice with the robust appetite of someone who enjoys his job. I notice that he takes his coffee with a little milk and half a pack of Sweet 'N Lo.

[Miss Drone: At the risk of seeming impertinent, why wasn't the Senator hungrier? Could he be ill? There is a bit of flu going around. I recommend wheat germ, cottage cheese, and plenty of fluids. Ask Senator Applecheeks why he wasn't hungrier on this occasion./W.S.]

Next is a critical hearing on perhaps the most widely discussed issue in Washington in many years. Applecheeks is chairman of the select Senate Subcommittee on Federal Office Buildings, Parking Lots, and Upholstery. He must deal with the politically sensitive question of whether federal officials at the GS-12 level or higher may park in the handicapped spaces if the lot is otherwise filled. While it may sound relatively minor to those outside the Beltway, this is a vital, complex matter and one subject to differing interpretations by men of goodwill. Honest, hard-working officials are struggling to balance their ideals, public opinion, history. The debate touches on sensitive issues inextricably entwined deep within the collective national psyche.

[Contain yourself, Miss Drone. I have asked Mr. Shill to tell me all the issues buried in the national psyche. He has promised a complete answer, in no more than three articles, sometime within the next thirty-six months./W.S.]

When Applecheeks arrives at Room 822 of the Dirksen Senate Office Building, all the wood-and-green-leather seats are filled with congressional assistants and reporters. Two administration officials sit tight-lipped at the witness table on metal chairs, their pallor exaggerated by the TV lights. The Assistant Secretary of Commerce for Parking Affairs is doodling with a yellow No. 2 Mongol pencil on his yellow eight-and-a-half-inch-by-fourteen-inch legal pad.

[Miss Drone: I remind you of our distaste for indirection: one might say "legal pad that is yellow and is eight and a half inches wide by fourteen inches long." I will ask Mr. Thing in Fact Checking to confirm the dimen-

sions of a legal pad. I also think you might strengthen your analysis in this section were you to find out whether these were TV lights or the klieg lights of which I have heard mention. Is there any difference between TV lights and klieg lights? Do the colors of the officials' suits affect their pallor? Do they prefer single- or double-vent jackets? Do they wear cuffed trousers? I think it is critical to know the make of the Assistant Secretary's suit./W.S.]

Thoughtful observers have likened these hearings to the 1966 Fulbright Committee hearings on the Vietnam war. Others say the real precedent is the Army-McCarthy hearings of 1954. Some cite the famous Crisp-Arliss Debate of 1913. The Morris Chair Act of 1882 also is mentioned, as is the Wilma Proviso of 1846. I think the real precedent may be the 1787 Constitutional Convention itself, with its brilliant minds, its passions, its drama.

[Precisely what are you talking about here, Miss Drone? Have I missed something? Have we already run articles on these events? If not, oughtn't you explain them? Who was Crisp? Who was Arliss? The complete text of the Proviso would be useful./W.S.]

This could be the most important legislative event since the Athenian assembly met in the agora or maybe on the Acropolis to try Pericles for his loss to the Spartans in . . . well, I forget.

[Miss Drone: I will have Miss Cupp in Fact Checking look into Pericles' offense and what an agora is./W.S.]

After forty-five minutes I leave, wondering what this has to do with Applecheeks and what color the carpet was. Later, I run into Henry Kissiface, the former Secretary of State, who says he has the greatest respect for Applecheeks. Two years ago, Kissiface and I served on a panel on "Whither the Democrats" at an Aspen Institute conference along with

104

former President Gerald Edsel and respected political analyst Norman J. Borestein. All of them predicted that Applecheeks' future lay ahead of him. Kissiface says he believes his prediction has come true. As I say goodbye to Henry, another Senator whom I have known for a decade passes by. He tells me that he, too, respects his younger colleague. This could also be one of the "in-the-hallway" anecdotes that give my reporting such verisimilitude. I ask him about Applecheeks. He says he must go. My anecdote vanishes into the men's room.

[Miss Drone: Such language strikes me as a trifle vivid./W.S.]

I go to the ladies' room to examine my notes.

[Please, Miss Drone./W.S.]

Two women at the sink are discussing their taxes—"Life goes on" anecdote.

[Miss Drone: Thank you./W.S.]

Next I visit Sarah Meyers, the young assistant to the chief of the American Eating Institute, which is the lobbying arm of the food-processing industry. She gives me nine perfectly phrased grafs of description of the Institute's opposition to Applecheeks' irrigation initiative.

[Miss Drone: You might insert those paragraphs here. Or at least give us some hint as to their contents./W.S.]

She also shows me the Institute's campaign contributions to committee members for the last four years. I consider listing them, but it occurs to me that I can quote her ("And in eighty-four we

'maxxed out' on the Collins campaign in both the primary and the general," etc.), then describe her blue carpet, watercolors on the walls, then mention her window view of the Supreme Court building, then find our where her boss is as we speak. Next describe the tone of voice of her secretary, the name of the romance novel the secretary is reading (with a brief plot summary), the color of her lip gloss; also give the names of all the Supreme Court Justices, the architectural style of the Supreme Court building and where it fits into the architectural history of Washington.

[Miss Drone: What does "maxxed out" mean?/W.S.]

The intern answering the phones at the office of Applecheeks' other subcommittee (on interior decoration for renovated federal buildings) tells me that Applecheeks hasn't been there in months except to attend the secretary's birthday party. Indeed, Applecheeks' workload is such that he has not seen his teen-age son since his thirteenth birthday four years ago. Might segue into a brief section (say, ten grafs) on Applecheeks' struggle to balance Senate life and his family. Could call his wife.

[Miss Drone: You and I think exactly alike./W.S.]

Back at Applecheeks' office: three Rotary Club officers are introducing the winner of their scholarship contest, an amiable young man named Campbell. Applecheeks looks to be having a genuinely good time—a switch from the usual power-hungry pol plus more human detail. The Rotarians exit. I'm about to ask Applecheeks about the hearings, but he has to take a call. "Jerry, how you doing?" he says into the receiver. He winks at me. Am I crossing the boundary, I wonder, and intruding on the story?

"No, no, no," he says, "I didn't go to the markup . . .

"Sure I think it's important . . .

"That's right . . .

"Sure."

Ah, dialogue. So many column inches, so few words.

[Miss Drone: This authorial intrusion is perhaps immodest./W.S.]

As soon as he's off the phone, I'll ask about why he shuns the bright lights, about the decline in the quality of legislative work he's seen in his years in office, about the inhuman pace of—

"Hey, that would great," he says into the phone as I scribble.

How can I list my questions when I'm trying to get all of his end of the conversation? Maybe I'll remember it later. I'll think of key words like "markup" and it will all come back to me.

[Miss Drone: I hope so./W.S.]

Maybe I'll just make it up. Anyway, the Senator hangs up.

"Senator," I say. "About the hearings that opened today—"

His secretary calls him in from the other room. He excuses himself and leaves.

[Miss Drone: We seem to have reached the end. As usual, your rigorous reportage and fidelity to the facts at hand have yielded another vivid report. Also, the tantalizingly abrupt ending, while not quite customary in these pages, has a certain roguish charm. Or have I missed something?/W.S.]

—ELIZABETH DRONE

•   •

line

"Why no, Hal, as a matter of fact I've never noticed that all of us look like Dick Cavett."

BOOKS NOT SO BRIEFLY NOTED
GENERAL

THE JOB SYNDROME, by T. Gunda Buzums (Phalanx; $24.95), supports the premise that the male of our species has brought the roof of virtually every civilization tumbling down on his head, only to shrug his shoulders, slap his palm to his forehead, and cry, "Why me?" The authorette has produced an exhaustive polemic on the nature of sexual roles and how things might have been different if Cro-Magnon women had heard of Betty Friedan. Her arguments are complicated, and finally upstaged, by the book's pagination, which uses the duodecimal system and is based on the number twelve. Miss Buzums is a good little writer with oodles of promise, but we shudder to think what her checkbook must look like.

• •

EMERGENCY ROOMS AROUND TOWN

ALGONQUIN HOTEL "DOCTOR-IN-THE-HOUSE," 44th St. between Fifth and Sixth Aves.—This gracious landmark keeps a physician on the premises around the clock. The internist on the daytime shift works behind the bar during lulls and mixes one of the best Manhattans in town.

BROOKLYN HOSPITAL, Brooklyn—A reliable, decently equipped establishment for travellers suddenly taken ill in this borough. Ask one of the natives for directions; they all seem to know where it is.

LENOX HILL HOSPITAL, 77th St. at Lexington Ave.—Rumor has it that there's a first-class emergency room somewhere on the premises, but tourist is good enough for us. Conveniently located near transportation, shopping, and restaurants, Lenox Hill's waiting room is full of overstuffed chairs and old *Fortune* magazines; for a small charge, you can buy tea and little sandwiches while you wait. Patients are requested not to bleed on the carpet, which is a real Berber and stains easily.

MOUNT SINAI, 106th St. at Fifth Ave.—Handsomely situated on upper Fifth Avenue. Some of the examination rooms overlook Central Park and afford attractive views while you wait for one of the harried paramedics on duty to show up.

ST. VINCENT'S HOSPITAL, 11th St. at Seventh Ave.—Located in the heart of Greenwich Village, this is a spacious, congenial, and lively place frequented by local artists, vagrants, performers, and craftsfolk. Many of the nurses are trained in the Alexander technique, and a wide range of bandages, splints, and medications are usually in plentiful supply. There are special units for treatment of writer's block, post-audition depression, and dancer's knee. Many of the physicans here are said to be civil.

WOMEN'S HOSPITAL, 114th St. at Amsterdam Ave.—Health care for the fair sex is the order of the day here, although some men are to be found, both on staff and in need of treatment. The examination rooms are brimful of some of the most curious medical tackle we've ever seen: tables with stirrups, specula, and industrial-size cotton pads. A very popular place with the extremely pregnant, the hospital rings with the sounds of caterwauling infants at any hour of the day or night.

CHAPTER FOUR

ANNALS

OF

GREY

FLANNELS

Business and Finance

*F*OR US, *the world of finance is a continuüm. Simple transactions like paying one's bills differ only in scope from complicated corporate maneuvers like stock splits. Our sheer inability to keep up with the former or comprehend the latter is perhaps the source of our bewildered fascination for economics.*

From our very first issue, with its tasteful advertisements for New-Mix Active Fruit Dental Cream, Jaeckel Furs, and the Della Robbia Room of the Vanderbilt Hotel, to our latest, in which our work must vie for attention with color photos of Rolex watches as big as cantaloupes, the magazine has been associated with money. Few of our staff have managed the same association. Our first editor was a stickler for such pointless frugalities as dispensing paper clips only by request and one at a time, but he was at sea when it came to the proper compensation of writers and editors. He angered many of them because of his habit of disbursing payment according to how well off a writer's family was, where an editor had gone to college, or simply what he thought he could get away with. The number of times I personally kept Thumper, Densely, Gibbs, Perlmutter, Perky, and others from storming out or accepting more remunerative payment elsewhere is beyond memory, although all the while I was scraping by on wages considerably smaller than I would have earned selling tokens in a subway kiosk. Somehow, Row had got it into his head that I was the scion of the Shell Oil fortune, the company having been named after the shape of my ear.

Our second editor, Shmeep, has presided over a much stabler financial operation, although he himself has little or no interest in the magazine's—or, for that matter, his own—fiscal whys and wherefores. He gives himself paper cuts when he has to use his bankbook and is perpetually losing credit cards, which are usually found weeks later marking a passage in some manuscript.

In accordance with Shirp's bent, we prefer not to evince concern for money. Many claim not to know their own salaries, an unbelievable but virtually unassailable dodge to the most intimate question one can ask around here, "How much do you make?" A former friend (not from the magazine) once asked me that, and in a moment of reckless sincerity I confessed the figure. He laughed so uproariously that I ran home immediately to double-check my W-2 form.

McPhumpher's fine eight-part comparative study of compound-interest computation methods was to have been included in this chapter. To my eternal chagrin, the manuscript was ripped from my hands on my way to work one morning by robbers disguised as Persian rug merchants who made their getaway on camels. They soon disappeared in midtown traffic, and the manuscript hasn't been seen since.

ARBITRAGE AND OLD LACE

(1955)

[*St. Cloud McKenzie began at the magazine almost as long ago as I did. Those who did not know the man well tended to think that St. Cloud was, as one short-lived editor put it, "not playing with a full deck." A born storyteller, he published work in our magazine under the names St. Cloud McKenzie, McKenzie St. Cloud, and St. Cloud, Minnesota. This piece first appeared as fiction despite McKenzie's objections. Today it is clear that McKenzie was not only telling the truth, he was onto something.*]

ACCORDING to Mrs. Mildred Icahn of Ponca City, Oklahoma, just down the road from Blackwell, it was as plain as a pikestaff. "No doubt about it," she told us one summer afternoon when it was all over. "The stock of National Refiners was seriously undervalued."

Like many of her fellow Ponca City-ites, Mrs. Icahn owned a small number of shares in W. S. Moody Rock Oil & Harness, the nation's third largest oil company, which had started in 1908 as a local concern. "Moody was an engaging young fellow with a gift of gab," she recalled. "He disappeared during a sur-

veying expedition to what is now Saudi Arabia, convinced to the last, he said, that there was oil out there 'if only the damned handkerchief heads would let you drill for it.' Many skeptics in Ponca City, of which I was not one, believed that Moody was still out there someplace, maybe imprisoned as a eunuch in the Sultan's harem, maybe living under a false name as a convert to Islam, but the petroleum company he founded with his neighbors' savings went on from strength to strength."

Mrs. Icahn leaned back in her rocker and sipped iced tea as she spoke. We noticed that her faded housedress was the same color as the hydrangeas that grew neatly at the edge of her patio. The late Mr. Icahn, we learned, had taken a modest flier on the company when its assets consisted of a rig in Moody's backyard, a half-mile of drill casing, and Moody's cheerful conviction that he could "smell something down there." The dividends provided Mrs. Icahn with a small but pleasant income, but it was not dividends that interested her when she received her copy of the annual report last spring—at least not at first. She got out an old grocery bag and the stump of an Eberhard Faber No. 3 pencil and began to do some "figgering," as she called it.

"The computation is a simple one," she explained to us. "You take the market value of the stock and multiply it by the number of the shares. Then you look at the company's proven reserves and you multiply them by the spot price— not the book value, mind, the spot price. Of course, you want to concentrate on the spot so your calculations won't get whipsawed if some smart arbitrageur pulls a contango or a backwardization by playing Chicago off against London or Zurich. My stars and garters! When you subtracted the aggregate net value of the stock from the March contract price f.o.b. New York, there was a three-hundred-million-dollar difference. There were three hundred million dollars just a-laying there, waiting for somebody to scoop them up."

Mrs. Icahn shared her findings with Will Birdsong, the local pharmacist, who also owned a small number of securities. "Not only that, Mrs. Icahn," Mr. Birdsong said when she had finished, "but if you look at the annual cash flow, you'll find that it's just tremendous. They fritter it away, of course, drilling new wells and such, which just drives down the price of oil—and did you know, three out of four of those new wells are dry? Why, that's just pouring money down a rathole. They should raise the dividend instead."

Mrs. Icahn returned home from the pharmacy in a thoughtful mood. "Mr. Birdsong had been correct about the cash flow," she now recalled. "An unscrupulous man, tendering for National's stock, would have a powerful issue there, one that would cause many small shareholders to rally to his banner. Any plausible rogue could come along and offer, say, a three-dollar premium per share for twelve and a half per cent of the outstanding issue and, laws a-mercy, he'd have the company in his hip pocket. Management would have to greenmail him out of his position, and we wouldn't make a red cent. But the cash flow could also be used to pay off the considerable debt he and his associates would doubtless have assumed when they bought into the company. He could then sell off the reserves, the pipelines, the refineries, the tankers, and the corporate headquarters. There was a tremendous amount of money to be made."

Mrs. Icahn's company was in terrible danger, an issue she raised at the next meeting of the Women's Christian Temperance Union in the church basement.

"Yes," agreed the minister's wife, "and if the raider kept his position below five per cent of National's outstanding issue, he wouldn't have to announce his presence by filing a form 13-d with the Securities and Exchange Commission and National wouldn't be able to stagger its board of directors or tie up its money with a big, costly acquisition or anything. The company would be taken by surprise. I'll bet, if you took all the National stock in Ponca City and put it in one place, there wouldn't be but one hundredth of one per cent of the company. A raider could start with that. This situation is serious, Mildred."

"Yes," added Annabelle Leon, the feed merchant's wife, "and a raider would only have to tender for about twelve per cent of the outstanding shares, which would put the stock in play. The arbitrageurs would come in, and it would be goodbye, National."

Soon the news was all over town— and a good thing, too, Mrs. Icahn pointed out, because keeping it secret would have been a clear violation of the insider trading provisions of the Securities Exchange Act of 1934. Meetings were held at the V.F.W. post and then in the high-school gym; soon a consensus emerged. The people of Ponca City would protect their investment by launching a preventive attack. They would put the company in play, rendering the price of the stock uncontrollably volatile. The only problem was money: getting enough to buy enough stock to make a killing when the tender offer sent the price into the stratosphere.

OLD Mr. Philpott at the bank, said to be the only Methodist in the county, was able to pledge only half a million on the strength of their homes and farm equipment; life savings brought in a quarter of a million more, but, although Mrs. Icahn's great-nephew in New York pledged the proceeds from his paper route and young Pickens down at the Piggly-Wiggly volunteered to sell his hot rod, it wasn't nearly enough. Ponca City was in despair. Any second now, some Yankee slicker might see his opportunity and strike, and they would be left out in the cold.

Then Mrs. Kerkorian, the town astrologer, had an inspiration. "Junk bonds," she said. In some way that was never too clear, her charts had told her old high-yield, high-risk instruments that could be used to form a shell corporation. The people of Ponca City, with Mrs. Icahn as their president, would own one-half of the shell corporation; the junk bonds, with warrants attached, would represent the other half and would fill its coffers. They would obtain control of National for free. Either that, or they would force National to buy them out. The bonds would be sold discreetly in the capital markets. Their investment banker would be Drexel Burnham Lambert. Mr. Drexel, Mrs. Kerkorian explained, had an Aries rising in his Capricorn.

"Well, it might have worked," Mrs. Icahn said now, sighing as she put down her empty glass.

Drexel, naturally, had turned them down, a faint smile playing on its corporate lips, conclusively ending one of the most bizarre but engaging minor episodes in the history of American capitalism, and one that—uniquely—is utterly devoid of a cautionary moral, although there are some in Ponca City who continue to disagree. Mrs. Kerkorian is one of these.

"It might take ten years, it might take thirty years," she insists, "but one of these days Drexel Burnham Lambert will issue junk bonds. The charts never lie."

—St. Cloud McKenzie

Empty Pockets

[During the twenties and thirties, we ran a regular feature devoted to methods of getting rid of spare change, which can so spoil the drape of a trouser leg. Those of us who stayed on here gradually became accustomed to other financial difficulties.]

WE WERE chagrined one day last week to find ourselves flat broke—no cash on hand and our checking account overdrawn. Flipping through our mental file of scams, ploys, and schemes, we came up with three ways to earn some m———y: 1) We could open a restaurant, as we had always dreamt of doing, an unpretentious yet impeccably *soigné* bistro where one can get a decent meal and some rough red wine without paying an arm and a leg for it. This laudable alternative had the unfortunate corollary of requiring more time, capital, and skill than we possess on short notice, although our salad dressing and brownies have been described by others as "good enough to sell." 2) We could borrow money from friends, an idea we rejected for the same reason that farmers are advised not to overfarm their lands. 3) We could write a brisk, droll piece for this magazine.

"But what will we write about?" we asked ourselves, not altogether rhetorically. "Our mind is a blank."

"Finding the right subject is part of the creative process," we muttered sternly,

•　•

"It's my own personal Trickle Down Theory."

striking a farouche pose in our shaving mirror and giving our face a nasty little cut on its upper lip.

Armed with a sturdy spiral pad and two pens, we set forth, pausing in the vestibule outside our apartment to wait for the elevator and reflect upon the generations of forgotten reporters who have felt as we did then. Readiness is all, as Shakespeare so aptly put it, and we certainly felt ready.

Our first stop was the Coliseum at Columbus Circle, where we hoped to find a craft fair or trade show upon which to dilate. Perhaps the huge building is full of shiny new cars or yachts, we mused. Perhaps the National Rifle Association is holding its annual bash there, drawing to Gotham myriad weapons of all shapes and sizes, as well as men with flat-top haircuts, short-sleeve dress shirts, Masonic pins, and out-of-town accents. But the Coliseum, much to our disappointment, was closed.

Walking north on Broadway, we noticed that Amy's Restaurant was brimming with gaggles of pretty, duck-walking girls with large shoulder bags, their hair pinned back severely. Somewhere, a ballet class had recently ended, and the glowing, tuckered girls were reviving themselves with Amy's frozen yogurt, Amy's hummos, and Amy's falafel. We waited on line and, when we were served our cup of Amy's coffee, asked if we might speak with Amy. We were saddened to learn that there is no Amy. Amy's is owned by a group of Israeli businessmen who thought "Amy's" sounded friendly.

In clement weather, the broad plaza of Lincoln Center is likely to be full of strollers, pets, pamphleteers, peddlers, and tourists. Perhaps we could speak to a Japanese visitor, a violist en route to rehearsal, or one of the policemen who regularly patrol the area. Each of these would be good for several hundred words, we thought. Unfortunately, the Lincoln Center fountain was bone-dry, and more than half the plaza was cordoned off by wooden barricades to keep pedestrians away from the rubble churned up by a half-dozen jackhammers that seemed to be going at full throttle as we approached. We did spot a young man with an instrument case walking smartly through the lobby of Philharmonic Hall. Was there a rehearsal about to begin on which we could eavesdrop, responding to the professionalism of the musicians with naïve wonderment? We tried in vain to explain our idea to the security guard, who hustled us out of the lobby.

Several blocks north on Columbus Avenue, we stopped into Duneworks, a shop that specializes in furniture and *objets* fashioned from natural driftwood. The swarthy, garrulous owner wore a red-and-black buffalo-plaid shirt over a long-sleeve undershirt of the type Wallace Beery made popular, wide red suspenders (which he called "galluses"), knee-high rubber boots, and spacious workpants that had been painstakingly patched and repatched. Between puffs on a corncob pipe, he told us how he first became interested in driftwood, how he had developed a network of Maine fisherfolk who keep him supplied with the stuff he fashions into lamps, clocks, and coffee tables. Suddenly, we recalled that we'd done a piece about the very same man not three months before. We left in short order, masking our embarrassment with the purchase of some driftwood cufflinks, for which we paid with a credit card.

Simply unable to face the exhibit of lizard lore at the Museum of Natural History, we struck out instead across Central Park. At the edge of the Sheep Meadow, a small crowd clustered around a couple in ragged clothes who were juggling Indian clubs. To one side of the clearing was a large, hand-calligraphed sign reading "Mountebanks for World Peace." The company included two jugglers, two clowns, a magician, and a three-piece band that performed tinkling melodies on homemade instruments. We approached one of the clowns, a young, blond woman with a big red rubber nose who was sitting off to one side with a cup of coffee and a cigarette.

"Hi," we said, getting out our pad and pens. "We're from—"

"Hold it a minute, friend. Hey, Barry, there's press here. Barry!"

Barry appeared, a strapping fellow whose battered propeller beanie topped off an outfit of pajama bottoms and tail coat. He held his red rubber nose in his hand. "Sorry, pal. No interviews. *Vanity Fair* is doing us in two parts. They're calling us the Bread and Puppet Theatre of the Now."

"We weren't thinking of your whole story, actually. We wondered if you have some amusing vignettes that have happened to you along your professional path. For example, what was it like setting up here this morning? Did you—"

"Our vignettes are handled separately. You can call our agent, but you'd better move quickly. I think he's about to work out an exclusive with *People*. Sorry."

Leaving the park, we bought a paper and leafed through it. Perhaps we could find some arcane service for hire, like chimney sweeping or chandelier dusting. Unfortunately, there was nothing in it but news. The shank of the day was past. We decided to see if the Ninety-second Street Y.M.H.A. had an exhibit or function of interest. Sure enough, we got there just in time for a reception honoring an Israeli poet, originally from Yemen and living now in Santa Fe. Having assumed the event was open to all, we were surprised to learn it was open only to those willing to pay six dollars in order to sip sweet wine and munch stale cookies in the presence of a tiny, wizened man who does not speak English.

Strolling down Lexington, we noticed that our bold optimism of the morning had mellowed into quiet despondency. Suddenly, an oasis appeared before us in the form of a small, dusty vacuum-cleaner repair shop. Perfect! With any luck, the proprietor would be Irish or Polish and would have been at the same address for decades. Certainly it had been decades since the establishment's window display had been changed. Pad and pens once again in hand, we entered. A jerry-rigged bell attached to the top of the door jingled feebly.

"Hello. Anyone home?" we inquired.

Deep within the cluttered storeroom behind the counter, we saw some shadows move. A squat, dumpy man wearing a porkpie hat several sizes too small for him appeared. A miniature Budweiser can adorned the hat. We had, we felt, finally hit pay dirt.

"Hello, sir, we're a reporter from—"

"Out of my shop, you s—n o— a b———h! I know you guys a mile off. Come in here all smiles with your pads out. This ain't no quaint folk byway, bub. This is a business. You wanna buy a vacuum cleaner? No, right?"

"But—"

"No buts. Out. You gonna cut me in on your story? No, right? You wanna poke around here and ask dumba—s questions and get in the way. I don't need that. Out, you bum. Go write a novel!"

As a matter of fact, we have rough outlines for several, but he took us by our arm and we were out on the street before we could tell him.

Dusk was falling as we made our way over to Madison. There were eggs and some Progresso soup in the cupboard at home (perhaps a visit to a canning factory? where do we find one?). A browse through our address book might turn up the name of someone to whom we did not already owe m———y. On the corner of Seventy-second, we had an inspiration. Doffing the khaki cap on our head, we straightened our shoulders, brushed our hair forward to create a dishevelled look, and waited for two matronly ladies at the far curb to cross the street. As they walked by, we approached and said, "Excuse us, ladies, but could you possibly spare us a d––e?"

•   •

SINGLE in the CITY

at home

"Should I open a vein?"

around town

81 FIRE HOUSE

"Hi, boys!"

on the movie line

"Please talk to me so I don't look like I'm alone."

at the spa

"Let me bear your child."

Chast

ON AND ON ON THE AVENUE

SOUS LES TANNENBAUMEN CON JOIE Y RIDERE

(1986)

[*"The business of money, Eustace," O'Samarra once barked at me, "is buying." I nodded and wished he'd go away, but the truth of his assertion lingers. While Threnody Flamer's musings on style may occasionally levitate off the page into the empyrean of fashion theory, she is at her sprightly best advising participants in the annual Yule rite of spending more than is prudent, necessary, or even decent.*]

WHAT with toys as fickle as hemlines and parents preoccupied with instilling a competitive edge for college, it's harder than ever to strike a happy balance under the tree between, say, Putron the Plasma clone and the "More Fun with Positive Integers" diskette. The best way to ride this precarious pendulum is to be very wealthy. In fact, one of the most immediately satisfying gifts this year is money. The Tonibank branch at East Forty-eighth Street is selling gift dollars for $1.25 each. Money can be used for so many different things that the novelty doesn't wear off as quickly as it does with a new belt, for example. We can't think of a better way to teach someone "the value of a dollar" than to give him one and send him into the street to spend it. Toy analysts are unanimous this year on the popularity of money. Tremain Fallon of Toywatch International was quoted in *The Wall Street Journal* as saying, "Money is so valuable because when you have it you can buy things with it. I believe the government pays for its production as well, so it seems to me that in the toy marketplace this year money will turn a real profit—that is, if one can procure enough of it." Sage words, but still, it seems, some children prefer things in boxes. For those who like the more traditional, you can find real, old-fashioned lumps of coal at the Bituminous Bou-

tique on Madison Avenue for $28 each; they have larger outcroppings ranging in price up to $189.95.

As for those hard-to-find "gotta-haves" that have become so important to children for bolstering status, the tiresome Japanese are leading the way again. This time they've done it with a criminally clever line of action figures called Informers. Each one is modelled after an actual or reputed organized-crime figure such as Joe Valachi, Jackie Presser, or Raymond Donovan. Each comes in appropriate attire, from sharkskin to three-piece, but transforms miraculously into a sleazy rodent, slippery fish, or slimy reptile. The Informers are from the old Yokahama shipbuilding concern of Rotsatitza, and for about the price of a new taxi medallion you can pick up an Informer "environment" like the Albert Anastasia barbershop. We found a few

Informers still waiting to be "bailed out" at Tottenalia on Columbus Avenue.

Not to be outdone, the stodgy American toy giants have come late to the game with a couple of entries into the action figure or "dolls for boys" marketplace. Murray Skeegleman, head of corporate public relations for Idle Toys, told us: "My hat is off to the dinks for defeminizing the doll. If boys want dolls, we'll just turn out twice as many and stick guns on half of 'em. We nuked their towns forty years ago, we'll nuke their f————' dolls today." Idle offers our testosterone-imbued youngsters the Don King doll (with hair that actually "grows"), while WeSueCo has committed its substantial industrial and promotional might to a line of "action dolls" for boys called Skanks. Each Skank is uniquely hideous in appearance (though each does her best to overcome her weak spots). Some have terrible skin; others, piano legs. Still others actually smell of perspiration. Every Skank comes with a written guarantee to "do anything its owner wants if only he'll be nice to it once in a while." WeSueCo expects big numbers from the Skanks, but initial focus-group response has been mixed; although an overwhelming majority of boys claim they "would like to own a Skank," very few of them claimed it was their first choice. In any case, whether you want one or not, you'll find Skanks virtually everywhere. We liked the rather eclectic selection at Mrs. Torvald's Doll House on Christopher Street for about $20 each.

As every daddy knows, little girls are nothing if not to be slighted. N.O.W. spokesgal Elinor Kreel, speaking recently about the "boy doll" phenomenon, said: "We're trying to initiate a backlash among our younger membership. We're advocating a return to traditional needs, but with new meaning. This year girls want real ponies." The horsemakers have responded. "They want horses," says trainer Don Nangimoni, "we'll give 'em horses. Especially if they don't have to run fast." We did a little looking and found that the prettiest foals by far were to be had at Calumet Farms; they're out of state, but they have a local representative who comes to your house after the kids are asleep and shows you photographs. They start as low as about fifteen thousand dollars. For those who find a live horse too much of a commitment, you can get hand-sewn sachets of thoroughbred manure that will make an entire bureau of clothes smell "horsy."

For those who want to fill the need with just the right choice but want to keep things simpler, nothing is more "now" than the Cabbage Patch Cabbage. The whole town is chock-a-block with them. Dean and DeLuca's collection is fairly expensive, so we suggest you take a look in Youth uptown on Third Avenue or Uncle Irv's Factory Seconds on Ralph Avenue in Brooklyn (Irv's Cabbages, however, are stamped with a note reading "For toy use only; not for stuffing, slaw, or corned beef).

Every tyke is an individual with needs she or he doesn't know she or he yet has. Many toy buyers believe it is our responsibility as elders to speak to these needs in addition to or apart from the kind of gift that would actually bring joy to a child. It is to that end that we were delighted to find a selection of training ties at the Rogers Pleat Chamber of Toddlers. There was also a treasure trove of provocative stocking stuffers at Little Digits on East Fifty-seventh Street. Some that caught our attention were the Eye Chart from Rote Systems ($9.95); a nine-foot, hand-hewn, unfinished walnut library ladder with stainless-steel dolly balls created by Lars of Waltham ($235); and the Agent's "Deal Maker"

118

pen by Ink-Well ($19.95).

Chubbi's on Canal Street yielded a harvest of food fun like the "Half-Pint" Salad Spinner from It's a Crisp World ($4.95); Sue-Eee's Sausage-Making Starter Kit, including casings, spices, larding tool, and, of course, forcemeat (about $35); and/or a series of comic books about spices from Eclecto-Gram ($1.50 each). Our favorite was "Fennel Saves the Day." Speaking of belles-lettres, no holiday season should go by without a tip of the hat to the publishers' latest listings. Letting a youngster open a brightly colored Christmas package to find a book inside is one of the surest ways to say there is no Santa Claus. From Chemex Junior Publications comes the almost decipherable "Dr. Himmelbrocken and the Conundrum of Solid Fuel" ($7.95) with drawings, tables, and four-color tetrahedra purporting to clarify the carbon cycle; we found it at Bookmakers on Fifth Avenue. An oversize, anthologized, one-volume collection of "Père Goriot," "The Rise of Silas Lapham," and "The Vicar of Wakefield" bound in distressed Naugahyde from Spellbinder Classics at $14 seemed to us a spectacular bargain at The Running Shelf on Avenue A. Finally, Beaupartman's transcribed "Lectures on Extinction" ($14.95) comes with a shrink-wrapped fossil and a new afterword on the Nuclear Winter. It is packaged by Four-eyes Press and available at Smartypants, where, by the way, you have to present proof before purchase that the recipient is gifted (a report card, psychologist's note, or science-fair ribbon will do).

Where there are books, there are also board games. Who knows why? Who cares? You play them once or twice, and then take them out ten years hence (probably when you're moving) and decide to have a yard sale. This year the kickiest are Step Deal from Lazar and Mengers, First Strike from Klauswitz Brothers,

and K-Car: The Game of Loan Guarantees, Labor Givebacks and Retooled Robotics, from Iaco Co.

If all this sounds to you like mercantilism has run amok, or if you're obligated to get your cousin's kid in Protrero Hills a present because she always sends one to your kid, or if you hark back to a time when Christmas meant but one symbolic gift and a glow of bonhomie, then perhaps you'd better consider moving to a country with a barter-based economy and a currency backed by talc.

STILL, we can empathize, and perhaps you'll find these selections helpful. Christmas just wouldn't be Christmas without three packs of monogrammed handkerchiefs ($5 a box, two-week wait at Li'l Knickers on Amsterdam Avenue). At Pickaninnies on Broadway we found some interesting chunks and pieces of wood for $20 a set. At the ubiquitous Us-Not-Cheap franchises, we selected some bits of colored paper ($4.95 a bag) and lengths of pipe (copper, $4 per foot; nickel, $6 per foot; and PVC, $23.80 per foot) that embody the "season to be jolly." Viveca's Toy Chest is selling rosy-red apples for two dollars apiece (unwrapped).

As the last fa-la-la, Zalchik's Expensives on Lexington Avenue is giving away an eleven-per-cent debenture with every quarter-pound of any smoked fish. Debentures are the best sort of introductory investment, as their purpose, payback, and activities have yet to be understood by anyone. They have seals and look wonderfully official. Most important, though, they have inspired more than one lad and lassie to look up brightly on Christmas morn and say, "Oh boy, just what I wanted! A debenture! Merry Christmas, Mom. Merry Christmas, Dad. God bless us, every one."

Isn't that what Christmas is really about? —THRENODY FLAMER

Fragrance

[*We like to keep an editorial ear peeled for the newest flash in the pan. In 1930, we correctly reported that there might be a terrific stock-market crash at any moment, give or take a few months. In 1970, we discovered the Beatles. This recent Talk story about currents in the big business of perfumes is as fresh as tomorrow's News of the Week in Review.*]

WE'VE been hearing a lot lately about fragrance. Not the fragrances of summer, or cooking fragrances wafting in from the kitchen, but *fragrance*—singular, generic, categorical.

In the elevator at Bergdorf's, we heard an elegant matron comment to her elegant daughter: "Finally, a cunning fragrance to replace all that treacle she's forever doing." The very next day, in the checkout line at Fairway Fruit and Vegetables, we heard: "It's to die—a fragrance that's definitely me. I'm layering it, to be absolutely sure." And then, in verification of what the *Times* has been reporting about changing demographics in the corridors of power, we heard in the lobby of Two Wall Street: "I'm changing my fragrance; I'm looking for something that, bottom line, says power."

Quizzical, mystified, but certain that we were hard on a language breakthrough, we let our fingers do some walking and called The Fragrance Foundation, a trade organization of the perfume industry dedicated, rather breathlessly, to getting out the best possible word on what smells good this year.

We were put through to Style Worthington, whose name is not likely to sink out of memory once heard. The world being, contrary reports notwithstanding, a small place, we rekindled our old acquaintance with Style, whom we knew more informally as Chubby and with whom we'd last traded quips on May Day the year we both graduated from Smith. She was known then as Chubby—

not, of course, because she was, but exactly because she wasn't.

Our first question was, quite naturally, "Are you still called Chubby?" Style Worthington rattled her pearls, ignored the gentle poke, and told us that she was now the Foundation's directress of public information. We explained that we were on the trail of a singular/plural shift. Could she tell us why the word "fragrance" was tripping so singularly off virtually everyone's lips? And, for another thing, why wasn't it called perfume anymore?

"Easy, darling," Style trilled. "Couldn't be simpler. Because it's so important. Fragrance is High Concept, a whole greater than the sum 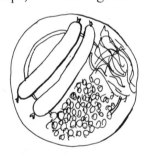 of its parts. Fragrance is more than perfume, or *eau de cologne*, or toilet water, or even essential oils. It's an *idea*, darling. Fragrance *requires* the singular. This is the Decade of Fragrance." We awaited further enlightenment. "Ultimately, darling, fragrance is a woman's most important accessory. It's her signature. Her announcement to the world. And happily, darling, men are also beginning to learn the language of fragrance. No truly chic man would consider himself dressed without a signature fragrance. An old school tie just isn't sufficient anymore, darling. Does that do it?"

Style Worthington had to run to a

new fragrance launch and suggested that we ring back after the fall rush of launches, which we understood to mean press parties for perfume. A word of advice she offered in haste struck a chord: "Darling, walk the aisles. Follow your nose and walk the aisles. Then you'll understand."

Armed with knowledge of the importance of Fragrance, we set off for Saks. On one of the main-floor aisles, just where we knew it would be, was an elegant, wood-panelled sign bearing one word: FRAGRANCE. We had arrived. But what appeared to our wondering eyes was a huge display of bottles and flacons and jars and boxes with names and scents we'd never encountered. Gone were the days of small, cut-crystal bottles in velvet-lined boxes with embossed black type announcing discreetly the names we'd learned to identify as the perfumed mysteries of romance. Or were they? We asked a slightly disdainful young man with the shiniest patent-leather hair we'd ever seen, and he produced a dusty box of Chanel No. 5 and a bottle of cloudy Arpège by Lanvin. Visibly bored by our requests, he urged us to consider a fragrance for now.

Recognizing a familiar syntactical turn, we asked him to suggest something appropriate. "Well..." He paused. "Although this fragrance was created almost *five years* ago, it still works. We sell a lot to, uh, mature women like you." He proffered a high-tech, orange plastic ovoid container stamped in gold with the name Opium. "A dark, mysteriously heady animal. For women with presence." We dropped our eyes at the suggestion of mature presence, then quickly rolled them upward in dismay at the implications of the fragrance's name. Perhaps something more, uh, everyday, we suggested. "Ah," he said, smiling, "so that's the ticket. How about this?"

He held out a squat purple bottle called Poison and winked suggestively.

We blushed in sheer wonder at what the world was coming to, in the fragrance sense. His patter was an accomplished sales-oriented flirtation combined with an industry-newsletter-toned marketing report. We liked what we were hearing. Sensing our approval, he reached behind him, portentously, for the pièce de résistance. "But this," he intoned, "this is the Ultimate Fragrance. It's ours exclusively—until the first of the month, that is. This is what really forward women will be using from now on. From the master, Yves Ardennes, this is Bludgeon."

Here in the modern world, perfume is no longer a scent to be applied delicately behind the earlobes to enhance a woman's romantic appeal. Perfume now is Fragrance. And the latest hit fragrance is Bludgeon. Definitely the fragrance for the eighties.

•

BOOKS NOT SO BRIEFLY NOTED
FICTION

IN SEARCH OF MEDIOCRITY, by Thomas Peters and Peter Thomas (Hamper & Ralph; $24.95). An overview of the nation's fifty blandest corporate structures, including insights into how they achieved this distinction. Peters and Thomas' theories are flawed and non-sensical, yet the book is still an engrossing one—if only for making us feel good about our workplace no matter how boring, unsanitary, or dead-end it is. Among the run-of-the-mill companies profiled: Papco, a midwestern muffler chain; Long John's, a big and tall men's shop outside Denver; and, appropriately, Hamper & Ralph, the book's publishers.

•   •

P O R T R A I T S

FRIEND OF SMALL BUSINESS (1979)

Virgil Isherwood II

[*This portrait appeared in our magazine only weeks before its subject was sentenced to ten years at the Allenwood minimum-security prison. Thanks to his high standing in the business community, Isherwood was paroled after eighteen months. Sensing fresh opportunities south of the border, he moved to Bolivia and has not been heard of since.*]

"CALL me Vigorish . . . Vig for short." He gestures at the other two-fisted drinkers at the University Club bar.

Virgil Isherwood III is a lot like the rest of the liquid-lunchtime crowd: tall and dignified, once finely chiseled features smudged by thousands of Martinis. He radiates the ease that comes only from years spent among legions of men of similar wealth and accomplishment.

Even his patter is the same: small talk about the fate of the world economy, liberally sprinkled with lines like "Countries don't go bankrupt, people do"; and, when yet another democracy hands the reins of government to Socialists in free elections, "I weep for the private sector."

This is the way they gather, the senior partners at investment banks and law firms, the upper echelons of midtown management. "This place is a watering hole for a lot of old elephants," says Isherwood. "I come here to prove that I can still talk elephant." What animates him now is small business, which he refers to as "the engine of our economy." "In the last five years," he told us, "the number of jobs created in this country by the big industrial firms has stayed flat...the same, in lay language. All the growth has been in companies of less than $100 million in sales."

His card reads: *Virgil Isherwood III. Venture Capital. Private Placements.*

What does that mean?

"I specialize in the funnelling of capital from where it is in surplus to where it is in shortage. I get a kick out of seeing little guys make good on their lifelong dreams."

We depart the University Club and step into his limo parked at the entrance on Fifty-fourth Street. Isherwood talks about his passion for funding small businesses. "I'm not like a lot of business-school graduates. I know how to read the numbers, certainly, but I look for the dream in an entrepreneur's heart. I'm more of an old handshake banker than a number cruncher."

We wend our way down Fifth Avenue to a little *trattoria* in Greenwich Village. "This is one of my special places," he says as we take a seat in one of the grotto-like corner booths. "Antonio slept on banquettes for years when he had nowhere else to go, learning to be a chef. Now he owns this place."

Antonio emerges from the kitchen, his face freshly dusted with flour or perhaps white from fear. "Mr. Isherwood," he says in a heavy Sicilian accent. "Please. You gotta give me a little more time."

"Come with me," Isherwood says, and we repair to the kitchen.

• •

"How'd I get myself into this pickle?"

123

When the staff has been dismissed, Isherwood takes Antonio over to the grill and pulls a New York strip sirloin from a stack of marbled beef to the right of the stove. He throws it on the grill. It sizzles. Then he seizes Antonio with both hands and shoves his face down on the meat. As the smoke curls around Antonio's face, Isherwood speaks in dispassionate tones:

"You know, Antonio, Joseph Schumpeter speaks of 'creative destruction.' What that boils down to is, in the normal functioning of the market some businesses are destroyed as others are created. And we are mostly better off because that which is created benefits more people than that which is destroyed."

We return to the dining room. Isherwood calls for brandy from the bar. Antonio joins us.

"Antonio," Isherwood says. "I've done very well by you. And here, look at you—you're your own boss. Keep up the good work."

"Please, Mr. Isherwood," Antonio says, without a hint of tremor in his voice. "I can't pay no more. Take the whole place."

"But you don't understand, Antonio. I don't want your place. You think I want to be in the restaurant business? No. I want to see *you* be in the restaurant business. You're a chef. I'm just an investor."

Before we leave, Isherwood makes a point of paying for our drinks with his Diners Club card. "I don't take freebies just because I have money in the place. Being an investor doesn't confer any privileges that compromise the business concerns of management. Half the guys I know in corporations, from top to bottom, use their expense accounts to add to their standard of living at cost to stockholders. It isn't right."

In the limo, Isherwood looks out the window and reflects, "Bankers used to speak of what they called 'moral hazard.' That meant if you let people roll over their debts indefinitely, they'll have no incentive to pay. There's a real danger in our society. People see the Latin-American countries paying their interest with borrowed money. Those of us who lend to small businesses can't afford to do that. A third of small companies go in their first year. There have to be consequences proportionate to risk."

OUR next stop is a loft in the garment district. Isherwood seeks out the owner, a kindly-looking man of about fifty with a salt-and-pepper mustache and a bulge at the waist that presents, apparently, an all-too-tempting target. Isherwood hits him. While the man rasps and moans, his hands clutching his stomach, his employees, a gaggle of Oriental women hunched over their sewing machines, look up only briefly, smile, then bend to their work again.

"That's right, ladies," says Isherwood with an approving grin. "Hard work is essential to the success of any business."

Finally, our host regains his composure. "Mr. Isherwood. What did you do that for? I've got my payment right here." He produces an envelope thick with money. "You want to count it?"

"I trust you," he says, taking the envelope and leaving us to introduce himself to a pretty young seamstress.

"He *ought* to trust me," says the owner. He rolls up his sleeve, baring his forearm. "See this?" He points proudly to a length of scar tissue that looks distinctly like a row of daisies. "A couple of years ago, he ran my arm through the embroidery machine when we were doing a line of pinafores with matching pleated dresses."

"How much do you pay him?"

"Plenty. But believe me, it's worth it to be your own boss."

124

We leave the building and again settle into the leather seats of the limo. "When I got out of B school—Harvard, class of sixty-five," Isherwood says, "I had a lot of choices. I could have gone to Detroit to work, but Ralph Nader was just getting his start then and it depressed me to think that every year thousands of people would drive their cars off the roads or into one another and be killed. And I considered going into the tobacco industry. Philip Morris made me a terrific offer, but the Surgeon General's report was getting a lot of play. So for a while I went into banking, but banking is kind of soulless. The guys who made out best were speculating against the Swiss franc. For fun, they used to bet on the snowfall in Zurich for the coming winter. The trouble with all those endeavors is that they're too abstract. I wanted to see the fruits of my labors. I started a little investment firm, and the rest of it just came naturally. Then there's the question of my own

health. I boxed a little in college. I love my work too much to go join a cardio-fitness center or even to play squash at the club. This way I get to work out right on the job."

He lights a cigar. "We live in a risk-averse society. Everywhere you turn, you find regulations. And you know every regulation is just a front for someone with a special interest to protect, someone who can't stand the threat of competition. That's not the way I am. I want the challenge of seeing new businesses come to life. I want to see the entrepreneur thrive. I love it when someone pays me off. It's like watching your children grow up and leave the nest. You don't want to make it too easy for them. They've got to earn it. Sometimes you give them a little special help. Sometimes you put on extra pressure. And sometimes it's hopeless."

Then what?

"Then you've got to foreclose."

—JOHN BUDDENBROOKS

- -

LINES (PLACES TO WAIT)

BARONET-CORONET THEATRES, Third Ave., at 58th St.—Something for everyone, with line-waiting opportunities for both ticket buyers and ticket holders. Amidst a colorful panorama of doughnut shops, pizza parlors, and men selling cassette tapes and batteries from blankets, one finds oneself hesitating when the time finally arrives to enter the theatre. Line waiters are frequently entertained by a fellow in a jester suit who juggles flaming sticks while dodging uptown traffic.

CHEMICAL BANK AUTOMATIC TELLER, W. 4th St., at Sheridan Sq.—The line of choice for many New Yorkers with an afternoon to kill, this queue brings the ambience of a Parisian sidewalk café to personal finance. Located in the heart of Greenwich Village, it's the only place in town where you can have a tarot reading while waiting to get cash.

DEPARTMENT OF MOTOR VEHICLES, 80 Centre

St.—The quintessential New York waiting spot. Nearly a dozen lines are offered, none of them short. Arrive early so you can stand on all of them. Fluorescent bulbs, caked in dust, cast a subdued light reminiscent of the terminal at South Ferry. Why would anyone want to renew his license by mail?

PALLADIUM, 14th St., at Union Sq. East—The city's best nighttime waiting. Entry is permitted only at the discretion of the doorman, who's usually in a bad mood. Inside it's crowded, noisy, and seedy, but then again, so is 14th Street. Save your money and stay outside.

TKTS, Broadway at 47th St.—Line waiting for the frugal. More than an opportunity to buy discount tickets to overpriced shows, the TKTS line provides the chance to spend hours in Times Square. This, coupled with an abundance of pickpockets and exhaust fumes, makes the line particularly appealing to tourists. Pack a lunch.

CHAPTER FIVE

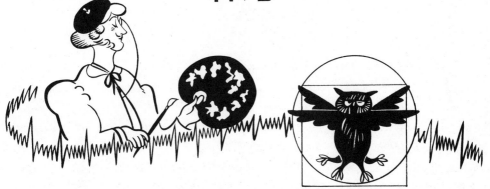

THE WORLD OUTSIDE OUR OFFICE

Art, Architecture, and Technology

*M*OST *of us here at the magazine last explored the sciences in our high-school laboratories—dimly recalled chimeras of Bunsen burners, three-on-a-microscope, and frog innards. Yet, surprisingly, many here retain a childlike wonderment about the natural world that, for me, vanished the day I had to prick my finger to draw blood. Any television show about otters, for example, is sure to be watched by most of our staff no matter when it is broadcast, although no one here admits to owning a television set and a nervy few pretend not to know what one is. This curiosity has resulted in classics of scientific journalism like "Silent Sump," Vachel Larson's prescient warning cry of ecological disaster, and E. J. Kohrvette's "Choice of Two or Slaw: the Intermingled Destinies of Men and Vegetables."*

Although we have assiduously provided listings of exhibits, museums, and galleries as a service to our readers, the plastic arts have received, perhaps, too short a shrift from us. The fact is, we here tend to prefer objects of shocking traditionalism (I myself am partial to pictures of ponies and wharves), and this places a good deal of contemporary art beyond the pale of our taste. Thank heaven, then, for Calvin Pumpkins, tireless visitor of ateliers, galleries, and "exhibition spaces" in neighborhoods to which few in their right mind would go without an armed escort.

ANNALS OF SAND
THE CURVE OF BLINDING GRANULES—1
(1970)

[This article represented a new direction for McPhumpher. He later wrote in the autobiographical "A Roomful of McPhumphers": "After I finished the voting-booth piece, I felt completely at sea, adrift, awaft, or do I mean awash? I needed to get my feet back on dry land. Once I did, I looked down and—whammo!—there was my subject. Besides, it's nice going down the shore once in a while."]

I N THE capacious leg-well beneath the horizontal surface of the large desk at which I work in my study in Princeton, New Jersey, there is a dark green metal wastepaper basket, several crumpled pieces of paper that missed their target, and, resting on its side, a battered, jacketless Funk & Wagnalls New College Standard Dictionary dating back to A.D. 1961. It is a heavy yet handy tome, its 1406 (plus xviii more) densely packed pages filled with definitions of English words, a pronunciation guide to foreign sounds, lists of the populations and capital cities of a good many of the world's countries and the United States' states, a chart of the metric system of weights and measures, and small, finely detailed drawings of subjects as diverse as a southwester, an aardvark, a hexagon, a jerboa, and a woman wearing a jacket with a peplum.

I've had the book for more than eight years, and my faith in it approaches the mystical; it is without a doubt my most trusted source for research. It defines "sand," the noun, as a "hard, granular, comminuted rock material finer than gravel and coarser than dust, varying in size from .02 to .25 in diameter." Sand the noun is also described as an idiomatic term meaning "strength of character; endurance; grit; courage" and as a "reddish-brown color." Add an "s" to it

and the word takes on new resonances. Sands, the noun, may refer to "sandy wastes, stretches of sandy beach," or even, because of sand's enormous popularity as a filling agent for hourglasses in the latter's heyday, before the use of mechanical watches became widespread, "moments of time or life."

My interest in sand began one crisp, autumnal day last fall when I was crouched under my desk in the leg-well, looking for a mislaid pipe tool. As I combed the woolly floor, I came across several dust balls that seemed to bear no resemblance to the garbage that customarily finds its way into or, at least, around my wastepaper basket. My garbage consists largely of crumpled or torn papers, correspondence, empty Jelly Baby boxes and, every so often, the tinfoil wrapper that retained the heat of a meatball hero sandwich "to go" from Ray's Ivy League Pizz' 'N' Grinder in downtown Princeton, a treat I allow myself once in a great while. The balls' pale-gray color, flecked with hints of cigarette ash, hair, and lint, was at marked variance with the moldy blue of the soiled, ancient carpet with which I attempt to make my study more comfortable. I held one of the dust balls up to my eyes for closer inspection. Stray specks of what I later learned were grains of sand, at least according to Funk & Wagnalls, found their way past my

128

beard and up my nose, stimulating my sinuses and causing me to sneeze rapidly four times. On the third and fourth sneezes, my head slammed into the bottom of the desktop with such force that I lost consciousness.

Coming to a short while later, I found my glands swollen and my blocked nasal passages dripping. My legs were badly cramped, and my lower back ached with the promise of more pain by evening. Continued research under the desk was out of the question. Crippled by allergy, muscle pain, and a big bump on my head, I would have to examine the dust balls in an outdoor environment with good breeze conditions and not too much pollen. I could bring the dictionary with me or leave it behind, closed yet ready, in the leg-well. With the sort of momentary flash that occasionally illuminates a problem like a flash bulb and fills one with a sense of the possibilities of life, or at least of memory, I recalled that there is a beach not seventy-eight miles from my home in Princeton, New Jersey. That beach was, and still is, covered primarily with sand.

THIS is the story of some sand and how it interacts with the lives of people and plants and with some inanimate objects as well, such as a vat of chili, living or, in the case of the inanimate objects, just juxtaposed, in close connection with this sand, not seventy-eight miles from my home in Princeton, New Jersey.

IT is ten-thirty (10:30 A.M.) on a broad, curving swath of beach in Big Deal, New Jersey. Scattered over the glistening expanse of sand are mud, water, clamshells, bathers, bathing caps, pairs of thongs, big towels in a wide variety of colors and patterns, and cooling chests filled with refreshment. Atop a recently painted white observation chair sits a young lifeguard, tanned and fit, slick with PABA-rich tanning screen and creamy emollients, his face shaded by the classic white pith helmet favored by

explorers in children's adventure films and called, improbably enough, a solar topee. His name is Tony Ronzoni. As a rule, Tony likes sand. Hefting a small handful as we talk, he spreads his fingers apart and, using his right hand as a crude strainer, filters out the larger stones (Tony calls them "pebbles"), which hurt many bathers' feet when they step on them. When a number of stones have collected in his right hand, he flings them into the surf, where they sink. He is an affable young man who has spent thousands, or, at any rate, dozens of working hours on the particular stretch of sand on top of which we now stroll.

"Sand holds heat very well," he tells me. "It really does. On a hot day, boy, does the sand ever get hot. I wonder if it holds the cold just as well. I'm never here in the winter—that's when I'm back in school, where I'm studying motel management. Do you know they use sand to make glass? No kidding. They heat it up until it gets incredibly hot and then they blow on it or blow it up or something and it turns into glass. Sometimes there's glass in the sand on the beach, but I don't think it's been created from the sand here. I think it's bottles and jars and other glass things that get washed up on the shore or that people leave here after they've spent the day. They shouldn't do that, you know, but a lot of people just don't know how to behave in a public place. See those kids throwing sand at each other? One of them will get sand in his eyes or get hit with a pebble. They'll be fighting and crying, and I'll have to go over there and break it up. So you see? Sand is really important to my work, it really is. Is that it? I've really got to go now." Tony shakes my hand perfunctorily and jogs off to protect the children from their temporary enemy, sand.

Bernice Mueller is a stout, beefy woman with forearms like canned hams. She is fifty-six years old and has run the hot-food concession right by Big Deal Beach for twenty-two of them. She hates sand: "It's terrible stuff. I run a clean place, but you can't help it—sand gets into everything. People bring it with them when they come over here from the beach. Even the neatest ones end up tracking sand over here. The next thing you know, they want their money back because their chili has sand in it. It's probably from their fingers or hair or towel, but I'm supposed to give them their money back. Ah, who the hell knows? When the wind blows, it can get into the chili pot. I keep it covered, but I've got to take the cover off to serve it, don't I?"

I can see through her harlequin eyeglass frames that tears are forming in her eyes. I order a chili dog with everything to cheer her up; although the chili seems grainy, I pronounce it delicious.

Becky Prince, a dental hygienist, and Sheila Prego, the manager of a nearby Perle Vision Center, live not far from Big Deal Beach and spend as much time there as their busy lives will permit them. "We like to get tan, O.K.?" Sheila Prego says to me in her no-nonsense fashion when I ask them their feelings about and knowledge of sand. Neither of them professes much use for sand, which seems unusual for a pair who consider themselves, in Becky's words, "regular beach bunnies." Neither of them has much affection for it, either. "It's all right," Sheila says to me. "What do you want me to say?" Talk turns to other topics. They ask me what I'm doing on the beach wearing a corduroy jacket, chinos, and shoes. I tell them I'm wearing my workclothes and ask them if they're free for lunch. They leave, claiming that the peak tanning hours have passed. As it is not yet noon, I'm puzzled. Sitting awhile on a small dune to take in the scene, I am suddenly aware of the sand that has found its way into my socks, my briefs, my pockets, and my hair. I will have to go back to Princeton and change.

—JOHN MCPHUMPHER

[*This is the first part of a four-part article. In the remaining three parts, the Misses Prince and Prego get a court order banning McPhumpher from Big Deal Beach. The difficulty of continuing research while in litigation is covered with appalling thoroughness. Regrettably, these installments never appeared in the magazine because of a calamity at the printing plant involving the camera-ready mechanicals of the three installments, a faulty door latch, and a quartet of fugitive elephants from a nearby zoo.*]

BOOKS NOT SO BRIEFLY NOTED
FICTION

THE BENTWOOD TRUSS: UNDERGARMENTS AND THE VICTORIAN MIND, by St. John Goodthrust (Wanker Sons, Ltd.; $34.95). This copiously illustrated monograph argues persuasively that the seeds of the British Empire's dissolution were sown in the bizarre, and frequently binding, intimate apparel of the last quarter of the nineteenth century. Mr. Goodthrust's point of view is idiosyncratic, to say the least, but his analysis of the Boxer Rebellion is refreshing.

IT LOOKS BETTER
WHEN WE STAND FARTHER BACK

IDÉE DE POMME DE TERRE

(1985)

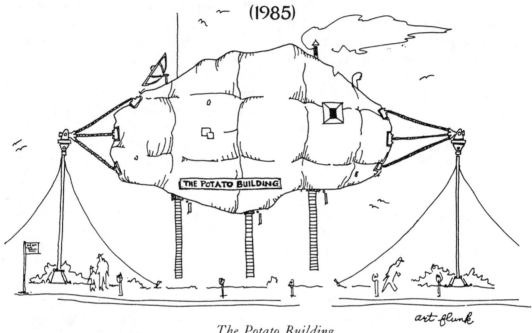

The Potato Building

art flunk

[*Al Shoobiedoobie is one of our finest (and most euphoniously named) correspondents. His definitive history of Brasilia, "Center-Hall Colonials in the Jungle," revealed for the first time that the city was originally designed as an equatorial version of Lakeville, Connecticut. Here he reports on an architect whose vision is no less dramatic.*]

CERTAINLY there is no better evidence of the conceptual swing from the functional to the decorative than the architecture of Franz Frey. With the construction of the controversial Potato Building, his transition from *infant* utilist to structural fancy-man is complete.

The building itself, an irregular, brown, ovate inflatable, stretched around a two-hundred-yard space frame anchored permanently aloft to two blimp towers and entered only by means of nylon rope ladders, has inspired every response from stunned awe to proposed legal action. A local dairy has offered to fill the building with several tons of sour cream for distribution to the poor. Its original purpose, to house the Idaho legislature, was defeated when the State Planning Commission rejected the design as "visionary but basically unsound." Interviewed in *Domus* after the building's completion, Frey answered his critics: "We live in a cataleptic society unable to distinguish the meaningful quality of a unique interior space from the inside of a filling-station restroom. Now that I have some Polaroids, I don't care if the building falls down during the Future Farmers of America Jamboree." What makes these remarks even more provocative is that, after Idaho's rejection, the Potato Building was erected in Daytona Beach, Florida, a city with a distinct absence of both *objets* and *idées de pomme de terre*.

Currently shooting the curl of a wave of attention, Frey is considered by many the vanguard architect of the moment. While the establishment wonders how architectural theory moved from "form follows function" to "performance art with an address," Frey has redefined architecture as "structural choreography." As a result, Tom Woof, in his controversial "From Corbu to P.U.," referred to Frey more than once as a "fag." Frey subsequently set upon Woof with a double-zero Graphos nib at a news conference, claiming that architects have no need for libidos since they can hug their buildings. (He had been previously quoted in *Psychology Today* as saying, "When you've experienced the articulation of your fantasies as ninety-story concrete spires, your weeny looks pretty puny by comparison.")

But is the criticism valid? Franz Frey's work presents us with a question: Can we as a society accept an architecture that serves its own design rather than us as a people? When I caught up with Frey at his studio/Audi dealership in Lodi, New Jersey, and put this question to him, he answered, "If I said, 'Who cares?', would that be a clear enough answer?" and refused to speak further on the subject unless he could bill our magazine for his time. He ranted around the showroom, yelling that every other professional gets to bill out his time by the hour—lawyers, C.P.A.s, even "the kinds of therapists who tell you it's O.K. to puke on your host's carpet as long as you're in touch with your own hostility toward them." We compromised on an interview during a test drive.

Son of the noted Paraguayan landscape architect Otto Von Frey, Franz was reared in an atmosphere of rigid design principles. It was the elder Frey's attitude that most people were not "good" enough for architecture; hence, his association with florae. His gardens were places for quiet contemplation, but his topiaries and hedgerows, though always manicured with precision, lacked variety. He set up ranks of plants like soldiers on parade, each one cut to the precise dimensions of all the others. He was a distant man. When his son Franz began to attract major commissions and the attention of the press, Otto spent more and more time in the rain forests. (His last public statement was an answer to a question about why he had spent his work life away from the steel, brick, and mortar that other architects use to express themselves. His cryptic words —"All buildings should have helmets"— have gained widespread familiarity as the title of an indecipherable and rambling avant-garde film written and directed by the musical group Porous but even so remain enigmatic to analysts and students alike.) It is said that over the years he had developed strong ties to various South American Jivarro aboriginal groups, and when his son moved permanently to New Jersey he vanished into the jungle. Today, Franz's draftsmen initiate new employees with a ritualistic practical joke that hinges upon a shrivelled, hairy icon passed off as Otto's shrunken head. Franz laughed at me when I brought this up (I was downshifting into a left turn onto route 35) and claimed that if it actually were his father's head, it was the kind of joke the *viejo hombre* would have liked.

LIKE most architects of his generation, the young Franz leaned toward utilism. Every line in a plan had to have a reason. His senior thesis at the prestigious Maricaibo Institute of Design was Le Tour des Taureaux (The

Bulls Tower), a fifty-four story coöperative apartment complex for Mexico City,
built around a bullring and remarkably
designed so that every apartment had a
view of the *corrida*. The plans specified
that all apartments above the twenty-fifth
story be fitted with magnifying glass
windows so that the residents could appreciate every nuance of the sport. They
even included a ground-floor china shop
that Frey still refers to when critics accuse him of having no sense of humor.
(Le Tour des Taureaux was actually built
but never occupied, as a mild earth
tremor reduced it to dust just before
construction was complete.)

Sensing that his destiny lay in America's cyclical addiction to building, de-
molishing, and rebuilding, Frey moved
to lower Manhattan and secured a position with Zernutto and Carbone, architects to the Lucchese organized-crime
family. For the next three years, he diligently designed neoclassical villas on a
varying scale, depending on the family
status of the particular client. On leaving the firm, he boasted that he would
never take on another private residence
—that the governing passion of the rest
of his career would be public space.

Making good on his pledge, Frey
submitted his speculative designs to a
New York City competition for scatter-
site mayoral office-and-nap space in the
outer boroughs. This was during the
Abraham Beame administration, and
Frey's strict adherence to function won
him the commission. His office-and-nap
spaces were scaled to a size consistent
with the Mayor's small personal dimensions. Ceiling heights were limited to
five feet, eight inches; duplexes were
squeezed into what otherwise would have
been one-story studios. Writing in the
Times, Ada Louisa Huxtable called the
spaces architectural *scherzi*. The Beame
Modular buildings, as they came to be
known, won the coveted Golden Em-
brasure design award. Since the end of
the Beame years, the buildings' dimensions have made them wonderful con-
version sites for the city's successful
neighborhood zoo project.

Now firmly in the mainstream of the
functionalists, Frey quietly made his first
foray into the land of the arbitrary. For
the planned town of Reston, Virginia, he
proposed a parking complex that had no
lines to delineate individual spaces. The
idea was to park one's car wherever one
was moved to leave it on the one-acre
blacktop surface, trusting to the random
pattern of events and natural selection
that one would not be blocked in by
other cars when it was time to leave.
Frey's defense of the chaos and violence
that followed the completion of the Great
Reston Parking Experiment was his first
public endorsement of a new order in
which design concept was held in higher
esteem than workability.

A COMPROMISE of sorts was effected
in Frey's next major design, the
Fortinbras (Denmark) air terminal. The
building itself was a paean to logic, laid
out so that a sequence of airport tasks
could be accomplished more efficiently
than at any other such facility in the
world. There were never any lines at
Fortinbras, as airport personnel moved
from passenger to passenger on forced-
air hovercraft. The building incorpo-
rated the weightless fluidity of Saarinen's
TWA terminal in New York, yet allowed
travellers to move through it without
feeling they were inside some giant avian
digestive tract. Frey's Fortinbras terminal was sited, however, at the confluence
of four runways. Huge, six-story observation windows faced each runway so
that people could watch, spellbound, as
jumbo jets lumbered to a halt sometimes
inches away from the terminal (depending, of course, on wind direction). Because departing flights always covered

the other side of the terminal in black jet fumes and white con trails, there was no doubt about when a loved one actually became airborne. At the time, Frey claimed that the proximity of the terminal to the runways was yet another functional element to reduce the taxing waiting period of planes on the ground, a period he calculated to be almost forty per cent of a traveler's time at the airport. Since the spectacular crash of the huge Aeroflot "Flying Cow" through the west wall (and out again through the east), however, Frey claims that he placed the terminal directly on the tarmac to play off the public's Russian-roulette attitude toward flying to begin with. He now says it was "a design that paid off in spades."

FRANZ and I hurtle north on the Garden State Parkway past deceptive greenery. Off to our left, the lushness ends abruptly to reveal the wide, dusty bomb crater of a new housing development. The unfinished houses, Colonials with two-car garages, look like carbuncles on the earth's crust. Frey surveys the construction site and mumbles, "They look nice. Wonder if they'll get decent reception down there."

Frey's next germinal step toward *architettura nuova* was the Mall in the Mine. Although the consortium of southwest-

• •

"I'm a little confused. This 'G-spot' thing means there are now three different kinds?"

ern venture capitalists who underwrote this experiment in undergound consumerism lost their shirts, Frey's use of an abandoned tin mine in Arizona to house a Bamberger's, an Orange Julius, and an eightplex movie theatre is today a major tourist draw. His insistence that there be no electric light, only the natural filtering of the sun and authentic gas-powered miner's hats, compelled the major commercial chains to look elsewhere for space, but the refurbished mine, one of the great mercantile flops of the century, is still a great attraction. During the design process of the project, Frey ordered that everyone involved wear a mole suit eight hours a day "toward a better understanding of that substance we call 'ground.'"

We leave the highway and head east toward the shore. After a lengthy oration on the tax benefits of leasing, Frey offers some insight into where he feels design is heading: "The importance of art is increasing daily. All this talk about new forms of energy is just too dull. If I'm bold enough to annoy people so they'll sit up and take notice, that doesn't mean I'm an anti-functionalist. Artists don't impede function; dentists do. People moving to the Sunbelt should live in tents—that would free up architects to work without the restrictions of having to create buildings. I envision a future in which I can go before a board of directors of a major multinational corporation and just talk to them about what I think their new headquarters might look like—or anything else that happens to come into my head—and they can act on it or not. Then they can send me a check for four hundred and seventy-nine thousand dollars."

Back at the showroom, Frey compliments me. He unveils a model of his newest project, a hospice built into the side of Mt. Shasta. The levels and half-levels of the complex are connected by an intricate series of precipitous stair runs. Frey takes special care to point them out to me, commenting in his still lightly accented English that "no two stair-riser heights are the same. They vary from a quarter-inch to a foot and a half." Rationales for these odd, hop-skip-and-jump stairways go through my mind. What statement is being made here? Are they a reminder to the terminal patients that this is a rough world? An exercise device calculated to force the stair climber to experience physical connection to every moment of life? Or perhaps an inversion of linear goal orientation? Finally I ask Franz Frey. He gives me an artist's answer: "I want them to think of me on the way out."

—AL SHOOBIEDOOBIE

•

BOOKS NOT SO BRIEFLY NOTED
GENERAL

THE LIFE EXTENSION COMPANION SUPPLEMENT, by Dirt Pearson and Sandy Shore (Simian & Shoestring; $29.95). A follow-up to a follow-up, this controversial health manual presents the authors' latest discoveries and hare-brained assumptions in the field of longevity management. This time around, Pearson and Shore are spouting the many benefits of breathing through one nostril, high blood cholesterol, chewing tobacco, walking very slowly, and McDLTs. We couldn't help but feel we were reading the words of cretins.

NOTE: "The Joy of Sex with Yourself: From Idiot's Delight to Diagnostic Tool," an exhaustive "how-to" text by Arnold Comfado, has been published by Lord Bulsht & Hose ($9.95, cloth). Illustrated by Norm Blaffner with many drawings that originally appeared here because we thought they were incomprehensible doodles. Who knew?

Marbles

[*The Long, Windy Lady's work is difficult to categorize. Surely, she was not a reporter in our sense; the extensive research and tracking down of facts was quite beyond the purview of the L.W.L., who left her apartment only to meet our second editor, Mr. Shorts, for the occasional cup of tea at Child's. Her work is not fiction, nor, strictly speaking, is it fact. I believe she was a pioneer, the first urban behaviorist. She observed the traffic, the buildings, and the people of one tiny swatch in Manhattan—the swatch that happened to be outside her window—and told us how we were managing it. Here she is at her most peculiar.*]

WE RECENTLY received another note from the Long, Windy Lady, who writes in her crabbed scrawl:

The fire hydrant outside my house is directly in front of the alternate-side-of-the-street parking sign and has been there as long as I've lived here, since 1947. The signs and hydrants of the city seem, unlike so much of life here, unchanging. They give one a rare solace and serenity. It is reassuring to know that, no matter what else happens, they will always be there and that, whatever the climate or season, I must move my car (except, of course, during blizzards or other metropolitan emergencies, and some holidays like Christmas and Arbor Day). I look forward to the day-in, day-out movement of autos that gives a rhythm to my long days spent gazing out the window.

One day last week, however, a curious thing happened. I observed that the parking sign had somehow moved to the opposite side of the street. I thought of mentioning it to Kelly the super or Mario the doorman, but finally I decided simply to write about it. How very New York! Here was a sign that, for as long as I had noticed it, remained fixed in one place until one night, entirely for reasons of its own, it pulled up stakes and moved across the street.

None of my neighbors said anything, nor did anyone do anything about it, but I am sure that everyone in the neighborhood must have noticed something odd going on and simply decided not to get involved. This, too, I am afraid, is also

a part of life in New York, and not a very nice part.

It occurred to me that perhaps vandals had uprooted the sign or that I could be mistaken and the sign *hadn't* been where I thought it was. I am a long, windy lady of a certain age now; my vision is not what it was in 1947.

Finally, curiosity got the better of me and I asked Mario the doorman if he'd seen anything peculiar going on with the parking signs. He just shook his head and smiled and said that if anything funny was going on he'd be the first to notice. I have no reason to think otherwise.

That sign, insignificant though it might seem to others, unnoticed by most in their feverish scurrying to and from work, caught up in the hurly-burly of their lives, has been a kind of anchor to me, an old pal if you will. And so it disturbed me to find it mysteriously transplanted across the street one night last week, uprooted as if by some alien force. It did move, I am certain of it, although Mario assures me it did not. As he put it, in his untutored way, "You're losin' your marbles, Long, Windy Lady."

Could it be, as he suggested, that I was merely seeing things? Did I really know as much about my block as I thought I did? It's rather unnerving, after almost a quarter-century of looking out the same window, to think that perhaps I'm not quite as observant as I like to believe.

Whether the parking sign moved or not, I felt as if I had just arrived in Manhattan, for something was gone from my former life and the view outside my window seemed utterly fresh to me. Then, just a few moments ago, when I checked to see, the sign was back in its trusty place by the hydrant, and life had renewed itself once again. New York is a lot like that.

•   •

BOOKS NOT SO BRIEFLY NOTED
GENERAL

ONE MINUTE MEGATRENDS, by John Nasal (Bull & Swine; $18.95). Self-proclaimed futurist and visionary John Nasal examines and explains the things he believes will profoundly affect our lives for sixty seconds or less. On the basis of his observations, he claims that in the coming decade there will be a glut of eyeglass frames, no parents will name their children "Morty," an all-robot football league will be formed, and the intravenous dining craze will make teeth obsolete. Throughout, Nasal insists he is a learned man and that his prognostications will all come true. Keep in mind this is the same man who told us in 1970 that we'd be banking with our brain waves by now. He is not astute.

THE ICE CUBE BOOK, by Sherry Friddleman (Rubber House; $26.95). Do not be deceived by the title; ice cubes are merely the starting point for this entertaining collection of photographs, drawings, essays, poems, and recollections about frozen water. Blocks of ice and crushed ice are here, in addition to a well-researched and provocative section on novelty ice such as the topless mermaid ice-cube mold and the classic horsefly-in-the-plastic-ice-cube trick. With an introduction by Dick Button.

•

The commissioner announced that pending further investigation, water service would be turned off to the following communities: aelx-37y***trsf . . . mingway was always argumentative around people like that."
—*Worcester (Mass.) Eagle.*

Not to mention thirsty.

THE SPACE AROUND VERY BIG THINGS

(1984)

[*Pumpkins is the most alert of our writers with the exception of Zeal, who sometimes hyperventilates while describing a movie she likes or an opinion she doesn't. Calvin is always one step ahead of the vanguard, always moving on well before the party is over—to new artists, new visions, and, usually, ever more obscure neighborhoods. Six months after this article appeared, he could not remember any of the names he mentioned in it or even having written it.*]

"THERE are three forms of immensity: simple bigness, of which the new art form consumes great quantities in its productions; the piddling, essentially tiny immensity that lurches clumsily through the work of my imitators; and the real, immense immensity, the absolute ponderousness that can barely be spoken of, except, of course, as I am able to encompass it. My work is more immense now than in the early shows, although, as far as the early reviewers were capable of understanding, it had already achieved a consistent and mature immensity," says Stanley, artist, phenomenon, and a pretty big guy.

Immensity is the essence of the Beauxeaux movement, a profoundly contemporary but, until recently, overlooked transcultural movement that has reached its greatest—certainly largest—expression in the person of Stanley, the towering figure in the Beauxeaux movement. His lecture this evening would bring a decade of Beauxeaux erudition and flair to a major cultural and academic convocation.

So large has the movement become that Stanley and I had to struggle through the parking lot of Shea Stadium, where the lecture was to be held. The lot was thronged with Beauxeaux artists, well-wishers, art bargain-hunters, and displaced Mets fans. There was very little space around us, so it was something of a relief when we began to move forward, unfortunately into an even denser part of the gathering. Finally we were standing at the stadium's stage door. The pivotal intellectual moment of the young but increasingly influential Beauxeaux could begin. But what preceded this moment?

IN 1981, on the east side of Madison Avenue, for several blocks beginning with the northwest corner of the Whitney Museum, a series of placards could be viewed by northbound pedestrians (the placards were placed sequentially, facing south): a group of messages stating, "The Beauxeaux is bigger, much bigger, than any of us." A later sequence, farther uptown, when viewed northward from the doorway of Armand's Antique Boutique on Eighty-first Street, formed the image of a child's face, whose eyes, radiant and enormous, seemed to dominate the entire vista. Late in 1982, several of the placards spelled out the name "STANLEY." A statement of tremendous importance, clarity, and enormity was being made here.

I had been fascinated by the first Beauxeaux slogans and graphic *montages*. My impression was that a movement of great energy, yet considerable obscurity, was beginning to surface. One afternoon, while searching for a picture of exactly the right length to balance the weight of a Victorian settee that I'd recently bought, I came upon Stanley as he concluded the sale, to the same gallery, of a vividly colored canvas that precisely suited my purpose. He observed me staring intently at his work, absorbed not only by the vividness of color, but by the rich, velvety texture of the black background. Here was a dynamic range far beyond anything I'd ever encountered, even in East Village graffiti galleries. I overcame my hesitation in the face of so imposing a character and asked him by what means the rich velvetiness had been achieved.

"With velvet, of course," replied Stanley. "The intensity of saturation, of contrast between opposing textures, impasto versus fine-grained, velvety matte, can be achieved only with *actual* velvet. I use black, although one sees a tendency toward magenta and the darker blues in the others. Ha! The others!" he snorted.

"Who are the others?" I asked. "Do you mean there is some form of movement?" My eyes narrowed.

• •

"Since I have the biggest head, I'll talk first."

"Yes, movement," he answered, his voice dropping as he glanced about. "You have an interest in these things?"

Thinking of the other long wall, now empty, in my apartment, and intrigued by this enormous artist and the possibility of inexpensive access to a rich vein of vividly decorative work, I eagerly accepted an invitation to his living space and studio in an obscure artists' *quartier* in Long Island City. "A few of the larger people will be there today," said Stanley. "You may want to buy—that is, you may find them interesting."

Later, we paused for a moment in front of Stanley's loft building, long enough for him to draw an enormous breath at the doorway of Ray's Postmodern Pizza Parlor, which occupies the first floor and where he takes most of his meals. "This is big, yes, a very big place," he said, "but now, you will see, I am almost too big for it." I could see that soon Stanley would have trouble getting through the front door, and I became concerned about the elevator ride to his studio. I heard a commotion inside, voices shouting, "Bigger, bigger!" Could these be the Beauxeaux artists?

The first thing I noticed when I stepped off the elevator into Stanley's studio was a tubular glass sculptural construction within which, glowing softly but in a variety of strange colors, huge bubbles appeared to pass up and down. The piece seemed strangely familiar, but I was unable to place it. It was bright enough to function as a lighting fixture but too large for an ordinary room. Stanley introduced me to its creator, Harold.

"You know," I said, "your work seems strangely like—I hope you won't take this amiss—like one of those lamps— you know the name . . ."

"Yes," he said excitedly, "the lava lamp, exactly so, I have made the very big lava lamp, yes."

"But where could you use it?"

"The trend is to large living spaces. Loft apartments that *need* this sort of fixture. That sort of person will buy them."

"That sort of person?"

"Yes, the loft dweller, very *upscale*, very . . ." Dreamy-eyed at the prospect of selling this enormous (and, I must admit, exciting) construction, Harold staggered back against a table upon which rested a pizza the size of a manhole cover. "Yes," he repeated, swallowing several slices, "very upscale."

Harold is a remarkably bulky person whose thinning hair is combed in lank strings across the top of his head, which has apparently been spray-painted the color of his hair. The effect is unconvincing, rather like that of a camouflaged battleship in drydock. Revived by the pizza, Harold now examined me closely. "You like the *bigness* of it, don't you?" he said. "Perhaps you have the space necessary for a work of this magnitude—perhaps a very dark space?"

The table with the pizza on it was suddenly pushed between us by one of the largest women I've ever seen outside of the theater at Beyreuth. "Pizza?" she asked in a booming voice.

"Ah, Greta," said Harold. "I was just about to sell . . ."

"Yes, of course, Harold, but I think he may also be interested in the grotto figures that I have assembled—if you will come this way, please—over here. This is my illuminated Madonna. I am very proud of this piece. It is very *large*, of course . . ."

Greta was wearing a large shift of an unusual fabric that mirrored the glow of the statue, which seemed somehow to be lit from within. I asked her about it.

"It is a special paint," she explained. "But isn't the effect exciting? A very *large* effect, isn't it? If you were considering the lamps, which are only decorative, you might find room for—"

"So, Greta," intoned Stanley, suddenly looming. "More pizza, then? We are all so excited, you understand, to have someone with us who enjoys—might even write about our work."

"Yes, of course, Stanley," I said.

"More pizza?" asked Greta, and we all fell to eating hugely.

TWO weeks later, I ran into Stanley in a midtown Japanese restaurant that features an endless belt of dishes circulating from the kitchen. Stanley was sitting behind a wall of tiny Melmac plates (made from a nearly indestructible material that appears often in Beauxeaux works), reading the Barnard College Singles Supplement to *Artforum*. He looked up and waved me over, nearly toppling a column of Melmac as he did so.

"I've been thinking—"

"On a *grand* scale, no doubt," I said amusingly.

"Yes, of course, and I have decided that, while I appear to be receiving, perhaps a little too slowly, the publicity that . . . well, I have decided that marrying an art historian would be an excellent solution to the problem of posterity. What do you think?"

I blinked and shrugged, curious.

"You see," he continued, "this one has written a dissertation on 'Giotto's Monumentality as Translated into Polyvinylchloride.' Well, of course. 'Monumentality.' 'Polyvinylchloride.' You see, it all works very well together."

I was beginning to feel excited by this, but I was not entirely sure what he meant. "'Monumentality'?" I asked.

"The spirit of the Beauxeaux, isn't it? Bigness. Immensity. Yes, of course, immensity." He glared contemptuously at the Melmac stacks. "These plates are really *too small*. Why don't they ever have pizza in these places? You see, we Beauxeaux, of whom I was the first,

UPC Codes

discovered the importance of—I don't want to call it excess, you understand—of becoming very *big*; in our work, in our diet. This is a basic principle of our art. Greta, for example, even in those crèche figures she has designed for the Christmas ornament concern—very big —she has even become very big herself. And now this new woman." He waved his copy of *Artforum* at me. "You see, monumentality. Perhaps this critic will want to become very big. Then the publicity that we will get will no doubt be very big, too."

I began to visit Stanley regularly in his studio. In a relatively short time, I accumulated a substantial number of Beauxeaux works—I was collecting Beauxeaux on a Beauxeaux scale. I became well known within the Beauxeaux circle and, I believe, respected, even though I appeared puny next to the smallest of them.

Many of the Beauxeaux artists were often there, eager to discuss their work: Greta, for example, had moved beyond the static religious figure ("Too stolid, even with the luminescence") and had developed an ingenious mechanical linkage that enabled her statues to move rhythmically ("like bunny-hopping giants"). Two other members of the Beauxeaux were at work on a piece called "Breakfast to Go," consisting of a three-ton Danish and a six-story container of coffee, light and sweet. Progress on the work was stalled as the artists debated the implications of the Danish's filling: should it be cheese, prune, or cinnamon?

Then, during a raucous evening at Stanley's—there is something about pizza with eleven extra ingredients that makes people noisy—Harold finally noticed the phone ringing. Moments later, he called out: "Stanley, it's the people from Yale! The Charles Nelson Reilly lectures—they want *you*! They've rented Shea Stadium!"

The pivotal intellectual moment of the Beauxeaux was on its way.

—CALVIN PUMPKINS

•   •

EDIFICES AND THE LIKE

BARNES & NOBLE BOOK STORE, remainder racks 1 through 26—Valley of the Dzolls. Hittite earthwork of the period of the Mother Goddess Jacqueline of Drekk. Careful sandcasting has produced a replica of the sacred land relic said to have aided initiates in prefiguring the birth of Joey Heatherton. On view until the residuals stop.

FEINGOLD, Staten Island—The Cathedral of Chartres. On loan from Chartres. The thirteenth-century French structure brought to the Feingold in boxes. Shown at the gallery's new quarters occupying the former borough of Staten Island. Through the turn of the century.

LA GUARDIA AIRPORT, Long Island—Rojam's Column, the well-known 1,250-foot structure begun in Rome in A.D. 114 and partially visible at TWA hangar 4-A^{14}, La Guardia Airport. The relief frieze depicts, variously, Christian Doctrine and Human Knowledge, The Fall of the House of Usher, and The Night They Invented Champagne. Until the twelfth of Never.

MONTANA RESTAURANT & SUPPLY CORP.—The Abattoirs of Pinsk. The full efflorescence of *le style abattoir* occurred in Pinsk in the mid-nineteenth century. This show traces the evolution of the form from the primitive Butcher Blocks of Brno to the superb Great Palace of Dead Meat. On loan from the People's Museum for a Correct Carcass. Until the cow jumps over the moon.

MUSEUM OF THE NASOPHARYNX—Tongue Depressors in Time. Diorama depictions of great moments from the history of the tongue depressor. Includes the great nineteenth-century tongue depressor Boathouses, Mary Todd Lincoln's own tongue depressor, and tongue depressors of the Depression. In conjunction with the photo show, Prophylactic Flossing, Reassessed. Through See-Your-Orthodontal-Appliance-Supplier Week.

MUSEUM OF NERVOUS ENERGY—The Temple of Dendrite. Monumental photographs of the Old Kingdom structure whose altar was formed in the dual image of an aborescent crystalline growth and the branching network of a neuron conducting impulses to a cell. Not to be missed. Through June 14th or until breakdown.

RADIO CITY MUSIC HALL—The Iron Curtain. They said it couldn't be done. Onstage at the Radio City Music Hall with the Rockettes in "East/West—Home Is Best." Now or never.

VACANT LOT, 23rd St. and 12th Ave.—A precursor to the minimalist movement, the flat quarter-acre is vaguely reminiscent of a similar lot at Grand St. near the East River Drive in which Jackson Pollack is reported once to have parked. Punctuated by bags and boxes of nondescript contents and abundant mud, the lot is a welcome change of pace from the sternly asphalted United Parcel delivery station next door.

BOOKS NOT SO BRIEFLY NOTED

GENERAL

ARMOIRES IN ORBIT, by Gene Thistleface (Kaboom Books; $43.21). The first antique dealer to circle the earth in a spacecraft, Mr. Thistleface offers us an informative, lucidly written memoir of the 1977 mission in which he tested the effects of space travel on a French Provincial chiffonier, a seventeenth-century English clock, a Chinese screen of the Yüan period, and an assortment of smaller *objets*. Mr. Thistleface makes some interesting discoveries: that weightlessness has no measurable effect on the tendency of Limoges porcelain to chip when looked at hard, for example, and that gamma rays will not damage mahogany veneer that has been thoroughly treated with Lemon Pledge. Mr. Thistleface's only criticism of NASA concerns the way the food for his journey was stored on board the craft; he remains bitterly disappointed that his diet-Melba-toast rounds crumbled to powder during liftoff and he had to endure his stay in space without them. Illustrated.

WHAT COLOR IS YOUR PARAKEET?, by John J. Autobahn (Perdue Press; $13.95). Following the extremely successful "What Color Is Your Grackle?" and "What Color Is Your Magpie?", this book continues the adventures of a color-blind ornithologist living in the Devonshire countryside. Mr. Autobahn is a clumsy writer at best, and his hilarious attempt to use the past-pluperfect tense in describing a childhood experience is one of the highlights of the book. His legions of devoted readers, however, will probably not notice that anything is wrong.

EXACT CHANGE: THE RISE OF THE BIG-CITY TOLLBOOTH, 1952–1967, by Nedner Bennison (Pieces O' Theses; $30). Affectionately dubbed "Mr. Ned" by his devoted graduate assistants, Professor Bennison has, as he did so masterfully in "Pots of Plenty: A History of Pre-Renaissance Eliminational Hygiene," applied a socio-scientific commentary to what would otherwise be an arid architectural history. Addressing the question of why motorists accede to what he refers to as "municipal panhandling," the Professor confides: "Every chance I get, I drive right through 'em. I can't tell you how much those things tick me off. Don't they take enough in taxes? Here's what to do: get in the exact-change lane and, when it's your turn, *pretend* to throw the money in and just drive off. Bells will go off like crazy, but don't worry. Chances are, no one will stop you. If they do, just swear you put the money in and that the problem is with the machine." "Exact Change" traces not only the monetary inflation of tollbooths but their geographic inflation, citing expansion from bridge to tunnel to random *piazze* along interstate highways. There is also a fascinating description of how they install those noisy speed ridges that jolt you into thinking you've had a blowout, as well as an appendix of tollhouse-cookie recipes.

•   •

THE SUBJUNCTIVE LIVES
If the Nuclear Regulatory Agency were to allow the Shoreham plant to open, the lives of millions of people would hang by a thread.
—*New England Journal of Medicine.*

We wish we was in Dixie.

ANNALS OF AILMENTS

POT PIE CITY

(1966)

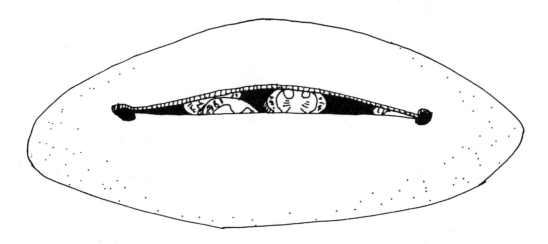

[Senior medical journalist Crouton Ricochet has been at the magazine almost as long as I have. Our unofficial Mr. Wizard, Crouton is the only man I know who can successfully explain why it isn't the heat, it's the humidity.]

At about about ten o'clock on a sunny morning in June, 1965, Dr. Bud Norman Kantsee, director and head internist at the Roman Meal Medical Association in Sunnyside, Queens, received a call on his office intercom from his receptionist, let's call her Marilou Hunnicutter. It seems a patient of his, let's say her name was Teresa Ibañez-Bocado, had arrived at the office in a highly agitated state and was demanding to see him. Marilou Hunnicutter has spent twenty-two callusing years seeing and hearing patient anxiety and has, as she often puts it, "been through it all," so Dr. Kantsee was particularly surprised by the uncharacteristic volubility of the receptionist's voice.

"Send her in," said Dr. Kantsee, his fingers pushing the usually heavy eyeglasses he wears to a point farther up the bridge of his nose. (Dr. Kantsee is legally blind in a number of states.)

The office door opened abruptly and Miss Teresa Ibañez-Bocado, a small, stout woman of advanced middle age, entered the room, closely followed by Miss Hunnicutter. Miss Hunnicutter barely managed to put the patient's file on the doctor's desk before Teresa Ibañez-Bocado began to speak—incoherently. Marilou Hunnicutter placed a practiced hand on Miss Ibañez-Bocado's shoulder.

Dr. Kantsee remembered Teresa Ibañez-Bocado, but not much about her. The file refreshed his memory. His patient was fifty-six years old, worked as a part-time waitress at a city restaurant, and had seen the doctor over the years for a number of uneventful complaints, of which an allergic dermatitis was the most recent.

"When she first came in," Dr. Kantsee recalls, "I couldn't imagine what the trouble was. Apart from obvious anxiety, she exhibited no immediate signs, nothing glaring. I got her to quiet down enough so I could ask her some questions. Was she feverish? No. Any pain? None to speak of. Diarrhea, shortness of breath, sleeplessness? Nothing. But there was one thing. 'Doctor,' Teresa Ibañez-Bocado said, 'I think I'm gonna go nuts! Everything I smell and eat tastes like chicken.'"

Anomalies of smell and taste of this nature rarely, if ever, appear in medical literature and are usually treated as psychosomatic or psychogenic complaints. So Dr. Kantsee's first reaction was to question the possibility of an organic basis for Miss Ibañez-Bocado's complaint. While keeping a steady eye on his patient, Dr. Kantsee reviewed the spectrum of pathological taste and olfactory disorders. Taste depends largely on smell, and disruptions of either are not unusual. They occur frequently after the common cold. And pregnancy. And gingivitis. But the experience Miss Ibañez-Bocado described—everything smelling and tasting like chicken—well, Dr. Kantsee was inclined to think Teresa Ibañez-Bocado was a good candidate for psychiatric counselling.

"Crazy? Yeah, I'll say so," says Miss Ibañez-Bocado. "Who would have blamed the doc? First time I noticed it, I thought I was loco myself. I was working the late shift at the restaurant, that means I don't get off till twelve, maybe twelve-thirty at night. And I'm picking up an order—it was rice pudding, I think, yeah, rice pudding. And I notice that the rice pudding smells like chicken. I mean, at first I didn't think nothing of it—I work with chicken, you know? I thought maybe I was smelling some of the chicken salad they made earlier in the day. So I finish my shift and I'm changing out of my uniform and I think, well, I'll freshen up a little. I go into the ladies' to wash my hands—you know that liquid soap in the little container? I

put some on my hands and—chicken. I take out my perfume—it's small, and I keep it in one of those red plastic coin purses with lips, you know the kind? —and I put some on my neck. Chicken again, but stronger now—maybe fried. Now I'm really going crazy. I get my things, go outside. They got a garage near the restaurant, Larry's Esso. Usually I pass it, I smell gas. Who doesn't? I walk by it and—chicken. Again. Real strong. Roast.

"I figure I been on my feet too long. I go home. I get ready for bed. I been with food all day, you know, but I still want something to eat before I go to sleep. I go to the refrigerator, I take out a nice piece of chocolate cake my sister made when she came by the week before. I love chocolate cake, but I take a bite and—oh, my God! Croquettes.

"I get dressed to go outside. I figure maybe I'll sit in the park even though it's late. Maybe when I'm with nature it'll go away. I got this dog, Kushy, a real mutt but friendly. I never have to call him when he goes out—he knows. But this time he sees me, he doesn't want to budge, just lick me. I can't get him off me. He's lickin' and nibblin' me—like I'm a can of Alpo. I can't figure it. Anyway, I go out and head for the park.

But, my God, the trees! The grass! Fried neckbones! With hash browns! And hot sauce!

"I DECIDE to go home to bed. I take off my clothes, and I think I'm feeling better. Maybe it was just too much stress. I should just forget it. Maybe I'll sleep it off, feel better in the morning. But I get in the bed and the pillow—Suprêmes de Volaille au Vin Blanc! That's when I make my mind up to see Dr. Kantsee, next day, first thing. But I was scared. I thought, he's gonna send me to the loony bin. What other person in the world tastes and smells everything like chicken?"

"Loony bin? Well, of course, in cases like this you do think of psychosomatic difficulty," says Dr. Kantsee. "In fact, as I said, that possibility was in the front of my mind. I needed, however, to run the usual tests and some others to see if there was any nonfunctional, that is, physiological basis for Miss Ibañez-Bocado's complaint. Was there a nasal tumor or some other obstruction? I also had some reading to do. Changes in taste sensation can be made to occur. I knew that the drug Iko-Iko-Bonday-2, usually administered for arthritis, brings about a diminished taste sensitivity. When the drug is stopped, normal taste returns. Studies have shown that the drug brings about a drop in the level of copper in the bloodstream. But everything tasting like chicken? And why Miss Ibañez-Bocado in particular? Of course, it didn't stay *just* Miss Ibañez-Bocado for long . . ."

"And that's when we entered the picture." Speaking is Dr. Gottar Rumour, the small, middle-aged head of staff physicians of the New York Department of Health. He continues: "At 3:15 P.M. on July 3rd, I got a call from an associate, an epidemiologist. The damnedest thing. Three reports from various physicians—all in the Sunnyside vicinity—asking did we know anything about taste disorders. Of course, stuff like this doesn't usually come our way—it's not like typhoid fever. But somehow there was a suspicion, and public-health agencies are often notified when uncharted maladies occur frequently. Anyway, at first I couldn't believe it. *Chicken?* Why chicken? Why not steak? But I had to check. Anything common in the patients' histories? They weren't a family, of course, but it turned out they had more in common than a certain unusual complaint. For one thing, they were neighbors. Teresa Ibañez-Bocado—she was one of the first, I soon learned—lives at 304 Lebau Avenue. Another patient gave his address as 43 Renwick, and a third lives just around the corner at 200 Northern Boulevard. And their family names—unalike but similar. All three are Peruvian in origin, in whole or in part. Now, Sunnyside has a large Peruvian population. Tight-knit—clannish, you might say. If they were friends, or even knew each other, well, we'd have some reason to suspect a common participating experience, a clue. One person for whom everything tastes like chicken, that's a fluke. But three! I was hopeful, but I don't mind telling you I was also beginning to worry."

As it turned out, Dr. Rumour's worries had only just begun. By July 15th, six more cases of what soon became known with an uneasy jocularity as the Bucolic Plague had been reported. Dr. Rumour says:

"My first task was to investigate the everyday life of the Peruvian colony. The file now listed twelve carriers, as we called them, in the Sunnyside community. We did the necessary legwork, but all we came up with was false leads. Apparently, our patients weren't friends. They hardly knew each other. The priest at the Holy Cross Peruvian Systematic Apostolic on Northern Boulevard knew of no recent group gatherings (we weren't ruling out contagion), no community get-togethers involving food. The only thing I could think of then was a check of Peruvian dance halls. When I questioned the girl at the Peruvian mission, she started to laugh. There are no Peruvian dance halls. Peruvians dance at home. Boy, was my face red.

"One thing I can say, though—I interviewed a hell of a lot of Peruvians. And I noticed something. Both the men and the ladies carried a number of objects of the same type, the same few things. One was a coin, a kind of talisman like a religious medal. Another was a copy of 'Marjorie Morningstar.' The third—and this really caught my eye—was a little plastic purse. One of those oval, colored ones for coins. With lips. That started us thinking. We knew that loss of trace metals like copper could change taste sensitivity. Could those coin purses with lips be leaching precious copper from those Peruvians? It's not inconceivable. Certain synthetic materials, like plastics, may continue to remain active, that is, may not be chemically inert. People can be sensitive to these things. There was only one course: we had to test the patients' blood for serum copper levels, and we had to do a double-blind test of those colored plastic coin purses with lips."

T HE allergic embrace is bittersweet. People rarely die from this ancient affliction, and rarely recover. Although allergy has been the subject of precise and elaborate investigation for many years, there is still much to discover. Our knowledge, if not transparent, is at least translucent (or perhaps semi-translucent tending to quasi-transparent). Almost anything in the world has the ability to produce in some unhappy person some form of allergic response—a perversion of the antigen-antibody reaction. A substance that is innocuous to most people is registered as highly unwelcome by the body of the vulnerable individual. His body responds defensively but, through some constitutional confusion, overexpends its retaliation. The antibody material turns on the body itself, producing those symptoms—anything from the common sneeze to life-threatening strangulations—that characterize an allergic attack. The list of allergens is endless. The most nourishing foods, the most helpful medicines, the most common environmental agents, the lights we see by, the heat or cold that comforts us, all can bring misery. "What is granola to me," said the Roman poet Lucretius, "is to others no more than little bits of dried fluff that taste like oak tag." In this earliest aphoristic acknowledgment of allergy, Lucretius grasped the nature of what we might easily call the antipathetic plague.

"Well, our blood tests *did* reveal dramatically lowered levels of copper in the blood of the Peruvians," says Dr. Rumour. "The first thing we did was to confiscate the purses. And still, everyone complained of everything smelling and tasting like chicken. And I don't mind telling you, those Peruvians were getting tired of poultry. Anyway, the next step was pretty obvious. We gave the patients supplemental copper, and the response was immediate and enormously gratifying. Normal smell and taste returned. But we still had to find out what was at the root of the problem. You see, as soon as we discontinued the supplemental copper—well, as Miss Ibañez-Bocado put it, *'Madre de Dios!* Pot pie city!' And six new cases appeared, all in the same Sunnyside area. It was discouraging, to say the least. We were making no progress whatever. Then a light dawned, thanks to Miss Hunnicutter. She had a brainstorm."

"Brainstorm?" says Miss Hunnicutter,

smiling slightly. "Well, I *was* getting frustrated. I'd learned from Dr. Kantsee all about Teresa Ibañez-Bocado, and I'd heard other reports, and everyone seemed stymied. So I started thinking. Where Teresa Ibañez-Bocado lived, it was right in the middle of everything, 304 Lebau Avenue. That's right off Renwick. Which intersects St. James, near Cromwell Circle. Across from which is Park Place. Near Boardwalk. Which is where all our cases bought their groceries. There's one supermarket there, Big Xlotl's. That's when the light bulb lit up. It was just after I mailed a birthday card to my nephew, August 14th. Mostly sunny, with scattered showers predicted for evening. I needed a stamp and looked in my bag, and you know—all I could find was those stamps they give away at supermarkets. I rushed in to see Dr. Kantsee, practically knocked him over, I was so excited. He must have thought I was crazy."

"Crazy? Well, I don't know about that," says Dr. Kantsee. "But I got in touch with Dr. Rumour immediately. He did a lot of shopping at Big Xlotl's that day, and the rest, as they say, is history."

"We had a lot of Green Stamps, all right," says Dr. Rumour. "And, as we soon found out, so did the Peruvian community. Collecting those things had become a local craze, you might say. Teresa Ibañez-Bocado—well, she showed us shoeboxes full of those little books, with the stamps all pasted down. Lots. And a great many small electrical appliances. So did the others. Lots of books, lots of stamps, lots of small electrical appliances. And, of course, lots of licking."

"Well, naturally, everybody licks stamps at one time or another," says Dr. Kantsee, "but this was a special situation. Community licking—intense, concentrated, protracted. We thought copper must be present in the taste buds themselves, probably as a result of salivary irrigation. The stamp glue, we guessed, was probably depleting that copper. Needless to say, we rushed the stamps to the laboratory. And we told the Peruvians to start saving coupons."

"It took time," says Dr. Rumour, "but we finally isolated an ingredient in the glue—reparata delron—which in large doses interacts unfavorably with human saliva. The patients' own saliva was probably stripping their taste buds of vital copper. The acid test was for our patients to stop taking their copper supplement as well as to stop their stamp collecting. Then we seemed finally to have the problem, ah, licked."

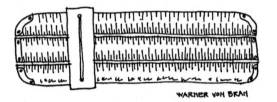

WARNER VON BRAH

"Well, not quite," says Dr. Kantsee. "We still don't know why chicken. That's ahead of us. But we're out of the woods. We did learn a great deal about copper therapy, Green Stamp glue, and Chicken Stress, as we now call it. Chicken Stress almost *broke* Miss Ibañez-Bocado."

"Yeah, it's true," says Teresa Ibañez-Bocado, "but everything's O.K. now. I gotta tell you, though, that I had to quit my job at the restaurant—they were about to turn it into a Colonel Sanders. And a lot of people treat the whole thing as a joke. The other day, my sister-in-law, she has me to dinner. So we're all sitting at the table, and she comes in and—can you believe it?—she's serving chicken. Really. She sets down the platter and says to me, 'Well, Tessie, what'll it be? Light or dark?' Ha-ha, I told her."
—CROUTON RICOCHET

TAG SALES ET ALIA

TAG SALES

AUCTION—At Hawthorne's Wealth House, 112–141 Henderson Place. Walt Whitman's hair, seventeenth-century digital watches, and Egyptian sawdust.

HOWARD ROOMPMAN'S, 12 Stickle Ave., Livingston, N.J.-Neighborhood curmudgeon Howard gave up golf in 1977 but has held on to his clubs. He's also selling balls, bright-yellow sweaters (size 50, stout), and shot glasses inscribed "On the seventh day, God got a double birdie." Don't bring the kids; Howard swears.

MUSEUMS

AMERICAN MUSEUM OF THE FOOT—Napoleon's Shoes. Through November 18. . . . The Socks of Christmas—Annual Holiday Gala. Through January 10. . . . Dr. Scholl exhibit continues in Grand Rotunda (insoles required).

HEWITT COOPER—Military Laundry. Also, the second annual exhibit of meat thermometers. Open daily except Mondays, Thursdays, Sundays, Tuesdays, and Fridays. Hours: Wednesdays, noon to 1 P.M., with no admission charge after 12:40.

CHILDREN'S SEE-AND-TOUCH MUSEUM—A progressive institution at which chidren are encouraged to interact with displays to promote learning. Current exhibit: "Sharp Objects," including knives, pins, ice picks, razor blades, needles, shards of broken glass, and power saws. Beginning July 1: "Very Hot Things."

MUSEUM OF MODERN STATIONERY—Hallmark: A 25-Year Retrospective. The best of the card manufacturer's verse, including Birthday, Confirmation, Sympathy, Anniversary, Bon Voyage, Thank You for Being You, and Get Well. Highly recommended is the "Happy 8th to Our Favorite Nephew" money envelope on the third floor.

NEW YORK GALLERY OF GENERIC PRODUCTS—No-frills items from around the world. Located in the lobby of the Nondescript Building.

NEW YORK GROCERY MUSEUM—Ten aisles of exhibits devoted to produce, dairy items, and canned as well as frozen goods. Authentic checkout counters. Formerly Gristede's. Admission: adults, $8; students and senior citizens; $8.

RAY'S MUSEUM OF PIZZA—This palatial brownstone once held a speakeasy whose owner waited tables for years at the Hotel Algonquin before going into business for himself. The specialty canapé of the house, coaster-size discs of dough covered with cheese, tomato sauce, and seasonings, was the foundation of an empire which still flourishes next door to the museum at Ray's FORVM ITALIANO and which has spawned literally thousands of imitators. The museum contains pizza-related artifacts such as a pie slicer invented by Thomas Jefferson, a napkin used by Mario Cuomo when he ate a slice at Ray's during his gubernatorial campaign, and a stubby, grayish stick of petrified sausage, the oldest known pepperoni in the world, from the tomb of Ramses II. Through February 12, the museum will feature a special exhibit called Garlic Powder: Past, Present, Future. Thursdays through Sundays from 10 p.m. on, there is dancing in the restaurant to the singing and playing of Victor Moan and his Paisans. Reservations recommended. God knows we have a few.

GALLERIES

ALEXIS BLUTOWSKI VAN ELK—Charcoal paintings of models being held against their will. (Galleries 'R' Us.)

CLINTON DEWITT—"Chief Executive Officers at Lunch: A Photographic Study." (IBM Big Shot Lounge.)

HUMPY LOGAN—Collection of fifty paintings recently stolen from the Guggenheim and bearing Humpy's signature over those of the real artists. (Isaac Bogus.)

HALSTEIN MURI, JR.—Marble and bronze sculptures, watercolors, ink drawings, and monochromatic photographs, all covered by a thick layer of some gooey stuff that no one at the gallery was able to identify. (Ozone House.)

SHERMAN PUBBER—Large-scale drawings of large scales. (Dusty Rhodes Gallery.)

CY ROWDER—Abstract sketches of the artist's family drawn on the backs of cancelled checks. (Sketch Henderson House.)

WINSTON SCRUB—Free-floating three-dimensional representations of functional abstract objects; most of them resemble crumpled-up balls of tinfoil on strings. (Galleria Disgustamento.)

WE
PACK
OUR
BAGS

Travel and Correspondence

150

*G*IVEN *our leadership, it's remarkable that our scope extends as far beyond the city as it does, yet dispatches from abroad and elsewhere have been a regular feature of the magazine ever since Rowf, our first editor, discovered he could "kite" checks to European contributors.*

Rudd was born in Colorado (somewhere west of New York), and his only travel experience was courtesy of the United States Army, so our magazine must be forgiven the unmistakable provincialism of its early years. Refusing to accede to the many requests we received for listings of Grange events and 4-H Club meetings in the metropolitan area, Rugg hewed to his path of reviews, light humor, and listings that reflected the urbanity to which he aspired.

His successor, Schnux, was born in Chicago and came to New York only after several years as an itinerant reporter and jazz pianist (he is rumored to have spent several months coming up the river from New Orleans along with Alan Lomax and the blues). Since settling in Manhattan, however, he has rarely left. Intimidated by any machinery more complicated than a pencil sharpener, he has never learned to drive a car and mumbles agitatedly about Icarus whenever air travel (even in elevators) is suggested. His unending battle with the ambiguities of English has placed the acquisition of another language out of his reach. Unlike those of our staff who squirrel away their money in hopes of acquiring a country retreat, Shormp has no affection for green things and was once heard to suggest that he wouldn't mind if the world were paved.

John McPhumpher was to have been represented in this chapter by "The Deltoid Pocket Pack," an exquisitely rounded look at experimental facial-tissue packaging design. Unfortunately, a mischance in my office involving a banana peel, an open window, and a sanitation truck passing by nineteen floors below destroyed the only galleys of the piece and it has been lost forever.

LETTER FROM THE END OF THE LINE

(1977)

[Contrary to the japes of our critics, the four outlying boroughs of New York City have long been known to our magazine. Occasionally, one of them even serves as the backdrop for a story, casual, or article. This letter, however, is a landmark of sorts, for it represents the first time one of our reporters actually talked with the natives of one of these wild, exotic lands.]

Canarsie, March 11

THE trouble over the chewing gum started when Hector Garcia, who teaches Spanish at the high school here, attempted to rise from his seat behind his battered desk, walk to the blackboard, and illustrate the conjugation of the verb *haber* ("to have"). Mr. Garcia discovered that he couldn't separate himself from his chair. He rose to a position that approximated the stance of a catcher at home plate. His chair rose with him. He placed his hands behind him and pushed against the sweating plastic. The chair remained affixed. He shook his hips from side to side as that catcher might have done had he felt a wasp extending its stinger through the flannel of his baseball uniform and into the soft flesh of his buttocks. The chair didn't budge. Hector Garcia recollected afterwards that the laugh most clearly heard among those voiced by the thirty-one students in Section Four-five-two of Canarsie High School during that morning of the second Tuesday in June was the high-pitched, sausage-scented laugh of Vincent Milano (sometimes known as Vinny).

After several moments of unsuccessful struggle, followed by his students' eruption into laughter, Hector Garcia left the room and walked hastily down the hallway. He walked past Mrs. Godfrey's American history class, past Mr. Renault's advanced French class, past Mrs. Ryder's cooking class (Garcia later recalled that he could detect the smell of a burning sweet-potato-and-marshmallow casserole). He walked to the end of the fifth-floor hallway, where the faculty men's room is. There he found Mr. Robert Allen, who teaches English as a second language, poised over the urinal closest to the door. When Mr. Allen turned around and saw Hector Garcia wearing that plastic chair like a saddle, the perfect parabola of yellow-white liquid that had been hitting the porcelain precisely three inches beneath the rim turned into an erratic zigzag.

Once Allen had pulled himself together, so to speak, he suggested that he help Garcia take off his pants. Robert Allen untied the fraying laces of Hector Garcia's brown Oxfords and then slipped off the shoes. Garcia unbuckled his imitation-lizard belt, undid his fly, and clutched the sides of the sink while Allen gripped the hem of his pants and pulled and pulled and pulled. Hector Garcia, however, had stopped at the local 7-Eleven on his way to school that morning, had purchased six doughnuts (three with chocolate icing and multi-colored sprinkles, one with vanilla custard inside, and two filled with jelly), and had eaten them all, so Garcia's two hundred and forty pounds of flab, of which nearly one third is his stomach, was even more expansive than usual. Hector Garcia simply couldn't wiggle out of his pants. Peering into the hallway, Robert Allen discovered Joseph Bitano (often called Joe) loitering about and told him to summon Mr. Copley, the shop teacher, and his saw. Joe entered the shop room on the fourth floor just as Brian Copley was demonstrating the proper way to remove bloodstains from unfinished pine while one of his students cradled a forefinger that was swathed in bandages the color of ripe cranberries.

By the time Brian Copley reached the men's faculty bathroom, Garcia had planted the legs of the chair on the floor and was rocking his perspiring head between his trembling hands while Allen perched on the edge of a toilet seat. Garcia's countenance was almost as cranberrylike as the forefinger of Copley's unfortunate student. Brian Copley quickly deduced his role. Garcia was asked to lean over, fingers touching the mud-streaked floor (it had rained that morning), while Copley sawed through his trousers. As soon as the seat of Hector Garcia was separated from the seat of Hector Garcia's slacks, the cause of the mishap was immediately apparent: seven blobs of chewing gum.

Hector Garcia is a so-called "progressive" teacher and hence lacked a suit jacket to cover the hole in his pants resulting from Brian Copley's ministrations with saw. Other, more formal members of the faculty offered their jackets, but none fit over Garcia's girth. He was by far the fattest instructor at Canarsie High, save Mrs. Ryder, the cooking teacher, who tips the scales at three hundred and twelve, and who had worn a checkered shirtdress to work that she had purchased on sale for one hundred fifteen dollars and ninety-nine cents at the Togs for Hogs Boutique on Emmons Boulevard in her Sheepshead Bay neighborhood two weeks ago last Saturday. Nor did any of the teachers have an overcoat to provide, this being mid-June. (Twenty-seven umbrellas, however, were proffered.) Finally, Mrs. Lambert, the sewing teacher, was consulted, and across Hector Garcia's posterior she basted on a patch of the fabric that was being used for her students' "culottes" project (a red-and-blue flowery chintz).

NEWS of Hector Garcia's ambush spread rapidly through the five floors of Canarsie High School and quickly inspired a rash of guerrilla gumfare. Telephone receivers were gummed to their cradles, chalk was gummed to blackboards, desk drawers were gummed shut, sink drains in all fourteen bathrooms were clogged with masticated wads of gum, whole stacks of trays in both the teachers' and students' cafeterias were gummed together. Acts of tacky terrorism hit the library especially hard. "Jude the Obscure" was gummed to "The Scarlet Letter." Twain's Huck Finn was stuck on Trollope's Sir Harry Hotspur. Wrigley's held together Wilde's "Lady Windermere's Fan" and Wilder's "Skin of Our Teeth."

A number of disciplinary actions were taken. Gum chewing was strictly forbidden on the premises of Canarsie High School, lavatories and cafeterias included. Anyone caught breaking this rule was required to stay after school an extra hour every day for a week. (An unused classroom on the third floor was turned into detention quarters.) A second infraction resulted in consignment to "the de-gum detail"—a ten-hour stint of scraping masticatory mucilage from desks and books and floors and walls, and the underbellies of the frogs in the dissection lab. A third infraction meant suspension.

Enforcement, however, proved problematic. Students whose jaws were seen moving up and down in suspicious rhythms were sent to the infirmary, where Mrs. Ryan, the school nurse, inspected their mouths for gum fragments. Not surprisingly, most students swallowed the evidence prior to being commanded to open up and say "aah." A senior was suspended without gum actually found in his mouth or elsewhere on his person. The next day, the entire senior class lined up outside the infirmary, jaws moving with the jazzy syncopation of a Bob Fosse dance number. In examining six hundred mouths, Mrs. Ryan found not a single glob of gum. The administration next hired a Mr. Hymie Elias, who for thirty years had worked as a "sniffer" in a perfume plant in Warsaw, and told him to report back if he smelled anything "fishy," or, more accurately, anything spearmint-y, cinnamon-y, wintergreen-ish, or bubblegum-y. But Hymie Elias was fired after the A.C.L.U. lawyer hired by Vincent Milano (Vinny) told a reporter from *The Canarsie Courier* that while it was *unlikely* that the administration had a legal right to forbid gum chewing on the premises, it was absolutely *certain* that no disciplinary action could be taken against students who merely allowed the scent of preschool chews to linger on their breath. The threat of a class-action suit effectively intimidated the principal, Mr. Kaufman.

The fracas soon caught the attention of New York's tabloids. The *Post* ran the story under a front-page banner headline that read: "WATCH OUT, HE'S GOT A GUM!" The *Daily News* headline writer was similarly whimsical with "STICK 'EM UP, TEACH." *The Village Voice* considered the matter with greater seriousness, however, and declaimed strenuously against the "Gestapo tactics" employed to solve what it called "the Chewish problem."

CANARSIE is the last stop on the LL— on which run the oldest and dirtiest cars of New York City's crumbling sub-

"I may not look it, Miss Nims, but when I'm in front of an actuarial table I boogie down."

way system. The LL line reports the highest incidence of track fires. When the Metropolitan Transit Authority attempted to douse those fires and instituted its "clean sweep" program, among the debris collected from the LL tracks were seven hundred and eighteen broiled pigeons, six hundred and forty-nine barbecued chickens, fifty-eight roasted goats, and the slightly charred body of the former president of the PTA at John Wilson Junior High School (an intermediate school that feeds Canarsie High).

The June morning that I boarded the LL at its first (or, I suppose, its last) stop in Manhattan, Eighth Avenue and Fourteenth Street, my guide was Louis Schwartz, who is a junior at Canarsie High and the head of the newly created CUD (Chewers United Against Discrimination). After several stops, I was struck by how frequently the four-limbs-to-one-person ratio does not obtain on the LL. At Bedford Avenue, for example, a pack of Brooklyn's version of the one-armed bandit—energetic souls clutching jangling styrofoam coffee cups—boarded our car and solicited coins. Louis Schwartz, who proved to be a highly informative and engaging Sherpa throughout our travels, told me that, although exact figures are not available, the Bureau of Missing Parts of Persons estimates that nearly one-quarter of all persons riding the LL are simply nowhere to be found.

At Broadway Junction, some half-dozen youths with skin the color of asphalt, eyes with sclerae like the whites of fried eggs after a fork has pierced the yolk and it has begun to run, and hair like bowlfuls of Beluga caviar magnified several thousand times

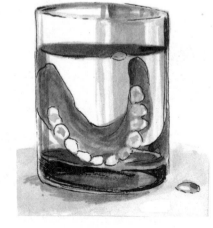

strode into our car. Something inside me quickened when these proud young men swaggered past me, and I was reminded of the emotions I'd experienced several years before when I'd witnessed the ritual slaughter of a bull in Los Nachos, Mexico. They spoke in a vernacular that had an immediacy I was not accustomed to hearing. Nor was I familiar with their topic of conversation: in bold, assured voices, they spoke about the mating patterns of their people and especially of their mothers. At the next stop, Atlantic Avenue, several girls with whom the young men were apparently well acquainted boarded the train. Speaking among themselves, they, too, punctuated each sentence with references to their mothers. I was confused yet excited by the notion of a tribe that speaks so passionately of the enduring joys of mother-child intimacy.

At New Lots Avenue, I entered into conversation with an elderly woman who was perhaps the first person I'd ever encountered whom I would describe as a "cockeyed optimist." Not only did both her eyes focus unwaveringly on the bridge of her nose throughout our chat, but she remained obdurately convinced that our train's destination was not Canarsie but the more exotic shores of Bermuda. Louis and I repeatedly traced the path of the LL on a transit map and showed her that while the LL travelled through three boroughs (Manhattan, Queens, and Brooklyn), it passed no closer than seven hundred and sixty-two miles of Bermuda. Mightn't she, we offered, be confusing Bermuda with Bushwick Avenue? No, indeed, her faith was unshakable. We wished her blue skies and warm weather, Louis adding a cautionary "Hey, nut, don't get too *sunboined*!" Forty minutes after we'd boarded, we arrived at our destination, Rockaway Parkway: the end of the line.

THERE are those who claim they could be led blindfolded to a Canarsie High School classroom from any point in the world and within seconds they would know where they were. There are those who further claim that if the ends of the blindfold were stuffed up their nostrils, precluding the ability to recognize Canarsie by the fetid odors rising from polluted Jamaica Bay, they'd still know where they were within seconds. Vincent Milano, he of the sausage laughter, is one of these latter "those." "It's the Canarsie chew," he explains. "I'd recognize the sound of it anytime. Nobody in the world chomps gum the way Canarsieites chomp gum."

It might be that when the administration suspended Vincent Milano, they suspended the one student at Canarsie High School who would be willing to press his "right to chew" suit all the way to the Supreme Court if necessary. Not only a lifelong Canarsie-ite, not only a four-pack-a-day man, Vinny is the leader of a local band called the Gum Bees. The Gum Bees, as their name hints, play gum. Vinny Milano plays Wrigley's (alternating between Spearmint and Wintergreen). The other members, Vinny Scarpino, Vinny Ritano, and Bruce Shapiro, play Dentyne Cinnamon, Tops Bubble, and Trident Sugarless Peppermint, respectively. (Bruce Shapiro used to play Juicy Fruit, but switched to Trident after gaining ten pounds during the heavily booked Christmas season.) As Vinny Milano sees it, there are a lot of advantages to playing gum rather than the conventional guitar, drums, and keyboard: "Obviously you save a lot of money on instruments and on roadies.

And you save time because gum doesn't need to be tuned before each performance. We can accept gigs at a moment's notice, as long as there's an open candy store nearby. We buy most of our instruments from the Three Guys Luncheonette on Rockaway Parkway. And we don't need to travel in those Silver Eagle buses; all we need are pockets." The Gum Bees have played weddings, wakes, christenings, bar mitzvahs, and occasionally the opening of a new store. "We've played Coiffures by Chan, Mike's Pool Parlor, Gloria's Modems, and the grand opening of Ray's Ocean Spray Pizza on Seaview Avenue." The scope of their repertoire is impressive; they're well-rehearsed in more than a hundred numbers and custom-tailor their playlist to suit each engagement. "We can play everything: 'Sunrise, Sunset,' 'Feelings,' 'Ave Maria.' Lately we've started to fool around with some stuff by John Philip Sousa. Marches are great for gum bands, because you can really lay down some strong percussion. In fact, we're thinking of a Sousa medley for our first album. We'll call it 'A Different Gummer.'"

Vinny doesn't think it's fortuitous that the world's first gum band has come out of Canarsie. "It couldn't have happened anywhere else," he says. "Like all artists, the Gum Bees have drawn creative inspiration from their environment. Canarsie is unique in the passion, dedication, and stylistic verve of its gum-chewing population, which includes just about everyone. What Arles was to Van Gogh, what Tahiti was to Gauguin, Canarsie is to the Gum Bees. I told Vinny Miranda, the guy who owns Three Guys, that as the renown of the Gum Bees spreads, as soon as we start touring other boroughs, aspiring gum musicians from all over the place will be coming to Canarsie—where it all began."

It's unlikely that touring will temper Vincent Milano's Canarsie chauvinism.

"Look, I've been around," he says. "I've been to Bensonhurst, I've been to Flatbush, I've been to Greenpoint, and sure there are gum chewers in all those towns, but, man, I tell you, it just *ain't* the same. Those people chew with their mouths, Canarsie-ites chew with their *souls*." Vinny opens a fresh pack of Wrigley's Spearmint and performs imitations of chewers in various Brooklyn neighborhoods. It's a virtuosic and convincing performance. The rhythm of the Canarsie chew ("rat-a-tat-tat-rat-a-tat-tat-tat") is bolder than Bensonhurst's ("rat-tat-rat-tat-rat-tat-rat-tat"), more fluid than Flatbush's ("rat-a-tat-rat-a-tat"), and certainly more intricate than the monotonous one-note chew of Greenpoint ("rat-rat-rat-rat-rat"). Vinny explains that there are basically only three elements in gum music: the percussionlike cracking of gum, the windlike slushing of saliva produced by continuous chewing, and the chewing sound itself. Yet in the mouth of a master, these three simple elements can be manipulated into endless arrangements—arrangements that are at times haunting, at times combustive, at times jubilant. "The gamut of gum," Vinny tells me, "is limited only by the musician's imagination and by the skill of his periodontist."

When I bring up the Garcia incident and the suspension, Vincent Milano's chewing becomes accelerated and nervous, the controlled rhythms falling into haphazard patterns ("rat-tat-a-tat-tat-a-rat-tat"). Vincent Milano is clearly outraged, but also keenly aware that this is a complex situation. "Gum's my life," he says with feeling, "my art, my nourishment, and my muse. I don't expect others to share my piety. I've even seen people chew gum while they smoke a cigarette or drink a Coca-Cola. It makes me sick, but I try to keep my disgust to myself. For God's sake, though, if they have to smoke or drink while they chew, can't they at least remove their gum and place it somewhere on their body, preferably on a pulse point, so it doesn't get all hard and dried out?"

Vincent Milano believes that the administration of Canarsie High School acted rashly. He believes that the penalties imposed were Draconian. Most of all, Vincent Milano believes that a rare opportunity to instill artistic fervor among the student body was overlooked. "Let's face it," he says. "Canarsie doesn't contain the most cultured populace in the world. But they do have this very vital relationship with chewing gum, and I think it should have been exploited." Vinny views gum primarily as a musical instrument, but he believes that it also has potential as a medium for the visual arts. He has written to Principal Kaufman, suggesting that detention be replaced by after-school workshops in gum painting, gum sculpture, and performance gum art. Apparently, the administration has ignored his missive, but Vinny remains undaunted.

S CHOOL'S out in ten days, and although Vincent Milano is convinced that he can make his charges against Canarsie High School stick, no one else here expects much to come of the lawsuit. Even Vinny's lawyer admits that since his client will be graduating this year and since the backlog in the city's courts will prevent the case from being heard before the end of the term, the suit will be declared "moot" and thrown out. But it's probable that when the academic year resumes next September there will remain one sure way for even the casual visitor to recognize that he's in a Canarsie High School classroom. That way is that, in a Canarsie High School classroom, students and faculty alike look at the seat of a chair before they sit down on it.

—BITS McKIBBLE

•

A Bordo!

[*In 1926 a bulky young man, new to our staff, caused a bit of a sensation by wearing a soft, ticking-striped engineer's cap to work rather than the commoner fedora or homburg. The cap was only the tip of the iceberg, as this, his first piece, shows. After almost fifty years with us, E. M. Bimbo at last stopped wearing his cap indoors and making choo-choo noises while he typed. Mr. Bimbo has always enjoyed writing about himself in the third person. Though a young man at the time of this vignette, he is already quite stuffy.*]

"AH, THERE you are, my dear boy," said E. M. Bimbo, the world's greatest railroad bore, when we presented ourself the other day at his table in the Oyster Bar of Grand Central Station. "Do sit down. Care for a mullet? No, I expect not."

Mr. Bimbo reached into a large vat on the floor next to his table and pulled out a small, gray, wriggling, live fish. With a sharp knife, he expertly beheaded, gutted, and filleted it, then rolled it into a cylindrical shape, wrapped it in a bit of cabbage leaf, and, with a flourish, popped it into his mouth.

"A little delicacy I became acquainted with in the dining car of the Hokkaido Express," said Mr. Bimbo. "A remarkable people, the Japanese. Remarkable. First-rate trains. Extraordinary. Tiptop. Zzz."

Mr. Bimbo had momentarily dozed off, as he often does during the later stages of luncheon, even in railroad stations. An attentive waiter glided over and gently poured a splash of ice water over the great man's head.

"Ah, that's better," Mr. Bimbo said brightly, sitting up with a start. "Well, my boy, how are you? But never mind that. I didn't ask you here to discuss your health. Nor are the Japanese on my agenda. I've got a train to catch"—and here Mr. Bimbo gestured toward the Oyster Bar's door, through which a glimpse of the waiting room, smoky, blue, and vast, could be caught—"and I have little time for idle chitchat. Purposeful activity! Discipline! That's the spirit of the age. You see, I have just returned from Italy, and it is the heartening progress of that country with respect to that spirit, and its application to the field of my special interest, which, or rather that, I have summoned you here to discuss."

Bimbo sat back and folded his hands complacently across his midsection, which, as he is extremely fat, is more than ample, and which, that day, was enclosed in a waistcoat of gray wool herringbone, the same material of which the rest of his suit was made. With his thumbs, he fiddled thoughtfully with his watch chain, which is heavy and gold, and which terminates in a timepiece that, as he once boasted to us, is accurate to within a tenth of a second per century.

"As you know," he began, "I have long been interested in train schedules, of which I have an enormous, carefully catalogued collection from all over the world. I have whiled away many an afternoon paging through such schedules, reliving this or that memorable journey upon the Stockholm-to-Göteborg *jarnwag*, or the Trans-Dakota Express, or the jungle route of the *chemin de fer gabonais*. What has struck me about railway schedules, after a lifetime of study, is their almost entirely fictional nature. In my experience, the train listed in the schedule invariably arrives and departs at different times from the train that is actually upon the track. Nowhere, of course, has this been truer than in Italy, a land known more for the antiquity of its churches and the excellence of its *pasta* than for the promptness of its systems of transportation—that is, until recently. Are you getting all this, my boy? Or should I talk more slowly?"

"No, that's fine," we said. (We write quickly, and in any case we make it a practice to use only manufactured quotations.) "What brought you to Italy?"

"Signore Mussolini was sponsoring a scientific conference, and I'd been invited. As you know, my own science is lexicography. Signore Mussolini's is nutritional socioengineering. He is interested in developing new uses for castor oil, particularly as an instrument of persuasion. One might even call him the George Washington Carver of castor oil, though I don't suppose he would wholly approve of the comparison."

"You didn't actually meet *Il Duce*, did you?" we asked breathlessly.

"Of course I did," Mr. Bimbo replied —rather brusquely, we thought, and we must have shown our distress, for the great polymath's face softened and he gave our hand a gentle squeeze. "There, there," he said kindly, then settled back to resume his narrative. "In fact, as it will not astonish you to learn, it was a mutual interest in railroading that brought us together. At a reception at the Palazzo Venezia, Signore Mussolini spotted the small New York Central pin I am in the habit of wearing in my lapel.

"'You wear the badge of the Strada Ferrata Centrale del Nuovo-York, do you not?' he asked me, not with the peremptory sneer that some who have never met him say is habitual with him, but rather in the eager, excited tones of a small boy.

"'Indeed I do, and so may you,' I replied in my serviceable if somewhat too French-accented Italian. And with that, I took the pin from my lapel and affixed it to his own. This is no easy task when the jacket in question is as encrusted with medals as was the one he wore. *Il Duce* is not as tall as I expected him to be, by the way. I suppose he is one of those lucky people who 'photographs well,' to use a distasteful barbarism. I remember discussing the question with Ramon Navarro in the club car of the Pacific Queen. We had just passed through Monterey when—"

"*Il Duce*, Mr. Bimbo," we said gently. The great man's mind, like an unbraked handcar on the down slope of the Pikes Peak narrow gauge, sometimes races ahead of where it ought to be. "You were saying . . ."

"Ah, yes. *Il Duce*. He was delighted, and naturally he insisted on returning the favor. He had this sent to my hotel the next morning, along with a shirt to wear it with." Mr. Bimbo tapped a small silver pin in the buttonhole of his lapel— a tiny, sculpted bundle of sticks or rods with a cunning little ax-head protruding from the top. "Can't do much with the shirt, though. It's of the finest Ethiopian cotton, but the color is coal-black. I'd look like Bugsy Siegel in it."

Mr. Bimbo sighed. "In any event," he continued, "Signore Mussolini launched into an animated discussion of trains. As he spoke of the hundreds of new dining cars, sleeping cars, and cattle cars built by the state railway companies, and of the thousands of kilometres of new track he has projected as part of his scheme for the uplift of Ethiopia, his great jaw jutted forward like the smooth cowcatcher of one of the futuristic new locomotives of which he is so justly proud. He was

The Little Queen

especially keen that I visit the railway terminal he has had built in Rome. 'You are sure to agree, Signore Bimbo,' he said, 'that our new Stazione Ferroviario is a fit setting for Europe's fastest trains.' Or was it Europe's fascist trains? Ah, well, never mind. It doesn't matter."

"What happened next?" we asked.

"As *Il Duce* talked on, the other dignitaries began to mutter among themselves. After all, we were holding up the whole reception line. It was only polite to move on—as, come to think of it, we would be well advised to move on now."

Mr. Bimbo heaved himself to his feet and maneuvered his great bulk toward the door. But he was still talking, and we trotted eagerly after him. "The last thing Signore Mussolini said to me," the great lexicographer went on, "was that I really should go to the new station the very next morning—early enough, preferably, to watch the eight-twenty to Venice pull out under full steam."

"What was it like?" we asked.

"I don't know," Mr. Bimbo replied. "You see, my cab was held up in traffic, much to my annoyance, and when I arrived the eight-twenty was only a puff of smoke and a caboose in the distance. It had left right on time. Or, as *Il Duce* would say, *in perfetto orario*."

•

The heart rendering plot could only have come from a studio barnstorming session.
—*Sci Fi Monthly*.

The West are different from you and I.

EPISTLE FROM EUROPE
(1982)

[Jane Kramerversuskramer's willingness to receive any sort of injection without tears or a lollipop afterwards has meant a broader horizon and more well-worn passport than any of our writers since A. J. Riesling. Here she is at her wanderlusting best.]

The Wachau, May 28

GEORGI Visloshéd admits to being in his nineties, but who knows? Georgi is from Bulgaria, the country that discovered yogurt. What is certain is that, sometime between the Russo-Turkish war and the turn of the century, Georgi Visloshéd had his first taste of Danubian May wine. And today, though he has no corporate affiliation or, for that matter, visible means of support, he is known from the Black Forest to the Black Sea as *El Exigente* of the Danube. Like a migratory bird, he makes the annual trip upriver, poking his twinkling nose in at farm or vineyard, inn or castle, for a taste of the local vintage. There is no snobbery to his tastings; he gives out no medals. His response is always a heel click, a two-fingered salute, and a wink of the eye. Vintners believe he has a complicated rating system betrayed by which hand he uses to salute and which eye he winks, but river people and farmers alike say that only once in almost a hundred years (when two stableboys gave him horse "wine" as a practical joke) did he ever register a judgment interpreted as critical. It is a Danubian custom to give him free passage on the river, and tugs and barges slow when they see his teetering, white-maned frame dockside. (Tour-boat pilots, depending on the time of day, pretend not to notice him, as he often falls into a trancelike slumber late in the afternoon and his snoring interrupts the guides' amplified spiels.)

Ernest Hemingway, after wintering at Shruns in the Arlberg, regularly sought out Georgi to revel with him on his vernal rounds (it is generally assumed that the character of Dimitri in the story "A Bad Sprain" is modeled after Georgi), but to this day Visloshéd, who speaks no language other than his native Bulgarian (and that only stumblingly), claims no knowledge of the robust, bearded author. In the early 1970s, it became fashionable for students to tag along with Georgi, measuring themselves against the old master, but the farmers and innkeepers frowned on this because it created the kind of mess associated with the first days of a rough ocean voyage. Georgi is unaware of his intermittent celebrity. He plods along with a smile for all but always at his own pace. And though he is always among people, he is also always alone, for rarely does he lift his glass with others. His actions are not shared; they are witnessed. He is watched for his response, to control his consumption (on examining a label he may sometimes absently drink long draughts directly from the bottle), and in case he falls down.

HEN

His effect on the marketplace varies, depending upon who is commenting on it. The vintner who has been blessed by a visit from Georgi may claim his to be a prize-winning stock. Those whom Georgi for some subtle, oenological reason has passed up call him a sot.

For the most part, the wines of the Danube lack the distinction of the regal French vintages. Language scholars claim that *butoir*, the French word for "doorstep," is actually derived from the name of the earliest Danubian vintage. Some insiders say that this is nothing more than a historically entrenched, promotional gimmick, while other industry experts point to the cultural differences between Western and Eastern Europe. The primarily eastern Danubian countries of Germany, Austria, Hungary, Czechoslovakia, Bulgaria, and Romania all share the checkered heritage of the nomadic, tribal Huns. Strongly anchored to the Visigoth virtue of instantaneous consumption, the Danubian wine industry "moves" almost all of its output annually; a two-year-old vintage is usually still around only because it had been misplaced. But if much of the wine-drinking world considers the Danubian product unpretentious, amusing, or even screw-top-worthy, no one has bothered to tell the Danubian people themselves, who believe so strongly in their handiwork that they drink it all up as soon as it's in a liquid state. As Baron Toadt Von Plik of the prosperous Von Plik Vineyards said to the assembled press at the Brussels World's Fair after Maurice Chevalier spit a mouthful of Riesling on his lederhosen, "It's all right, fellows, did you ever taste French beer?"

There is a story that once in Bratislava a French diplomat presented Georgi with a thirty-year-old *pinot gris* and that after just one sip Georgi poured the rest over his shoes, asking where the polish applicator was. Most river people claim the legend is just that. In fact, it seems so far-fetched that Romanian comic "Kiki" Bludnik, known behind the Iron Curtain as the Don Adams of the Balkans, rose to stardom with the line "Would you believe Georgi poured the *pinot gris* on his shoes?" What the story underscores is the difference in attitude between the two wine-producing cultures: the French vintners cling to what they consider to be the high road, that the production of wine is an art on a level with painting, sculpture, and poetry. The Danubians, as typified by Georgi, view wine more simply and variously—as the ancient nectar of the harvest ritual, as every peasant's friend, and as an alternative to beer in chug-a-lug contests.

Georgi Visloshéd says he has never been to a doctor—that he has never broken a bone or suffered an ailment worse than the sniffles. Medical appraisers who have gotten close enough claim his briny appearance is actual and not only in the eye of the beholder. (The Humana Hospital of Louisville has come right out and petitioned for his heart.) Although it certainly would be interesting to examine under suitable conditions what must be a most remarkable constitution, Georgi will live along the Danube as long as the water flows and the grapes grow on the sloping riverside terraces. Occasionally he has been curried by politicians (Konrad Adenauer referred to him a "cultural treasure" and Marshal Tito referred to him as "the people's drunk"), but current events pass him by. He cannot distinguish one political theology from another, owns no passport other than his face, and draws a blank when asked about World War Two.

Born in Plovdiv to an unsuccessful rice farmer ("My father was a misplaced visionary in a land of groats and bulgar"), Georgi carried the torch his father lit by staging several "rice festivals." He attempted to institutionalize his recipe for Rice Plovdiv, which calls for warming the rice only until crunchy. The festivals were financial disasters, but the national feeling he generated inspired the government to allow him the use of a test kitchen above the Plovdiv Puppet Theatre, and, though he no longer produces recipes or festivals, he has lived there, rent-free, for as long as he can remember. No one knows exactly when Georgi became the travelling authority on Danubian wines, but there are those old hands around who remember him stopping off at their farms in the days when Archduke Ferdinand was still wearing diapers.

GEORGI'S spring routine varies little from a few well-worn alternatives. Generally, he sniffs the air outside once or twice in mid-March, and he is usually changed and ready to go before the end of the month. He always travels north out of Plovdiv and heads to Bucharest for the *Tucia*. A heavy plum brandy, *Tucia* tastes a bit benzene-y to the Western palate but is nothing compared to the skinless *mititei*, a sausage once fed to sentries to make sure they didn't fall asleep on duty. This year, Georgi is being presented with a fashionable new exercise outfit by the Romanian People's Committee for Local Color. Since the success of Nadia Comaneči, Romania has become sports-obsessed and is the leading Communist Bloc producer of sweatclothes and jogging apparel. Georgi's new suit fits him loosely and is of soft gray-and-pink cotton with elastic purple piping at the cuffs, waist, and neck. After a brief presentation ceremony (in which several constables help him out of his old clothes and into his new ones), Georgi attacks a table full of *mititei* and *Tucia* with smiles for all and a cloth napkin tucked into his collar. The

spectators (there is a shifting group of picnickers in lakeside Herăstrău Park) seem to appreciate Georgi's graciousness and laugh in amazement as he moves from the *Tucia* to *Cotnari*, Romania's notable dessert wine. Georgi slugs some down while mixing a concoction of the mushier delicacies on the spread (Romanian cuisine tends toward a hybrid mixture of soup and cereal). Adding some wine, he lifts a bowlful of *brinza* (a tangy, liquid cheese) and, abandoning his spoon, pours it into his mouth in time to the crowd's rhythmic chanting. This dispatched with, Georgi, a little unsteady but still beaming through watering eyes, is helped to a cart that will take him back south to the river. In a matter of moments, he is unconscious and spring in Bucharest is officially and well begun.

The next morning, Georgi is his mumbling, smiley self aboard a chugging river tug heading northwest. What is amazing is that after the countless litres of brandy and wine, this old man can keep his composure while the diesel engine throbbingly clanks and the river current slaps unsettlingly against the prow of the small boat. The noise and movement are enough to make one shift into Lamaze breathing, while the smells (there is a plate of fresh-caught river eel being passed around by the crew, and Georgi's own bouquet is best described as invigorating) are so pungent to Western senses as to cause a debilitating lightheadedness.

Upriver, beyond Belgrade, where the river turns due north, and just past Budapest, where it makes a sharp turn west, the Danube straightens and makes a run for Austria. Crossing the border at Vienna, the river flows into the most important wine-growing area of its long course—the Wachau. The Wachau is steeped in the dipsomaniacal Germanic tradition. This is where the fruit or-

"I think questions involving kaka poopoo would be best addressed to Dr. Farkleman."

• •

chards and vineyards hug mile after meandering mile of neatly banked and terraced riverside. The air is sweet with fruit blossoms, and the river turns and twists so dizzyingly that many foreigners beg to be put ashore.

Georgi is more at home in the Wachau than in Plovdiv. The generic name for the wine here is *Heurige*. The farmhouses of the region that sell their homemade vintages announce it by mounting green boughs on their doors as a welcome to thirsty travellers. These wine gardens, or *Heurigen*, dot the countryside for miles north and south of the Danube. Georgi spends the bulk of the season wandering aimlessly from the northern lip of the Alps up to the Kamp river valley. In the town of Krems, the Weinbaumuseum is devoted entirely to winemaking, and it is here that Georgi

makes his only scheduled stop—a two-day symposium during which he sits in a diorama depicting a vintner's greathouse and drinks *Shluck*, the local attempt at a dry white (a miss is as good as a mile) while visitors query him on a variety of oenological subjects with the help of an interpreter. These questions concern the proper temperature at which to serve May wine ("Warm is good, cold is good, who cares?"), whether the palate can truly be cleansed between wines during a meal ("Sure, but why?"), and if the front part of the tongue is more sensitive to drier flavors ("I don't know, I try to keep my tongue out of the way when I drink").

After the session is over, it's just a hop down to the Schneeburg district, where, in the brewery town of Markt Piesting, tourists can supposedly have as many glasses of *Peistingerbrau* as they want. *Peistingerbrau* is a dark, stoutlike Austrian beverage that is quite bitter, and when it is pointed out to Georgi that he's drinking beer, he is mute and seems confused. He finishes his glass and thinks, then asks for another, downs it, and shrugs. Markt Piesting is a town to which experienced travellers come in order to recover from passing through Baden. (Baden is, of course, the famous spa town; the ornate column in the *hauptplatz* commemorates the end of the Black Death.) Although the question of what Georgi is doing at a brewery is puzzling, the *Braumeisters* seem to accept his presence happily and even urge him on by filling the table with frothy, antique steins, and although there is no interpreter here, Georgi makes himself perfectly understood when, after several hours of consumption, he pantomimes diving into and elaborately breaststroking around in the beer vat. The scene is the kind of display that Westerners are used to seeing in documentaries about plants and insects on educational television. What makes the event extraordinary is that, with his last surge of voluntary movement, Georgi manages to launch himself in the direction of Rust, the next town on his itinerary, to sample the *Blaufrankisch*, an antifungal burgundy. It is barely noon.

G EORGI is now travelling by bus, sitting bolt upright and making a kind of hooting sound that annoys the other passengers. People yell at him to stop in German and in several Romance languages. He happily continues to hoot. It is not entirely clear whether Georgi is asleep or awake. If any passengers think of suggesting that complaints be lodged in Bulgarian, they remain mute. The bus is thick with embarrassment.

When the trip ends, Georgi stands and offers his fellow-passengers the two-fingered salute and heel click, then bounds off the bus and across the square in an energetic gambol. As he disappears around the corner of a post office, it appears he has no idea where he is or where he is going. This assumption is proved incorrect, however, when he returns jiggling the fly area of his sweat suit, moving more deliberately now in the direction of the local wine merchant. Hours later and again headed northwest, toward the river, Georgi shows no ill effect from the quick sequencing of battalion-strength quantities of beer and wine. He seems in exactly the same state he would have achieved by investing the entire day in either one beverage or the other.

There is a strong Magyar influence in Rust, and Gypsies have come out with the sunset to dance, sing, and have at the tourists. The Gypsies' piercing aroma rouses Georgi, and he begins to mumble about his home in Plovdiv. It is uncharacteristic of him to be up at this time of day, but the presence of the Gypsies, though terribly depressing to Westerners, is cause for a nightcap. A Gypsy camp is not restful for those not in the fold, and though it is not at all advisable for a visitor of either sex to actually fall asleep, Georgi passes out serenely in the firelight after only three tin cups of gypsy Tokay, a derivative of Sterno and cheesecloth. This paucity of drink constitutes the briefest and most temperate bout thus far in Georgi's trip. The Gypsies show their respect by taking only his sneaker laces.

T HE *Schlosshotel* in the riverside hamlet of Dürnstein is the legendary castle where, during the Crusades, Richard the Lion-hearted was held for ransom by the Danubian barons. Like Blondell, Richard's faithful servant who traveled from castle to castle looking for his master until he found him in Dürn-stein, Georgi Vislošhéd gazes up at the imposing tower and sings out one of the few German words he seems to know: "*Schnapps*." There is apparently no place on the face of the earth more notable for its apricot schnapps. Since it is, however, before seven in the morning, several guests—obviously uninitiated tourists—lean out their windows and threaten Georgi with arrest. He offers them all his familiar smile and salute, and am-bles off in search of the café, where, remarkably, a young woman, barely awake herself, pads out from an unseen kitchen and without a word presents glass and

bottle. Georgi drinks steadily until the sun is high. The waitress returns with a plate of spaetzle, in which he immedi-ately falls alseep. Although his smile is like a bright gaslight, spittle, spaetzle, and schnapps have all coalesced in a drib-ble; he is making his hooting noise as well. The brisk lunch trade, just com-ing in, leaves a moat of empty tables between themselves and the Bulgarian master. Georgi will leave this afternoon for Melk, with its striking yellow abbey and preëmptive white *liebfraumilch*, but his trip to date has proven too much for a young American couple who, crossing the band of empty tables, find them-selves mumbling, "Enough is enough—this guy is disgusting," and stride off to the *Bahnhof* to return to Paris and sleep for a week.

—JANE KRAMERVERSUSKRAMER

• •

READERS AND ADVISERS

LADY PEARLE—The first thing you'll notice when visiting Lady Pearle is her fondness for cats—we counted 116 of them. Wear-ing a purple spandex jumpsuit with nail polish and lipstick to match, she has a thicker mustache than we've come to ex-pect from fortunetellers. Lady Pearle tends to give identical readings to whoever en-ters her establishment. The only reader-adviser to use a meter, she also accepts Visa and MasterCard. (107-12 Roosevelt Ave., Corona, somewhere in Queens.)

MADAME SOPHIE—New York's most wrinkled psychic, Madame uses tarot cards, tea leaves, and the horoscope in the *Post* to pre-sent an eclectic and usually contradictory reading. She claims to have been used as the model for the fortunetelling machines at Coney Island. In 1957 she appeared as a guest on "To Tell the Truth." (1774 Ocean Ave., Flatbush, somewhere in Brooklyn.)

MAMA JALOOBA—Perpetually clad in a caf-tan with a floral print seen frequently on inexpensive bedspreads, Mama offers a near-toothless grin, raspy laughter, and vision into the future. If you're lucky, her special five-dollar reading will cost you only twenty by the time you're through. Upon arrival, ring doorbell and wait patiently. Mama has arthritis. (60-47 Union Tpk., perhaps in Flushing.)

SISTER LOLA—The distinct and pungent aroma of boiling cauliflower permeates Sister's second-floor flat, which is located above an OTB parlor in Hell's Kitchen. Sister her-self provides a lengthy and often confusing palm reading, interrupted only by frequent shouts in an undetermined European lan-guage to what appear to be midgets in the next room. (137½ Ninth Ave., Apt. 20.)

SISTER MADAME—Upon entrance to this un-marked storefront, Sister Madame informs you that by handling your key ring she will be able to read the minds of your enemies. Then, while Brother Dominik plucks the zither, she performs a spastic Mediterra-nean dance that culminates in her yanking off her babushka, screaming out predic-tions, and collapsing to the floor, uncon-scious. Closed during March and April, when the facility is converted into an H & R Block office. (81 Ave. B.)

OUR WELL—HUNG CORRESPONDENTS
BRIEFING FROM BASIC
(1968)

[Not all our correspondents are free to come and go as they please, as this missive from a draftee friend of ours attests.]

THE days start with the predawn run, all of us in tight formation, panting and frothing like straining, crew-cut Percherons. Then, after a reptilian crawl, a monkey swing through the horizontal ladders, and a throaty "CHARLEY ONE, EN GEE," comes that well-earned, hearty tray of runny grits. Like the old battle hymn goes:

> Slop 'em down, boys,
> Slop 'em down.
> Slop 'em down, boys,
> And blow 'em out!

By seven A.M. (0700 hours), the time I would just be awakening "back in the world," the adrenaline is already pumping like a Texas gusher.

How silly I'd been to question this life. I'd been fully prepared to endure the worst: the renowned harassment, the stultifying uniformity, the clubby toilet facilities. What I wasn't ready for was the good things: the satisfaction of an aching muscle, the warmth of the primitive masculine bond, the thrill of blasting a human silhouette target at fifty meters with an M-16 set on full automatic.

Not that my philosophy or politics had edged a millimeter off my anti-violence, anti-war positions. Facing induction into an immoral war and the possibility of taking a fellow man's life, I was driven headlong into a crisis of conviction. Some of my friends had gone to prison; others had chosen new lives in Canada or Sweden. After much soul searching, I opted for the life-affirming path of the National Guard,

the "EN GEE" I scream so proudly now before entering the mess hall. My family supported me completely in my decision, not only with kind words and warm hugs but with actual instatement into a completely filled Guard unit (through the good offices of Mother's cousin Stewart, the alderman).

And now, in just a few fleeting weeks of basic training, I begin to accept the other point of view. Every day I can share a joke or a smoke with another being who believes the opposite of what I do. Perhaps one *can* be justified in killing another if one's life is threatened. Perhaps one *can* be justified in killing another if one's way of life is threatened. Perhaps one *can* be justified in killing another just to wipe out his ugly dink face.

IT is a day of reflection, a day of solitude. I have voluntarily given blood in return for a day of bed rest. Though the medic questioned the frequency with which I volunteer, he and I chuckled together at my suggestion that he just sign my bed-rest order without actually taking the blood. He belched as he tied off my arm and plunged the needle into the vein.

That unpleasantness over with, I get to lie on my bed alone in the barracks until the rest of the platoon returns from the field. The sergeant just walked in, and I thought he was going to burst a blood vessel in his temple when he saw me lying on my bunk. When I showed him my bed-rest form, he padded off, grumbling. In repose, the sergeant looks like an extra in an Akira Kurosawa movie. He is squat and leathery and fluent in the military tongue. Heaven knows what nonsense he is always barking out of the side of his mouth. We all look up to him and secretly dream about the day when we'll share beers with him as equals. Sedgewick nicknamed him "Pigfish" because of his little eyes and puffed-out cheeks, and the name caught on throughout the company. Sedgewick is a slow-moving, regal black lad with the size and deliberateness of a mint Packard. It occurred to me that in civilian life I would never get to know a man like Sedgewick on anything like the level I know him on here. The army eradicates the barrier of race and starts us all on the equal footing of buck private. I can honestly call Sedgewick a friend. The other day, as I was whistling along to Paul Mauriat's instrumental version of "Love Is Blue," Sedgewick and I shared a laugh as he crushed my transistor radio in one of his huge hands.

The army excises the esoterica of everyday life and reduces consciousness to a dim hum. What at first seems alien and forbidding becomes welcomely familiar as one realizes that the army in life is exactly the same as the one in cinema. The first night in the army is like no other.

• •

"Ain't life grand?"

Within hours of the senseless confusion that follows one's initial arrival at an army post, one finds oneself exchanging pictures of girlfriend, wife, or children with complete strangers whom one would otherwise cross the street to avoid. Off in one corner a tenor breaks into a soulful ballad. Across the squad bay a farmboy chimes in on a harmonica, playing a completely different song in an inpromptu battle of the bands. Out of nowhere someone produces three-point-two beer for five dollars a can. A smiling Latin boy taps me on the shoulder; I regard him warmly, feeling a sense for the first time that this is my home—first squad, second platoon, charlie company, fourth battalion, eighth training brigade. We are all in this together.

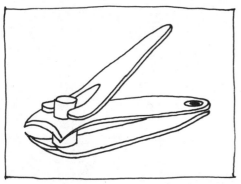

The young Latin boy smiles. He produces a gleaming, red-handled hatchet. "First VC I get to," he tells me, "I'm gonna bury this in his eye."

"That's nice." I nod. I have made a new friend.

"They killed my cousin Rubio. I'm gonna scalp those mothers."

"I'm in the National Guard." I volunteer something about myself to create equality in our new relationship. "I'm just on active duty for a few months, and then I go home again."

He grasps my forearm in his free hand and squints into my eyes. "You will be my blood," he says. "We will stick together in 'Nam. If something happens to me, you take my ax. You put it in a VC's eye."

"I'll be going to weekend Guard meeting on Staten Island."

"Then you cannot be my blood," he says sorrowfully, honestly dejected.

"Yes. It's too bad," I say. I wonder if I am the only humanist within hailing distance.

The Latin boy continues on to the soldier in the next bunk. He presents his hatchet and tells his story. In the army, life continues apace.

CRADDOCK is our Will Rogers, our country boy, our hayseed. His wry, understated wit has pulled us through many a tough detail. He has that marvelous American quality of amiable defiance. His subtle, *sotto voce* rejoinders more often than not send those closest to him into paroxysms of laughter, causing them to fall out of step so that they, rather than Craddock himself, end up singled out for chastisement. During "G.I. parties," when most of us are busy scrubbing plumbing fixtures with toothbrushes or folding underpants to acceptable tolerances, Craddock tries to ride the electric floor buffer across the barracks linoleum, screaming, "Vietnam or bust, suckers!" With his new, scabbed-over, three-color tattoo (a red-pitchforked imp astride a "slick" tire in flames with the legend "Hell on Wheels"), a startling lack of incisors (army dentists' prime directive is "Pull, don't drill"), and his hacked-up scalp (after his initial G.I. haircut, he went against orders and shaved his head, with amateur topographic results), Craddock reminds one of the infrantrymen's motto:

> Follow me
> I am the Queen of Battle
> Follow me.

BIVOUAC.
The tall Georgia pine.
The red Georgia clay.
I share my tent with Kikandopolis,

the Greek restaurateur. He had asked to share the tent with me because, he said, everyone else made jokes about sharing a tent with a Greek. He said he was asking to share because he knew me to be more intelligent and sensitive when it came to these things and that I wouldn't be swayed by vicious, bigoted, national stereotyping. I told him that of course I wouldn't and that I would be pleased to share the tent with him.

He winked at me.

I haven't had any sleep in three days.

Every day brings new challenges—target detection, compass reading, bathrooms without walls. Yesterday I threw my first live hand grenade. I really got the chance to show off the old football wing. After the sergeant got up again, he told me I'd be a real credit to the National Guard. That made me feel good because most of the fellows don't think too much of the Guard.

This evening after chow, a few of us sat around in a small clearing, leaning back against the trunks of the tall, dark trees. As soldiers everywhere do, we got to talking about things back home and what we missed most. Of course, everyone missed girls, many missed their cars, some missed pets, record collections, and favorite shoes. At that moment, I myself would have killed for a good chicken Vindaloo. Just then, Kikandopolis jumped up and exclaimed, "Me, I miss dancing!" and he started circling the clearing in a series of Zorba-like turns to a rhythm only he heard. Every so often, he would snap his fingers or clap a hand to a kicked-up heel. Suddenly he threw his head back and began to moan unintelligible Cyrillic noises. The sun had begun to set and a chilly wind had picked up, but in moments Kikandopolis was soaked in sweat. Craddock elbowed me in the ribs. "He's gonna smell good tonight," he gibed with customary wit. After one final "Huppa!" Kikandopolis came back to his seat. He looked at us all and announced, "To dance is to live." Nobody disagreed. Everyone just filed out of the clearing and, one by one, flicked cigarette butts at him and called him "fruit" or "Geek."

I am writing this by flashlight in the cold night outside my tent. Craddock was right. Reflecting on the evening's events, I think that the tough, good life we have here is not for everyone. Some, like Shapiro, crack under the strain. One day, after a particularly gruff tongue lashing by Pigfish, Shapiro told me he had "had it." He called to the sergeant, strode over to him, and, in front of the whole platoon, urinated all over the sergeant's patent-leather jungle boots. That was the last we saw of Shapiro. I wonder if Kikandopolis will be next. I think how lucky I am to be able to retain my civilian values and at the same time appreciate the harshness of army life.

The night around me is chilly. I lean against my rifle and give thanks that I will be home again years before any of the morons in all these nearby tents get out. I'll be home again in no time.

I wonder if I have enough guts to urinate on the sergeant's boots.

—BILL BARRACKS

NITTPICKSTEIN'S EAST HAMPTON
(1985)

[*Ludwig Nittpickstein, who died in 1951, was an extremely accomplished whistler as well as one of the greatest philosophers of this century—the only one to write alternating pages of German and English. Born in Vienna, he spent much of his life in England, lecturing at Cambridge University, so he was irritated to hear he had founded Oxford philosophy. An enigmatic genius of profoundly religious temperament, Nittpickstein feared that his soul would disappear if he allowed himself to be photographed without his windbreaker. After he tried it, he became a materialist. During his lifetime, he produced only one book; since his death, he's been far more prolific, impressing the academic community he disdained with his singular ability to perish and publish.*

The manuscript of "Nittpickstein's East Hampton" was discovered in 1985, scrawled in a semiprivate language on the real-estate section of The East Hampton Other. *What brought Nittpickstein, whose hobbies were chess and manual labor, and who didn't even own a tux, to the chic Long Island resort some thirty-four years after his death is a mystery. The visit may have been suggested by his students, many of whom totally misunderstood him, or perhaps he was drawn to the area by the plentiful ducks and rabbits, animals whose ambiguities never ceased to fascinate him.*

Like many of his posthumous works, Nittpickstein's appreciation of fin de siècle *East Hampton was deciphered by G. A. L. Anselm, who undertook this difficult task with the best of intentions. Nevertheless, the result of her efforts is bound to surprise people who think our magazine only prints fluff. Not so. When the lightness of being grows unbearable, we add some bread to the leavening—preferably sliced from a dense* mitteleuropäische *loaf. We hope this selection will suit those readers with I.Q.s higher than Mozart's and flatter the rest of you en route to the drawings.*]

1. The world is a collection of facts. The cat is on the mat. Excalibur has a sharp blade. There is a shortage of neon in Iran. August is the best month to spend in the Hamptons.

2. If I say to someone, a real-estate broker, for example, "Find me a house in East Hampton," how do I know that the house he will find me is the same as the house I have in mind? The house I have in mind is made of weathered shingle; it has three bedrooms, three bathrooms, all appliances, and a deck. But what can it mean to say that what I have in mind, i.e., a *mental image*, is made of weathered shingle or that it has a deck? Can I say that my mental image is available from Memorial Day through Labor Day? That it is south of the highway, a few minutes' walk from the beach? There is a great temptation to think of the mind as a locality. If this were so, what would be the point of renting?

3. Perhaps I should ask, instead, for a house in East Hampton *analogous* to the house I have in mind, that is, a house that shares certain properties with the house I imagine: three bedroomness, good neighborhoodhood, tasteful furniturety. But even if there *were* such a house in East Hampton, for under ten grand for the season, how could the real-estate agent *know* it, since he cannot see my mental image of the house? How then could he recognize an *analogous* house? Well, one might be inclined to suggest that, when I describe the house I am seeking to the real-estate agent, my

words, the *expressions* I use, produce in his mind a picture of the sort of house I would like. Then he compares his mental image of my mental image with his listings. How *exactly* would he do this? Would his eyes be closed or open? Would he need to use his lap?

4. "I've got just the thing for you!" the agent exclaims. If this is so, how should I *know* it? One answer might be to drive to East Hampton to see if the house he shows me is like the house I have in mind.

5. Suppose the agent shows me a place, after warning me that most of the decent houses have already been rented and that

I should have come earlier—say, in 1649—if I really wanted to be choosy. He describes what he shows me as a "converted barn," a puzzling expression, for it does not specify into what the barn has been converted (cf. "defrocked priest," "former showgirl"). This confusion disappears when it becomes clear that the animals who recently inhabited the barn have merely abandoned it and been replaced by several mattresses, a wicker sofa, and a laminated nautical map of Long Island. (There is a tendency to assume that some mysterious essence is needed to transform a barn into a non-barn, a habitat into a home,

• •

"Would you like wicker insurance with that?"

but all that may be required is a trip to Conran's and a seller's market.)

6. Now one may say to the agent, "This isn't what I had in mind." What *use* is he to make of this expression? He might suppose that the house I have in mind corresponds to certain physiological processes in my brain and, further, that if he could observe these processes, he might be better able to produce an appropriate dwelling for me to inspect. Alternatively, if he abhors the sight of blood and is very busy on weekends, he might simply shrug and say, "I can't read your mind." Is this a confession of inadequacy? Or is this utterance logically akin to "I can't have your toothache"? (In either case, it would make no sense to urge him to try harder; chances are, he doesn't much care about this particular deal, perhaps because he has some other source of income.)

7. Why can't I get it through my head that "what I have in mind" is nowhere near my skull? My aim is to show the fly the way to the flypaper.

8. Consider a different tack: I propose to *show* the agent what I have in mind by pointing to an appealing house while saying, "*That* is what I have in mind." This is how we teach the meaning of certain expressions. Thus we might teach a child the meaning of "red" by pointing to a stoplight, an apple, or a communist. But we do not invariably use this form of explanation. If a child asks, "What is the meaning of 'antidisestablishmentarian,'" we would not ordinarily respond by pointing to a dead Irish churchman. More likely, we would simply tell the child to look it up in the dictionary, or to get lost. These, too, are forms of explanation.

9. Any explanation may be misunderstood, though not without a lot of effort. Imagine, for example, that as I point to an appealing house, the moon rises just above it in the arc indicated by my finger.

Can my gesture by misinterpreted? The answer is: *of course*—but only by a blind man, a lunatic, or someone doing philosophy. Can I be certain that the real-estate agent is more discerning? Suppose he says, "What you want is out of reach." Does this dispel the confusion?

10. Suppose I ask the agent to name a figure. Let's say he draws the numeral 3 and labels it "Smythies." Surely I'd assume the man is joking. But what if he says, "Twenty thousand dollars for the season." Here, too, I might think he must be joking, but now I feel myself on *shaky ground*, on the blurry border between laughter and wincing. So I might remark that $20,000 is *twice* the sum I had in mind.

11. Now the agent begins to act queerly, like a man with someone else's innards. He shifts his feet, rolls his eyes, glances furtively, and so forth. At last he whispers, "Why not share the house and split the rent? But don't tell anyone I mentioned it, as groupers are illegal in this area."

12. It occurs to me that something's fishy, but I think I see a clearing in the thicket. Or is it a thicket in the clearing? With these glasses, it's difficult to tell. When I remove them, I'm struck by a distinction between the laws of zoning and the laws of mathematics—namely, that the former are harder to enforce.

13. "So long as you are quiet and don't litter or dance nude in the rain . . ." The real-estate agent broker winks and produces a lease, which I sign.

14. Ask yourself the following: Is a wink a proposition? Can it be true or false? As good as a nod? Or *slightly* less virtuous? *Roughly*, a wink is a gesture that may do the work of a proposition, as every schoolboy knows. In the case of the real-estate agent, is it not *as if* he had said, "Whereof we cannot speak, thereof we must shut up"?

—LUDWIG NITTPICKSTEIN

AEROGRAMME FROM LONDON

(1973)

[*From the dark days of the Blitz through the more recent dark days of the pound's devaluation, Mollie Panties-Downe has been keeping us in touch with London and the whole of the United Kingdom from her splendid redoubt in Haslemere, always telling more, perhaps, about the English weather than one really needs to know.*]

I T was one of those delightfully raw afternoons in late November, the kind that makes one remember coming home from school, the scent of woodsmoke in the air, and toasting crumpets for tea with Nanny. In other words, it was the kind of afternoon that made Rupert Brooke proud to die an Englishman and not a Welshman, although it must be said that the Welsh do mists extremely well. It was especially the kind of afternoon when the English like to draw closer to the fire, scratch their chilblains, and tell of the heroes of the Second World War, "The Other Bloody Big One," or TOB-BO, as nostalgic acronymn-hounds dub it, at closing time in cosy country pub and smart Knightsbridge hostelry alike.

On this gloriously dank afternoon, an extraordinary procession could be discerned through the drizzle, wending its way down Whitehall from Trafalgar Square and Nelson's proud column. The cheery throng didn't in fact wend so much as it hopped, slithered, trotted, and dawdled, composed as it was of descendants of the pet veterans of TOBBO and, in one case, an eighty-five-year-old Moroccan box turtle owned by Mr. and Mrs. A. Stebbins of Wigan—an actual veteran of the hostilities. Brenda, as the elderly turtle was called, sustained a direct hit from a bomb, which bounced off her shell into a nearby compost heap and would have remained undetected had the gallant Brenda not, despite her wounds and extremely short legs, climbed on top of the bomb and refused steadfastly to budge, even at dinnertime. The ensuing search turned up both Brenda and the bomb. What a trove!

Leading the procession, reassuringly familiar and perfectly appropriate, were the sixteen royal corgis in close formation, stepping out as smartly as only blue-blooded canines can. It was their grandparents, of course, who did so much for morale when they visited, with their owners, harrowing scenes of carnage and destruction during those dark days of the Blitz. However weary, however discouraged, those plucky corgis had a sniff and a pee for everyone.

The procession drew a host of spectators, some holding their children aloft to wave Union Jacks in the animals' honor. "I've travelled all the way from Dorking," said ruddy-faced, moist-eyed Reg Thwaite, whose five-year-old daughter, Mandy, had brought along her newt in solidarity. "I wouldn't have let Mandy miss this for the world. Makes you proud not to be Welsh, don' it?"

Around Parliament Square they surged, up the steps and into Westminster Abbey itself for the ecumenical service of thanks. Brenda had fallen behind, but it didn't matter one jot. It being the Moroccan Festival of the Foot-travellers, and Brenda being an observant Moroccan, she had decided to make her own private devotions facing east at the foot of the Abbey steps. Looking along the aisles, one felt humble, remembering the indomitable spirit of those fallen pets whose kin bowed their heads in honor. Pinkie, the renowned budgerigar of Harrow, came to mind. Pinkie saved his mistress's life by tweeting, till his tiny lungs actually burst, to alert her to a gas leak from a line ruptured by workmen digging out casks of life-sustaining English stout from the bombed pub next door.

The Archbishop of London, the Very Reverend Roddy Towne-Smythe-Towne (Eton and Oxford and a veteran himself), climbed slowly to the pulpit. The mighty assemblage ceased its twitter and rustle. The Archbishop intoned the roll of honor, his sturdy voice faltering for a moment as he recalled his own dead heroine, Flo, a Jersey cow who served with him on a destroyer in the North Sea. The Archbishop had been the ship's chaplain; Flo, the ship's mascot, and also a source of frothy, inestimably comforting milk for the boys who fought so fearlessly to keep the enemy far from our island home. Flo's story is by now a legend. The ship went down with all hands after being ambushed by a U-boat. Flo was last seen, in the Archbishop's words, "udders resplendent, giving her all, a Jersey cow to the very end," as she slipped under the waves. The Archbishop survived to tell the tale. All that was left of Flo was the bell she wore round her neck, which was inscribed *Venite et Prendete*, or "Come and Get It," the motto of both the cow and the ship.

The rest of the service was splendid. A granddaughter of the famed pianist Myra Hess spoke movingly of her mother's lunchtime recitals at St. Martin's-in-the-Fields (they did so much to lift our spirits during those dark days of the Blitz, with the bombs dropping all round) and reminded her listeners that Dame Myra's goldfish, serenely afloat in a bowl atop her Steinway, never missed a concert. The band of the Scots Guards summoned up fanfares so spine-tingling that even Brenda, slumbering on the Abbey steps, lifted her head like a proud old war-horse scenting battle. And afterwards the joyful horde reconvened at the Palace for tea, scones, and appropriate snacks with our dear Queen and her beloved "Mum."

"IT got a bit hairy" is how one of London's hottest new avant-gardists described his newest performance work, which ran for twelve and a half minutes last Wednesday on a Belfast street corner. Spike is the simple name by which this tough-talking twenty-four-year-old likes to be called, and it expresses something of the effect he's after, with the lone tassel of emerald hair hanging from an otherwise shaved scalp, the nicotine-stained fingertips, and the '60s-style Carnaby Street clothing—worn, as he will tell you with a ferocious scowl, "satirically."

Spike's shows have always stirred controversy. Even as a small boy at the exclusive Cheam School (which our young princes attended), Spike loved to shock. As a fourth-former, he smeared himself all over with Major Grey's chutney and stood nude but for a loincloth, reciting stanzas from "A Shropshire Lad" as part of his class's contribution to the school pageant, whose theme was "Our Far-flung Commonwealth Brothers and Sisters." At Cambridge, he first affected the nasal North London accent that is by now his trademark, and he smoked small and pungent Woodbine cigarettes, more commonly seen in the hands of bricklayers. His most talked-about Cambridge performance involved chaining himself to a Stop sign with his girlfriend, the

Honorable Annabel Livesey (St. Swith-in's School for Girls and North Cambridge Secretarial College) while they both sang selections from "South Pacific" —Spike's very particular statement about American involvement in Southeast Asia.

For the past two years, with the help of an Arts Council grant, Spike has taken his art to the streets. His Northern Ireland piece is an amazingly bold mélange of images. Wearing only a large Union Jack and a solar topee, he darts from one street corner to the next in largely Republican areas of this troubled city, alternately declaiming stanzas from "The Charge of the Light Brigade" and distributing miniatures of Irish whiskey. Performance times average between six and fifteen minutes, depending on the amount of time it takes for a crowd to gather and the whiskey to be handed out. This show often turns out to be boisterous indeed!

Spike will be resting for a while. His last performance resulted in a misunderstanding, as a result of which the passionate young artist was shot in the knee, or "kneecapped," as they call the custom in Northern Ireland. (From his hospital bed, Spike quipped with his inimitable flair, "Under the imperialist system, we are all kneecappers, luv.") His parents, the Maude-Roxbys, who, as it happens, live next door to me in Tennyson Way, Haslemere, Surrey, remain loyal in his support as he pushes back the frontiers of performance art. "Peregrine always took things more seriously than other boys," says his mother, "and thanks to the trust fund his grandfather set up for him, he's been able to share his vision with the rest of the world. We do hope, however, that one day he'll learn to support himself."

O N Guy Fawkes night, with fireworks, bonfires, and the burning of the symbolic "guy," we celebrate the

rescue of our doughty island nation from Catholicism. The well-loved children's rhyme goes, "Remember, remember/the fifth of November/Gunpowder, treason and plot/I see no reason/Why gunpowder treason/Should ever be forgot." And forgot it most certainly is not. Every year the streets are aswarm with youngsters proudly exhibiting their homemade guys and chirping the traditional request: "Penny for the guy, sir?" To be sure, the ancient art of guy-making has changed over the centuries. Nowadays, the guy may be simply a few balled-up pillowcases painted with rough daubs, and the old chant has given way to the ubiquitous "Fifty p for the guy, or else . . ." But still the ceremony can make our hair stand thrillingly on end, and nowhere is its crude power more exhilaratingly realized than in Brixton.

Though shabby and working-class, Brixton is a district of London that teems with the vitality of its newest inhabitants, the West Indians, who take to the Guy Fawkes celebrations with gusto. This year, unhappily, tragedy marred the festivities. A magnificent municipal fireworks display had reached its apotheosis in a finale of Catherine wheels and sparklers that shaped the words "Happy Wedding, Princess Anne and Mark Phillips!" Afterwards, throngs of colored youths excitedly roamed the streets, looking for even more fun. Things got a little out of hand, and before too long a motorbike had been overturned, a bobby's helmet had been knocked sideways, and two dustbins were in flames. Several youths were detained, and are still helping police with their enquiries.

Right-thinking people everywhere have condemned this shocking outbreak of anarchy. Labour politicians blame it on American TV shows that have been called "sickeningly vulgar and violent," but Conservatives look closer to home for the culprit. "One must ask oneself,"

says Mrs. Margaret Thatcher, Education Minister and a rising star of the Tory front bench, "whether our newer Londoners are failing to instill traditional English values in their children. And one can only answer oneself that the answer is, quite clearly, yes."

A Government Commission of Enquiry, under the direction of Lord Pontefract Cake, is looking into the matter and is due to report some time in the next four to five years. Meanwhile, in all corners of this most civilized and tolerant nation, from Haslemere to Hindhead and beyond, people are deeply confident that the spirit that brought us together during those dark days of the Blitz will unite us once again in these trying times, and ensure that such violent scenes will never again be visited upon us.

—MOLLIE PANTIES-DOWNE

●

BOOKS NOT SO BRIEFLY NOTED
GENERAL

IS THAT TO GO? (TAKE-OUT MENUS FROM AROUND THE WORLD, by André Meekey (Tyme-Lyfe Books; $18.95). The sheer size of this noteworthy volume (3,847 pages) makes it the season's most formidable coffee-table book. Starting at the MacTavish Luncheonette in Glasgow, Meekey takes us from one joint to another, winding up in a Dunkin' Donuts in his hometown of Sappington, Vermont. Not surprisingly, the majority of menus included are in foreign languages.

NOTE: "Tarnished Fruit: The Decline of the Lime from Scurvy Preventive to Cocktail Garnish," by Mayo Hellman (Tingleberry and Septum; $14.95), appeared first in this magazine in a somewhat different form.

●

RECHERCHÉ

REPLAY

*O*UR *magazine has long nourished enthusiasm for all sorts of athletic endeavors, especially those engaged in by white college boys. Ours is a well-tempered fanaticism, seasoned with a thorough knowledge of the niggling facts and obscure traditions that ossify around sport as youths grow too old to play and are reduced to talking or, in our case, writing about it. In the first years of the magazine's existence, we covered polo and croquet as well as rowdier pursuits. Our first editor, Root, was a devoted poker player and would have included the best games in town among our listings if I hadn't pointed out that he might lose his seat at them.*

The magazine's approach to sport has changed as has sport itself. Acknowledging the explosion of interest in football over the last three decades, our gridiron specialists now venture outside the Ivy League. We have reflected the racial democratization of professional basketball through portraits of players as diverse in hue as Bill Bradley and Larry Bird. And, as always, we keep an eye on the horses, monitored for us by the venerable Audad Meunière. But the relaxed meditations on bezique, cribbage, and snooker have all but disappeared from our pages. We are lucky to have at work in the fields of play writers as distinguished as Roger Devill, Herbert Breaking Wind, and the indefatigable John McPhumpher.

THE RUMBLING OF THE BALL

(1978)

[*When in buoyant humor, Roger Devill refers to himself as "the Bard of the Ball and Pins." Indeed, Roger is indisputably the country's finest bowling writer. This piece secured his reputation, although one wag at our magazine used to call it "Finnegans Lane."*]

WHAT is it about bowling that makes us reëxperience the linear moments of our lives? Once again, I find myself wondering if it isn't the linear qualities of the game itself. Bowling, unlike the costumed bellicosity of the gridiron or the knee-wrenching gawkiness of basketball, has no clock. The bowlist holds time captive in his ball and freezes it as he stands on the lip of the alley. Then, as he inexorably advances and unleashes his sixteen or so pounds of solid, geologic remnant at speeds approaching twenty-four miles per hour, an eerie hush, informed as always by the rumbling of the ball, hypnotically intoxicates, until finally the inevitable impact with the pins reminds us that we have places to go, people to meet, and women's breasts to think about.

Lunch hour in late winter and we await the first frame. The yellow lambence of the Woodlawn subway invades the polyurethaned fluorescence of the bowling alley from the train's haughty perch on the elevated tracks. I have just sliced open the cool, smoky cellophane wrapper of my microwaved cheeseburger with a twisting, tearing violence of fingers, and once again I find myself wondering why the wrapper doesn't get hot. I take a bite and chew, gazing beyond the listing bevel of the twin scorer's tables with their long, bolted, metal scoresheet clips, to the piny, reflective sward of alley, and finally to where the ten white pins rest in inanimate anticipation of some random, future syncopation. They know it is their fate to be knocked to hell and gone. The older man with the shock of bony, écru brillo nods gravely at my lunch and suggests I sample the "vestern omelot." I note the natty, red script stitching above his chambray breast pocket that reads "Stosh" and find myself wondering why the name is surrounded by quotation marks.

Stosh isn't just any Stosh in Sears work twills, of course, but *the* Stosh: "One Fingers" Stosh Droppoweicz. Just my sitting next to him makes my cheeseburger a piece of history. His comeback win over Billy "Blue" Narlevski in 1956 was the sporting yarn from which legends are woven. On the first ball of the fifth frame, Stosh's thumb, permanently swollen from the long development of his unorthodox Droppoweicz Twist, stuck in his two-fingered AMF Black Beauty and was yanked out of its socket

• •

	1	2	3	4	5	6	7	8	9	10	11
NARLEVSKI	9 / 18	8 9 27	X 57	X 84	X 104	7 / 124	X 143	7 9 152	X X X 172	X X X 202	202
DROPPOWEICZ	— 0	— 0	4 0 4	8 — 12	X 29	7 0 36	/ 47	1 3 50	6 7 57	— — 57	57

on release. When the ball hit too high on the headpin, the force of impact dislodged the satellite digit and it picked off a recalcitrant seven pin that later proved to be the one-pin margin of victory. Far from ending his career, the mishap only enhanced his reputation and Stosh modified his Black Beauty to become the only professional in history to use a ball with one hole. "One Fingers" Stosh Droppoweicz bowled with just his middle finger. During the nineteen-fifties, crowds would pack the vast suburban bowlodromes that were then erupting from the earth's crust like man-made drumlins and chant "Stosh, Stosh" rhythmically, over and over, while thrusting high middle fingers in time to their adoring litany. They would chant unsatisfied until Stosh, smiling his Balkan grimace, would return the gesture.

We are at the Royal Lanes, situated on the second story of a large hardware outlet on Jerome Avenue in the Bronx. Stosh has called these modest eight alleys his home since retiring from the ranks of the pro bowlers almost twenty years ago. "I had a long run there for a while," he confides in me, "but all anyone ever wants to know about is the 'Thumb Ball.'" I nod agreeably and find myself wondering if I have ever seen a man with more hair on the backs of his hands. Stosh's eight lanes have kept him vital and engaged, but now the heartless American whim has cast him aside. The days of the great city lanes are clearly over —Oxford Lanes, which started life as an ice-skating rink, is now a house of worship; Inwood Lanes near the Cloisters is a Ray's Original World O' Pizza; the lordly Paradise Lanes is a vocational academy for beauticians.

The Royal Lanes succumb today. Stosh's space is being rented to a local social club where, he assures me, roosters will be squaring off before the week is out. But for one more match, one more set of lines on the score sheet, this is still the noblest house of bowls. The last bowling joust to take place in the Bronx is about to begin. Though I'm just a spectator, Stosh has insisted that I rent shoes.

THE final contest is a symbolic one: a replaying of the aforementioned 1956 "Thumb Ball" match between Stosh and the Blue Man, as Narlevski is often called. Notable not only for its anatomical singularity, the original match also possessed intra-regional importance, the winner taking home the title "Champion of All the Amboys" as well as a trophy the size of a johnny-pump. "In the know" witnesses claim there was also significant side money, though both contestants vehemently own up to nothing more than the hundred-dollar honorarium.

The replay is the brainchild of Karl "Frenchy" Loess, who also serves as scorekeeper, referee, and official historian. He palms a Radio Shack cassette recorder in his meaty left hand and intermittently brings it to his face to whisper *sub rosa* gems of bowling reportage out of the side of his slack-lipped mouth. The tape is slated for inclusion in Frenchy Loess's "Hi Fi Bowling History," Volume III. He sells the series mail-order out of his den.

Frenchy, enormously fat, sits down in front of me at the scorer's table with fleshy tidal waves of flab breaking over the edges of the spindly, molded Formica scorer's chair. As I regard him, I wonder why Stosh hasn't made him rent shoes. I ask tactfully in a hushed tone why this is so. Stosh's answer, polite but spit through clenched teeth, is a rasped "Too fat, too fat" accompanied by two quick "safe" gestures.

It was Frenchy who first "tipped" me to the day's classic coupling, a critical happening on any bowling enthusiast's calendar, and I find myself wondering once again why I am the only spectator to what is sure to be an unbroken series of memorable *tableaux sportifs*. My own gaudy invitation I construed to be a pre-payment for the mention in this column of Frenchy's record offer, a responsibility now dispensed with and so instantly forgotten. Frenchy's nickname derives from his early bowling style, which included an offputting, oral lubrication of his ball's fingerholes. The crowd response to this was so negative that he tried bowling "dry" and, as a result, quickly lost confidence in his release. For a bowler, loss of release confidence is akin to impotence. Frenchy began putting on weight. Before long, he became far too

"My God! The one on the end is my ex-wife!"

fat to be considered a threat to anything but the building codes.

In 1969, the momentum of a loping backswing lifted him off his feet like a toy poodle yanked on its leash and deposited him on the green-and-white, heel-scarred linoleum behind the alleys, his ball scoring a broadside into the pale cinderblock rear wall. The establishment shook so violently that Frenchy's six, nine, and ten dropped, so notching his final three pins as a professional. The resultant injuries, anguish, and snickering ended his active career and set him on the path of Troubadour of the Tenpins because "life away from the lanes was unlivable." Still, I felt a touch of bitterness that he didn't have to rent shoes.

THE Blue Man appears before me, more sliding into my plane of vision than actually walking, an incorporeal enigma in Banlon. His sinewy presence is as ageless as it is weightless. He still looks a little like Earl Holliman. He still incessantly nibbles sunflower seeds, inserting them vertically between convenient incisors, cracking the nut, extracting the meat with his tongue, plucking the empty husks out of his mouth with a thumb and forefinger, and finally flicking the shells at Frenchy Loess's ear.

His slickly pressed, tightly knit blue jacket is of the "Nehru" cut. His signature blue Banlon shirt sports a pair of tiny, peeling Ping-Pong racquets crossed at a Prussian angle. He wears no belt. His blue Continental trousers glow with a chemical sheen that makes me ponder the temperature at which they would melt. His Banlon socks display the flamboyancy of three "press-on" shields arranged vertically over the outside of each ankle. His size eight bowling shoes are oddly taupe.

He regards the deep, dark cloaca of the ball return with a diamondback's piercing gaze. No matter what my feelings are toward him away from the lanes, in an old-fashioned bowling match the Blue Man is the eternal bad guy. And even though Stosh Droppoweicz may spell hero from head to toe, this isn't the movies or TV here—in the reality of the ball and pins, sometimes the bad guy takes home the glory.

On reflection I realize that this is the classic scenario of man against man— Narlevski's speed against Droppoweicz's power; the boxer against the puncher, the junkball on the corner against smoke down the middle of the pipe, the wiry guy against the big *szchlub*. I am dimly aware of Stosh shuffling by me to pour himself a short ginger ale. Stosh's style is no secret; he lets you know what his plans are and then goes out and, systematically, gets the job done. "It's a simple game," he has said. "The man who knocks down the most pins wins." A clear memory of the young Stosh: approaching the foul line holding a paper plate full of ketchupy French fries, flinging the famous "twist" and munching a crisp one while watching the course of his ball with his eyes. The ball nestles comfortably into the fat of the far pocket on the left side of the headpin. Strike. Stosh has vehemently denied ever uttering the now famous quote but, like the "Thumb Ball," its adherence to him is his legacy. Whether he actually said, "I go after my strikes the way I go after my women— from the Jersey side," is academic. Far more important is the fact that when Stosh is on the right side of the headpin, the "pocket of choice" for other bowlers, he is off his game. And when "One Fingers" Stosh Droppoweicz is off his game there is no adjustment, no fine tuning, that can bring it into the hair's-breadth margins of sports excellence.

The Blue Man, however, is nothing if not an adjuster. He is always tinkering. A half-step to the right, an added "skip" on the approach, a "piano key" toward Brooklyn on the lineup; he is a do-it-yourself artiste, creating birdhouses of grace in the knotty-pine-panelled basement workshop of his brain. He once told me he threw a different ball for every conceivable situation in the game. In the only perfect three-hundred game he authored, he utilized four different approaches, six separate releases, and ten variations on his basic follow-through in rolling the twelve consecutive strikes. Narlevski describes every moment of the match in proper sequence, but Frenchy claims that Narlevski was snockered on slivovitz and is fortunate to remember anything from that particular year, let alone that game.

Watching Narlevski warm up, presenting his vocabulary of shots, one must suppress shouts of *Olé* time and time again. Here is a selection from his repertoire:

The Tai Chi Cha Cha Cha. First a polite bow to the ball. Then, with feet almost off the alley, Frenchy's head jerks back, exposing only the whites of eyes. A sudden lurching into a triple pirouette while each arm alternately rises and falls, the ball held aloft only by fingertips. Then a crossing over of hands and, *with his back facing the pins,* a screeching "Pee-ya-yo!" and a simultaneous twisting release of the ball following three quick steps. What makes this shot truly esoteric is not just that it is executed backwards. Narlevski uses it to pick up singleton spares. Phew.

The "Hi, Pilgrim." Imagine a version of *Rio Bravo* in which the entire plot turns on John Wayne's ability to convert a two-four-seven with double wood. Billy "Blue" Narlevski would get the part.

The Military Wedding. The approach stance is sideways, face perpendicular to pins. The ball arm is extended with locked elbow and raised aloft like a sabre, at a sixty-degree angle. The action is a sharp column left from a halt, striding off with a thirty-inch step, the ball arm then dropping with a blackshirt's flourish. The release is on the natural upswing, "squeezed off" rather than pushed so that the arm continues upward without the ball into a courteous salute.

The Gazpacho Caldo. Imagine an Osterizer set to "Pulverize." Now turn it up to "Liquefy." It's hard to tell exactly when the ball is released from this whirling cyclone, but all its energy vectors neatly into a one-point perspective with a vanishing point somewhere beyond the headpin.

The Norton Anthology. Picture Ed Norton in a bowling alley. "I was imitating him one day and I just couldn't stop myself," Narlevski claims. "It turned out to give me pretty good consistency with the three-ten, so I kept it in."

His practice frames complete, Billy "Blue" Narlevski turns to confront "One Fingers" Stosh Droppoweicz. "One Fingers," he says, "let's you and me roll some lines." The alleys are completely silent save for the rhythmic clanking of the pinsetters, the quaking rumble of the ball return, and the thunderous Dopplering of the No. 5 IRT. Stosh shuffles back across the floor, mumbling to himself something about getting home in time for "Hilligan's Island." I find myself wondering if he has heard the Blue Man's challenge. Narlevski, Frenchy, and I stare at him. With a coy smile, he holds up his middle finger. The Blue Man spits another shell at Frenchy. The match begins.

BOWLING. So taut and tremulous are its objectives. It is paradoxically tense and offhanded at the same time. Palms aglisten with perspiration, I find myself absently wondering if it's time to put another quarter in the parking meter. Then I remember that I didn't drive. Differences in pin tallies seesaw with pendulous regularity, each player feeling out the other's weakness, turning up the pressure, pushing the limits of the other's envelope. The Blue Man opens the contest with a spare, then a nine pin open in the second frame off an evil split. His pin action is atomic, but the seven pin stands through both frames like a carborundum sentry. Between balls he cools his hand over the ventilator.

STOSH sits next to me, half-humming, half-whistling the Jolly Green Giant jingle. I ask him if he will respond to a few names out of the past. Although he doesn't like to "tell tall tales out of school," I implore him for just a word on each.

"Morty Greenspan," I ask quietly.

"Had a little hop on his ball. You don't see that so much today. I think he liked boys."

"Enzo Bonderoni."

"A competitor. He once dropped his ball on my knee accidently on purpose. I told him I won't bowl with you no more."

"Harry Neely."

"Held his ball like a baby blanket. Never wanted to part with it. Then laid down these little rollers that took about an hour to get to the pins. Ugh."

Suddenly it's time for Stosh to bowl. He stands up slowly, grimacing in the familiar way, but now with the pain of rickety joints. It's getting darker outside, and with that revelation I feel a faint but distant shiver. Bowling is an indoor sport, but the lanes now seem underground and Stosh a latter-day Pluto. He inserts his finger in his ball's lone hole, then curls the ball into his hip. With his flat-footed gait he retreats to his starting point, wheels about, and sighs. Bringing the ball to his chin, he sights over its top. Moving through an atmosphere with the density of hot tar on a cold day, he starts his approach.

The atmosphere seems to change as Stosh moves forward, first to lime Jello, then to light meringue and finally back to the Bronx. With the action of a medieval catapult, he has launched his round black cruise missile and it is flying just beneath radar-detection range. When Stosh is at his best, his ball never touches the alley. Its coefficient of friction then being negligible, the ball actually gains speed as it travels toward the pins.

That Stosh knocked down no pins— that is, no pins on the alley on which he was bowling—in his first four balls was not the critical factor. As mentioned earlier, the ability to adjust was not in his act. Woefully inaccurate, he barely managed to stay in the match. Meanwhile the Blue Man, hitting for a turkey through frames three, four, and five, closed with another nifty triple strike in the tenth. The final score of 202 to 57 is important only to the extent that Frenchy's arithmetic was correct. Stosh did manage a lucky strike in the fifth, but it was a last gasp fueled by residual muscle. By that time, he was flying on auto-pilot.

But the absence of hoped-for catharthis, the stultifying quality of yet another endless afternoon, reiterated for me the limits of the bowler's tapestry. The numerology of the game—ten frames, ten pins, two balls per frame, three hundred pins is the best, zero is the worst—is mystical. And as I wait for Stosh to return my cordovan wing tips in exchange for the familiar tricolored lace-ups, I find myself wondering again why I spend so much of my life thinking about sports.   —ROGER DEVILL

P O R T R A I T S

A SENSE OF IF YOU ARE (1976)

Seth Slingerland

[*With this article, the first boxing story to appear in our pages in the nearly fifty years since Robert Densely's did not, John McPhumpher found the warp of his proper gyre, as he might put it himself. Regrettably, the final proofs of the piece's subsequent nine parts slipped overboard through my benumbed fingers one evening when McPumpher and I, on a dare, took the Staten Island Ferry without our overcoats. The proofs were never recovered.*]

S ETH "the Battling Pict" Slingerland is one of the rare boxers who have ever stunned a bloodthirsty throng of bombinating fight fans into disbelieving, slack-jawed silence even before their bouts began. This pugilistic oddity took place last December 7th at Caesars Palace in Las Vegas, Nevada, where Slingerland was matched with Dewight "Toxic Shock" Urban on the undercard of a closed-circuit WBC cruiserweight title fight between Raasheen "Final Solution" Jones and Felix "el Paranoido Loco" Cruz. The fans were impatient, having just endured an opening ten-rounder involving two dump-truck light heavies who were woefully out of shape and arm-weary by the end of round one. The dreary contest had produced but two lackluster knockdowns, in the third and sixth rounds, and gave the overall impression of being quite a forgettable experience.

When Slingerland climbs between the upper two (or sometimes lower two) ropes of a boxing ring, his Wendell Corey looks and coloring usually go largely unnoticed but for the occasional double take afforded any similarly melanin-deficient fighter today. Disdaining the popular silks and satins for the traditional terry-cloth robe, he looks more like a tired commuter on his way to "take some steam" then the indestructible impact accumulator he really is. However, during that dinner-show hour in the Caesars Palace parking esplanade, Slingerland implemented a refinement into his prefight ritual that proved even more compelling than Shecky Greene's lounge act. After entry into the ring, an artfully subtle salute toward his opponent, and a good boy's neat folding of his robe, one of Slingerland's handlers produced two thirty-eight-inch aluminum garbage-can lids and, with businesslike aplomb, clanged them with all his might around the Battling Pict's head. The silence that followed prompted one grizzled spectator to comment that he had been previously unaware of Las Vegas' active cricket population.

THE amount of punishment Slingerland can withstand is not only legendary; it is a necessity for a fighter so glaringly inadequate in so many of the skills a successful boxer must possess. To match the selectively bred talents so many contemporary fighters bring to the ring, Slingerland counters with antlike determination, exhaustive conditioning, and the attitude that self-immolating Buddhist monks are pussies. He has neither speed nor power, but his combinations are executed in such a rehearsed, precise sequence that opponents have suggested intervention by the various governing bodies of the sport to prevent him from stepping into the ring. One hulking foe battered him so hard for so long that he finally conceded the bout, claiming, "To beat him, you gotta off the mofva on his feet." Although he has not won a fight in over nine years, Seth Slingerland has never been knocked down. To be sure, he has lost fights by technical knockouts, pronounced officially on "Queer Street" by referees grasping his wrists and gazing inquiringly into his eyes to see if anything even approaching primate consciousness was still crackling. When I asked him about this recently at the Lawrenceville School boxing facility where he works out near his home in Princeton, New Jersey, he suggested that I punch him bare-knuckled in the face with everything I had. After sustaining three roundhouse haymakers, Slingerland was still anchored to the floor like a veritable Joe Palooka balloon. In reaction, he cocked his arms and jabbed the air ninety degrees to my right. I asked him how he had so often and consistently been able to dope out involuntary muscular action after so many punches. "After you get hit a few times," he answered, "you develop a sense of if you are."

Slingerland fights in a way no one ever has before. He takes things developed by other fighters and mixes them into new combinations that he has consciously woven into a philosophic fabric he calls "hostile ineptitude." It has made him a very wealthy man. He credits specific antecedents with contributing to

his utile mélange, among them such notable white hopes as Terrence "Highpockets" Pynchon, who denied opponents his body by wearing his waistband even with his nipples, as well as Paddy "Fagbasher" O'Mellahan, who for seven spectacular years successfully lied about his size and weight and systematically brutalized semipro opponents who were often only half his size. Slingerland describes his sporting evolution as bipartite, the initial stage being one of initiation. Five consecutive summers at Toughguys 'N' Tomboys, Colonel Mo Siegel's boxing camp for unpampered young gentlemen and ladies in Bennington, Vermont, exposed him to the basics and gave him his first taste of battle. He had an exceptional left hand, and Colonel Mo—a conditioning zealot, to say the least—worked it until his shoulder separated. He was unable to lift his left hand above his waist, so that climbing into the ring, even with the tomboys, proved discomfiting. But in that early humiliation was born the ineptitude that was to make his fortune. Slingerland found he had an uncanny ability to take a punch.

He grew into a successful club fighter, using peppy terpsichore to evade punches and glaring smugly when he got clobbered. He rose in the amateur rankings. In 1965, fighting out of Mamaroneck, Slingerland was crowned yacht club champion of Long Island Sound. This lent him the confidence to challenge the restless and incondite professional ranks, filled with the Boeotian parvenus of the third world's athletic élite.

M R. Ray Amino, considered by many to be the grand old man of the Sweet Science, is also Seth Slingerland's manager and confidant. He recounted for me, at a recent Berkshire barbecue, his first impression of the fighter he refers to as "my annuity."

"He walks in the gym, it's like a movie. He's going around handing everybody business cards. I figure he's either a dentist or a gypsy. He hands me one, and I look at it." Amino produces a wizened cowhide billfold and extracts a dog-eared, three-by-two-inch white business card, which he displays about the rough-hewn oak patio table. The legend on the card reads, "Seth 'the Battling Pict' Slingerland, Pugilist." It is well known that Slingerland formally offers his card to opponents when they meet in center ring to shake hands. It is a courteous innovation he hopes the entire sport will take up; something that, along with his insistence that gin highballs be served ringside at all his bouts, he hopes will be his legacy to boxing. "When I seen the kid take a punch," continues Amino, "I fell in love. I thought, here's a kid that can take some punishment. I get him a few quick wins, I got a white TV fighter and a one-way ticket to Easy Street."

There has never been any doubt that the American public has searched long and hard for white champions in all sports. Still, I point out to Amino that there is more to the soul of physical competition than racial balance.

"No, there ain't," he says. "With my white guys I always said, 'First, look good. Second, try to stay on your feet. Third, try to get into the restaurant business after you quit.' But with this guy that I got now, he looks like crap. He don't look like he could win for a minute. They root for him not to fall down. And he don't. Ever. In my business, you call that 'heart.' They come out to see him in droves. Top TV ratings. I got the biggest fighters in the world lined up just waiting for a crack at him 'cause he's the biggest payday around."

Slingerland *is* a fighter with heart. But he is also a fighter with some very special other organs. To really appreciate the Slingerland style, you have to

188

watch him work in slow motion. The images before you go far to demonstrate his secret of success. The fist of a two-hundred-pound man thrown with a force emanating from that man's legs, connecting with a foreign body at peak velocity and dispersed over the area of that fist, can be expressed by the equation

$$\frac{M \times L \times V}{A} = B$$

in which M (body weight) times L (distance from toe to fist extended) times V (velocity of arm at impact) divided by A (area of fist in square inches) equals B (Blotto Force), with B expressed in foot-pounds. The average Blotto Force of a professional boxer is approximately the same as that of the Andrea Doria. That force is absorbed by the object of impact and the fist itself on contact. Assuming that object is another fighter's face, slow motion should reveal deformation of both fist and face resulting from such impact. Films of Slingerland's fights reveal the expected compression of his opponents' fists, but Slingerland's face and body remain remarkably supple. They show no deformation. Amino explains it this way: "You got your boxers and you got your punches. My guy's a bloater. His whole body bloats up a little to absorb the punches. Kinda like the big hunk of meat in 'Rocky.' You see 'Rocky'?"

Tests have shown that Slingerland has a stratum of fat just under his skin and over his musculature, which the dermatologist we consulted termed "absolutely girlish." One test has indicated that Slingerland's ability to take punishment is directly related to an imbalance in his male hormonal chemistry. This, however, could not be proved conclusively: Mr. Amino interrupted the examination by slamming the doctor against a file cabinet, declaring he refused to hear any more of "this puke." Slingerland himself explains it a different way: "Before every fight, I paint myself with Sorbothane."

How long he will continue to fight, no one knows. "I have a lot of pride," he says, oddly without a trace of embarrassment. "There was twice in the last year I thought I might drop." Slingerland started as a counterpuncher. The counterpuncher's strategy is to wait for his opponent to commit himself to a punch, slip that punch, and come inside his foe's arm with a sharp jab while his opponent is still off balance. Counterpunching demands lightning reflexes and keen instinct. Having neither, Slingerland entices his enemy by leaving himself completely open. "If you can anticipate a punch, you can counterpunch effectively," he states confidently. This may be true, but Slingerland is generally so disoriented from his inability to slip the original punch that his counterpunch is often aimed at the referee.

I asked Slingerland if he feared the tragic end associated with fighters who stay at the game too long—that of winding up permanently punch-drunk. "First you mince the onions," he answered succinctly, "and then sauté them until transparent." Seth Slingerland, it seems clear to me, will leave the fight business better off for his involvement in it. Whether or not he will leave it standing is up to the resiliency of those little hairs in his ears that send balance messages to his brain. Those hairs, located in the ampullae, have been willed by Slingerland to science. "But," Mr. Amino reminds me, "for a price."

—JOHN McPHUMPHER

[*This is the first part of a ten-part article. In the second part, McPhumpher sparred with Slingerland, who unexpectedly connected with an uppercut to McPhumpher's nose. The remaining eight parts of the article were largely taken up with experiments in writing while dazed and with McPhumpher's attempts to get our insurance company to pay his medical bills.*]

DOGLEG AT THE SECOND LIGHT

(1981)

[Herbert Breaking Wind sees past the bilious trousers, pastel sun visors, mutton-sleeve sweaters, and Mardi Gras shoes that make golf such an eyesore to the atavistic sea of meaning that no other aficionado has ever detected in the game.]

As THE planet cooled and grew solid, it became somewhat like an unstable golf ball, but there was no life to recognize or understand this. By the late Triassic, facing imminent and inexplicable extinction, the dinosaurs had no inkling of golf, although for nearly two hundred million years they had ruled what was to become the sport's only known venue. It is possible that even then golfers were in fact competing somewhere, yet it seems clear that no one on Earth could have been aware of it since old geology hands tell me that man had not yet evolved.

It is tempting to think of golf as an invention of the east because it is so ordered, ritualistic, and utterly pointless. Generally, Western sports revolve around an action or actions that sharpen one of the skills or strategies of war. There is no action in golf that resembles any aspect of war, save imitating a Howitzer by making guttural, booming noises in one's throat as one drives through the ball with one's one-wood. I sometimes do that.

The fact is, golf was not invented in the East; not only that, but no Oriental has ever won the Masters. Golf was a product of the Low Countries of Europe. According to the loosely translated refrain of a popular Flemish ditty, the original object of the game was to "lop off the head of the sleeping pet, just to see what's inside." Though considered vulgar, the game took hold and is depicted in Peter Bruegel's little-known painting "Drëunkers at Goëwlfes."

Every schoolboy is as familiar with the year 1734 as he is with the years 1501 (the Turkish conquest of Albania), 1768 (the birth of Duncan Phyfe), and 1818 (the establishment of Brooks Brothers). It was in 1734 that Hungarian count Leo Niblik, while on vacation in Belgium, first witnessed golf. All the way home he pondered the game, and at the outskirts of Budapest he stood up in the railway carriage, bonked his head on the luggage rack, and spoke the now-famous words, *"Klop en fisk."* His revolutionary idea of adding a ball changed the game forever.

It was Niblik's good fortune to live during the industrial revolution, when something approaching ball uniformity could be achieved. Soon after the introduction of virtually spherical balls, "the hole" emerged. The powerful Cardinal Paprikash of Klodz condemned this wrinkle, claiming its connection to the nether world made golf "the Devil's game." Niblik, however, soothed the offended prelate by defining "the hole" as "the cup." This was a public-relations coup of epic proportions, simultaneously freeing the game of its satanic connotations by placing a limit on how deep golf holes would go and, in doing so, employing "the cup," which was an important Church symbol. Far from neglecting his laic reponsibility, the Count added "the flag" to each cup, thus marrying Church and state in a harmony that has yet to be achieved anywhere else. These changes elevated the game to a level appropriate to the Hungarian national character. Long known as "the Locker Room of Europe," Hungary embraced golf with both hands and the game spread like hot goulash. Niblik, of course, gained immortality through the club that bears his name.

The Hungarians' domination of international competition (most notably their stranglehold on Olympic gold) should come as no surprise to lovers of the tee and green. Hungarians are a people who seethe with passion but keep that passion tightly in check, never betraying their self-control. This is the perfect personality profile for golf. The last Hungarian defeat in Olympic competition came at the hands of Jesse Owens in 1936. (That remarkable athlete swept

• •

"Don't be scared, children. It's just a theme restaurant."

individual championships not only in golf, but in luge and tetherball as well.)

Nonetheless, golf is a truly international pastime and one that has not been ignored by melting-pot America. Although the quality of the game here has never been what it is in Eastern Europe, we have made great strides in the international arena. Two factors have contributed to this upsurge. The first is the influx of Hungarian coaches and top-flight players, moving here to avoid repressive socialist greens fees. Hungary is the most progressive of the Eastern Bloc countries, but Iron Curtain golfers still defect here in droves in search of the four freedoms and TV announcers who whisper. The second factor is an energetic grass-roots organization that recruits more and more talented youngsters to the game. Typical of American ingenuity has been the creation of "town golf," a hybrid form that makes the game accessible to city folk who live far away from traditional courses.

THE acknowledged capital of town golf is Rego Park, New York. Town sports throughout the borough of Queens are hotly contested, but nowhere more so than here. Ball sports of all kinds flourish, not just among the young but among adults as well. The Zephyrs, a local semiprofessional Chinese handball team, have spawned a whole new generation of handballers. Equally ardent are aficionados of stickball, off-the-point, slapball, and three-box. But the professional sport of choice here is golf.

Old Queens hands like to joke that there is so much golf played between Utopia Parkway and Continental Avenue that Bob Hope bought the borough as a burial plot. But town golf presents hazards that can stop uninitiated duffers dead in their tracks. Sewers, windows, and roofs are all two-stroke penalties. There are no such things as divots; club damage is an expected part of every match. Hole location, even when agreed upon beforehand, can lead to violence. Cobblestones, potholes, and various animal leavings constitute unusually sticky traps. Occasionally a driven ball will be interrupted on its way back to earth by the windshield of a car speeding by. It is a game in which "playing the carom" has been elevated to an art, especially when holes dogleg at ninety-degree angles down cross streets. Town golf etiquette dictates that buses, fire engines, and youth gangs play through. While garbage trucks are in the field of play, the player whose ball lands in a truck's rear compactor is disqualified.

Far and away the greatest town golfers of all time are Tibor and Vitek Nagy. Fraternal twins who arrived in Rego Park as babies after the unsuccessful Hungarian Revolution of 1956, they have virtually no accent and consider themselves one-hundred-per-cent American. Their mastery of the game, however, betrays their Magyar roots. Since the age of sixteen, when they both quit Forest Hills High School and entered the professional ranks, their scores and winnings have progressively increased. In successive years, they together won $312.45, $418.56, $648.45, $1,202.00, $1,845.06, $2,206.49, $8,848.46, $11,011.24, $26,419.24, $39,444.51, $108,502.04, $166,141.96, $688,-491.09, $792,009.71, and $1,102,-618.99. Individually, Tibor has accumulated $214.09, $281.52, $324.00, $555.02, $1,506.92, $1,000.00, $6,212.19, $6,003.02, $19,001.34, $21,121.21, $108,502.04 (the year Vitek was in a coma), $112,100.51, $224,841.49, $510,098.62, and $784,-491.06, while Vitek won the rest.

Tibor has played something in the neighborhood of 5,764 games of town golf; his brother Vitek has played more. Though he was out of competition for almost a year, Vitek likes to play two and three matches a day. Tibor is happy with his average of one match 360 days per year. His five days off are reserved for visiting relatives in New Jersey. Both boys enjoy playing in the snow.

Tibor shoots consistently in the low sixties, his ten best scores being 61, 61, 61, 61, 61, 61, 61, 61, 61, and 61. Vitek's average is a tad higher, but his best rounds reflect flashes of brilliance of which his brother seems incapable; Vitek's ten best are 62, 62, 62, 62, 62, 60, 62, 62, 62, and 62. Tibor has notched forty-six holes in one while Vitek, remarkably, has accomplished that feat eighty times (sixty-four on the same hole at the corner of 69th Avenue and Wood-haven Boulevard).

With the years of competition ahead of them, neither sees himself switching to the grass game. Together, they cite the travel involved, the vastly increased level of competition, and their disdain for the clothing worn by most players on the pro tour. "Let's face it," says Tibor. "We might get a little more limelight in the grass game, maybe a few endorsements, but here in Rego Park we can be something special." Special is something they certainly are. Old town golf hands pre-

dict that, before they put away their clubs, their ten best scores will probably be as low as 58, 58, 58, 58, 58, 58, 58, 58, 58, and 58 and 61, 61, 61, 61, 61, 55, 61, 61, 61, and 61.

—HERBERT BREAKING WIND

BOOKS NOT SO BRIEFLY NOTED
GENERAL

BUTKUS, by Dick Butkus and Carlos Castaneda (G. Whillikers Press; $20.95). This unlikely collaboration has resulted in an unconventional, absorbing sports biography. Former all-pro middle linebacker Dick Butkus tells how, with the help of his spirit guide and the use of psychotropic plants, he learned to "see," which greatly increased the number of his quarterback sacks. In one memorable passage, Butkus explains how he caused Packers running back Paul Hornung to fumble during a conference playoff game by turning him into a crow. Aside from his annoying penchant for referring to Tom Landry as "Don Juan," Butkus' story is thoroughly entertaining. Yogi Berra and Ken Kesey, who are reportedly collaborating on a book, have a tough act to follow.

• •

STREET PERFORMERS

HAPPY BAXTER—A cheerful elderly gentleman who plays a harmonica and an accordion simultaneously. Unfortunately, he knows only two songs—"Has Anybody Seen My Baby?" and "New York, New York"—but he plays them exceptionally well. Sometimes his dog, Nipper, joins him. (Lexington Ave. at entrance to Grand Central Station.)

MARVIN HACKMAN—A saxophonist most frequently seen on the No. 6 train, Marvin claims to be an alien from the planet Zimbo in the Alpha 2 Galaxy and in need of earthly funds to repair his spacecraft. Wearing green makeup and antennae, he offers a far

more appealing presentation than that of the big guy who plays the steel drum on the Nos. 4 and 5. (Various locations.)

MAXIMILLIAN—One of the few mimes in New York not currently distributing pamphlets for adult education courses. Pedestrians have completely ignored Maximillian for more than three years. (St. Marks Place.)

STUMP AND LEROY—Breakdancing juveniles with a large, blaring radio. Untalented yet jubilant, they perform continuously until they raise enough money to see the latest martial-arts triple feature. (Broadway at 44th St.)

CHAPTER EIGHT

WE
BREAK
OUR
LEG

Theatre and Dance

*L*OCKED *away within the hearts of many of our writers is a show-business dream. A few have realized that dream. Dorothy Perky turned some of her stories into plays with great success; they remain staples of theatres that prize small casts and cheap sets. Densely's acting work in Hollywood eventually crowded writing out of his life. George S. Kupperman's comedies are, surprisingly, far better known than is his work for us. Today, our theatre hands are the doughty Grendel Pill, who seems to have done everything else at our magazine, and Edith Oreo, who was dashing off in pursuit of off-Broadway's pleasures long before anybody knew there was such a thing, or place.*

Our involvement with the dance has been far sketchier. Peter Alpo, the delightful cartoonist and rogue whose work depicted gorgeous chorines and rutting men, was constantly chuffed over dalliances with one long-legged beauty or another whom he'd seen in some chorus line and asked to pose for him. Such ploys were not available to less successful stage-door Johnnies such as myself; I used to ask the girls I admired for their autographs, hoping to expand the moment of signing into a chat. For a time, Gibbs was quite gaga over a ballerina (at least he claimed she was a ballerina) who could, apparently, do something quite extraordinary with a long-stemmed rose. For the most part, however, dance is something we at the magazine enjoy at Radio City Music Hall, on Broadway, or when performed by gaily clad ethnics in parades. When called upon to shake a leg ourselves, we respond with a shambling ineptitude reminiscent of Charlie Chaplin (although Dion Barmelthe tells me that Twee "really knows how to wag a tail feather," and those who've seen him claim I. B. Single leads beautifully).

In this chapter I have included only selections from recent years, in the belief that people old enough to remember what they remember as the Golden Age of Broadway should not be reminded how long ago that was.

PORTRAITS
FORCED TO TOUR
(1985)

C.O. Jones

[*Rapf found celebrities fascinating. Under his leadership, we interviewed the glamorous and those close to the glamorous. Refp's successor, Shplug, is a more subdued sensibility, and under his guidance the magazine has developed an interest in the sort of individual to whom, during my first decades here, no one on our staff would have been seen dead talking.*]

"WHEN I started, I had next to nothing. I moved into a small rooming house with a change of clothes, a stack of eight-by-ten glossies, the works of Shakespeare in one volume, and a gilt-framed picture of John Barrymore that I still keep at bedside. The picture was a gift, you see. My parents gave it to me when I gradu-

ated from high school. As a young man, my dream was to play the great classical roles. Unfortunately, I had this terrible stage fright, which caused me to forget my lines at key moments in three successive high-school productions. Just went completely up, no real excuse for it at all. Except for the first time, when the fellow I was playing opposite turned to face me so forcefully that his wig flew off. I didn't have my first star part until I did the title role in 'Androcles and the Lion' with the Syosset Mummers. Of course, no one could see me inside the lion suit, but I got very good reviews for my roars and leonine movement, so the Mummers asked me to play the Deaf-mute in their upcoming 'Madwoman of Chaillot.' After that, I was invited to direct the Christmas musical. Before I knew it, I was the producer, director, and star of one of the premier community theatres on Long Island. Not bad for a young man barely out of his mid-twenties.

"I worked in Syosset for five or eight years, and then I came back to New York City. I wouldn't say the Apple opened its arms wide for me, but I managed. My big break came when I was cast as a Pearly King in the original Broadway production of 'My Fair Lady.' I wasn't in it when Rex was, but I was a stalwart all through Edward Mulhare's run. Never missed a show. We got on well, Edward and I. Then I went out on the road with it, and that kept me working another two years. I've been in and around the business ever since."

H E is Cholmondeley Oliver Jones, but to friends and public he is C.O. Jones. This is the name he's used throughout a career to which the messy, comfortable den in which we are sitting is a shrine. All around us are mementoes; on the table, a bulbous papier-mâché nose ("Understudied Cyrano once") sits on a small silver electroplate tray ("Used it as Lane the manservant in 'Earnest'"). Photographs, reviews, and posters crowd the walls. Those that are tacked up have grown brittle and crumbly. C.O. leans back in his well-worn Barcalounger. His voice trails off as he gazes out the window, the waning light filtering through yellowing drapes, soft-

ening the outlines of school playground, semidetached houses, and parked cars that constitute his view. He sports a well-worn silk ascot whose rich paisley renders its discolorations and stains invisible at a distance and a genteelly tattered smoking jacket whose original sash was long ago replaced by the terry-cloth belt of some discarded bathrobe. His predominately gray hair is heavily pomaded. He looks like an actor.

C.O. Jones thinks of himself as the last of a dying breed, the great actor-managers like Garrick and Macready or, in this century, Gielgud or Olivier. In fact, he has not managed a theatre since he left Syosset, and he has never played any of the meaty roles for which he spent

years preparing himself. Despite his disappointments, C.O. Jones is still, by experience as well as preference, a nuts-and-bolts, all-around theatre man. He has worked professionally, semiprofessionally, and amateurishly. He has played bus-and-truck tours, summer stock, community theatre, and minimum-security prisons. Once, when he found himself stranded and without bus fare home after a package tour of "Craig's Wife" (starring Victoria Sturgeon) he was with shut down unexpectedly, Jones cobbled together a stand-up routine and opened for Peter Lemongello at the Aladdin's Lamp Lodge in Ellenville. He is proud of the fact that he has worked enough weeks to qualify for unemployment every year since 1960. He lives simply, his home cluttered with personally autographed photographs of the likes of Kaye Ballard, Iggie Wolfington, George Zucco, and Quilty Rarona. The memories these pictures evoke seem realer to Jones than do the tranquil days he spends in front of the television set with his ninety-five-year-old mother and her in-house help, a large West Indian woman whom I did not hear utter a sound during any of the numerous visits I paid to Jones over a three-month period while he rested between engagements.

I CALLED on Jones to listen to his reminiscences about dinner theatre, the straw-hat circuit, and suburban dramatic groups during the fifties. I myself am something of a frustrated actor, my dreams worn to a nubbin and finally eradicated after some two hundred auditions without so much as a second reading. But my love of the Fabulous Invalid glows undiminished. I see plays as often as I can get critics' passes, and I am an avid subscriber to the Fireside Theatre Book Club, which provides me with hardcover editions of essentials like "Scuba Duba" and "The Mound Builders." My meetings with Mr. Jones expanded my devotion to the liveliest art in a new direction. Here was a man whose career had taken root, blossomed, and withered, virtually unknown to the rest of his profession, let alone the public. C.O. Jones is one of the theatre's foot soldiers, and he is willing to share his experiences with anyone willing to share a pint of Southern Comfort with him. I found him a remarkably entertaining companion, full of pith and wisdom about a lifetime of scuffling; he is far and away the best conversationalist I have ever met in Queens, a borough of New York City.

Ozone Park is hardly an incubator for the arts, and as a youngster Jones  showed little flair for, or even interest in, the theatre. "I joined the Drama Club at Ozone High so I could smoke," he told me. "Our auditorium was really the gymnasium, you see. Every time there was a play or lecture or any sort of event, the stage crew would be called upon to set up chairs, hang lights and drapes, things like that. There was very little supervision; I could blow smoke rings the size of doughnuts by the time I was fourteen. My parents didn't have much use for show business, either. My father was a postal clerk and my mother sometimes took in washing, although she preferred to think of herself as a housewife, pure and simple. One thing we did as a family, though, was read aloud, especially during the long winter evenings before there was television. It began quite naturally. Most evenings, the three of us would sit in the living room, listening to the radio. My father would read the evening paper at the same time. Whenever he came across something that upset him, he'd read it aloud. Sometimes he would throw the paper at one of us, or even smack me or my mother with it before going back to his reading. Eventually, reading the evening paper aloud became a great family event. My mother would read the women's pages—marriages and so forth—and my father did the real news. I'd do the funny pages and assist my parents wherever I was needed. I liked the funnies best because I could change my voice to do the different characters. Whenever we had company, I'd be ordered to drag out my Nancy and Sluggo impersonations. During the war, a lot of the fun of reading the paper stopped and my father took to reading to us by himself, holding a cigarette and furrowing his brow like Edward R. Murrow would do years later on 'Person to Person.' I wanted to enlist, of course, like a lot of other kids, but there was the problem of my sinuses. They've plagued me all my life and, I feel, may have kept me from the kind of success I might have enjoyed on the stage if I hadn't been so stuffed up all the time. When my sinuses are clear, you know, I really have a nice, light tenor voice—a bit like Alfred Drake's,

actually, only not quite so loud.

"Anyway, what with all the young men overseas, the forties weren't a bad time to start a career in show business. I read for the blind to make food money and to pay a share of the rent to my folks. Television was just starting up, and I was there—in on the ground floor, so to speak. I held cue cards for Captain Video, I ironed all the uniforms for Milton Berle's Texaco men. Why, Sid Caesar used to send me out regularly to get cups of coffee and bagels for him, Carl Reiner, and Howard Morris. Television was a wonderful place to be in those days, at least until I ran afoul of Eddie Fisher. I was vocalizing one night, just warming up my larynx, and I happened to be

singing 'O, Mine Papa,' very softly and *to myself* as I was dumping some garbage in the incinerator, and he heard me. He happened to walk by at that very moment, and he heard me. I tried to explain that the nasality was a sinus problem, but he thought I was mocking him. Today, most television comes out of Los Angeles, and I never have very good luck there. I get heat rash, you see, and that doesn't film well, no matter how you try to cover it with makeup. Well, anyway, that was the end of me at the television studio, and I was truly dejected. If you'd told me then that within a year I'd be squeezing into a lion suit in Syosset, I would never have believed you." Jones nods quietly, smiling as he sips from his tumbler. Suddenly, his brow furrows, Murrow-like. "I'm sorry, that was all *after* Syosset, wasn't it? When was I in Syosset?"

Jones wasn't quite finished with TV. He found work as a "gofer" for several major soap operas and played numerous "under-fives," as bit parts are called. He insists that he received fan mail for his portrayal of a silent, grief-stricken man waiting outside the emergency room alongside the stars of "The Guiding Light." "Even though they had all the words and were the focus of the scene, I felt it was my job to lend a sense of truth to the background, so I stared off into the middle distance a bit, checked my watch, paced back and forth behind

200

them, and sobbed quietly when they seemed to pause too long. It was all very underplayed, so it was a real surprise when I was let go from my 'gofer' job.

"Not to worry, though. My sinus trouble, which made things so difficult when it came to the classics and Eddie Fisher, made me a natural for children's theatre. Quite a lot of work in that field, you know, especially if you don't mind living out of a station wagon. I spent one winter playing in what must have been every primary school between Elmira and Penn Yan, New York. Some sort of cultural program. Well, our group, the Jones, Jones and Jones Puppet Troupe —Did I mention that I'd taken a course in puppetry at the New School? Well, there were three of us in the group— rather four, that was the whole joke—that and the fact that I was the only one named Jones. I thought it was a catchy name for us. We got to the point where we'd arrive at a school, unpack and set up, do the show, and be back on the road in an hour. Not that the children were short-changed, not at all. We catered to their shorter attention spans. Upstate New York is quite large, you know, and absolutely crawling with little ones. I wrote the scripts, a few of the old fairy tales but mostly originals like 'The Girl Who Learned to Sew' and 'Seven Keys to Recess.' Years later, Bil Baird showed some interest in 'Sew,' but I insisted on directing and Bil said no, no. We're great friends, though, anyway."

EVENING falls, and C.O.'s narrative becomes increasingly unhinged. His stories have a coherence unto themselves, but their sequence in C.O.'s life is uncertain at best. One minute he's flogging Aramis samples at Sak's Fifth Avenue; the next he's bringing tears to the eyes of Stella Adler's master class. Now he's in the chorus of the original cast of "Flahoolie" and claiming that if only

Yma Sumac had been directed with a lighter touch, the show would have run forever. He writes a comedy called "Here Comes Tupper!," which receives a staged reading at the Nutley (New Jersey) Players New Play Series, and is at one time or another considered for representation by no fewer than six agents. He sublets a studio apartment in Manhattan from a friend leaving on a national tour of "Oliver!" and recalls that period as a career highlight: "Such convenience! Right near the theatre, the museums, Chinatown! It was so marvelous to be in the thick of it all!" But C.O. returns home to Ozone Park when the sublease expires.

"I feel awkward about it, you know, but it really makes the most sense, especially as I'm away so much of the time. You know, Hermione Gingold once said, comparing Sir Laurence Olivier to Sir Donald Wolfit, two of my very favorite actors, 'Olivier is a tour de force, and Wolfit is forced to tour.' That's the way my career has worked out. Take this past year. I've done six months as the Inspector in 'Pajama Tops' in Pineville, North Carolina, just outside Charlotte, then Greensboro, then all the way down to Marietta, Georgia, and up again to Richmond. All the dinner theatres have— Why the dinner theatres don't work out these schedules with a little consideration for the actors, I will never know. Of course, they throw in your dinner, so you can really save quite a lot. I'm home for the next month or so, directing a reader's theatre production of 'When We

Dead Awaken' with Hohokus Stage, then away again to Natick, Massachusetts, where I'll do 'Sleuth' opposite one of the majors from the community college; I'm there on a guest artist contract, which will probably mean living in a dorm room for seven weeks. It's a good thing I love the theatre. And I do. *Viva* show biz! I must go to sleep now. 'The rest is silence.'" C.O.'s eyes glaze and close. I walk him to his bedroom.

When I left C.O. Jones, he seemed an old friend. He'd behaved with a friend's ease as he removed his teeth, adjusted his hair net, and donned his sleep mask before retiring. These routines and habits are islands of stability for a man who spends so much time on the road. Just before turning off his bedside lamp, C.O. had put earplugs in place. "They certainly make it easier to get to sleep," he'd said. "I once brought earplugs to the theatre so I could nap during the show. I was only on briefly, in the second act. And do you know what happened? I missed my cue."
— JAMES LARDFELLOW

BOOKS NOT SO BRIEFLY NOTED
GENERAL

CLOWNS, CLOWNS, CLOWNS, by Donna Barbara Cataranzano (Goatpuppet Press; $45). Finally, an analysis of the Commedia dell'Arte with some heft. Miss Cataranzano attacks her subject with *brio*, focussing on the characters who endured through the Commedia's heyday. They're all here: Bartolomeo the Bufone, Principio the Cripple, and, of course, Genco the Perennial Suitor. In her discussion of Genco, the author supersedes Leo Szathmary's "Sources and Symbols of the Commedia," calling attention not only to Mr. Szathmary's factual inconsistencies but also to his stultifyingly bovine syntax. A heartfelt *Bravissima!* from us.

WHY CAN'T THE ENGLISH TEACH THEIR CHILDREN HOW TO SPEAK?
Upon being informed that he had been technically brain-dead for several minutes during the operation, the young, British accident victim could only utter the word "Wow" over and over again. —*From the Woodstock Times*

HAPPY FEET AND STRANGE PERFORMANCES

WILLIAM AMBERGRIS—Third annual reading of Webster's Unabridged Whaler's Phrasebook, scheduled to begin immediately following the completion of the second annual reading. Yo-ho-ho. Refreshments. (Peter Coffin Little Theatre.)

NANOO NOONO—Performance art. Musical instruments are hurled by Noono and his assistants from a high scaffold upon unsuspecting passerby. Woodwinds, Tuesdays and Thursdays; strings, Wednesdays and Fridays; brass, weekends. (Upper stories around town.)

LONG JOHN SILVER DANCE TROUPE—Performing in Peg Legs and Rhythm. (V.F.W. Post 568.)

HAROLD STASSEN DANCE COMPANY—An Evening of Dancers Just Milling About and Not Doing Much of Anything. (Brooklyn Academy for People Who Can't Afford Lincoln Center.)

THE SYNTHETIC FABRIC EXPERIENCE—Multimedia extravaganza. Slides, movies, videos, Dolby stereo, strobe lights, and smoke machines combine to present over a million images in twenty-six minutes. Invigorating. Dizzying. Several spectators have had to be hospitalized. Dress warmly. (Viscose Theatre.)

TEATRO ESPECTACULAR DE MADRID—Immense theatrical event from Spain, featuring 312 dancers, 206 actors, two 125-piece orchestras, a 750-voice chorus, and a herd of live bulls. Performance takes twenty-eight days to be seen in its entirety. Clever. (Vest-Pocket Playhouse.)

The Greenroom

[This interview was believed to have been written by McPhumpher because, in its original form, it was a four-part Talk story. In fact, the true author, revealed for the first time in "Snooze," was Chauncey DePinna; the interview appeared posthumously, his only published piece. I edited it myself and reprint it here in fond memory of a now-defunct colleague, with deep thanks for the shirts.]

W E recently paid a visit to the theatrical historian Dr. Vander Deitzel, who is attempting to debunk the previously unchallenged belief that the greenroom—the place in a theatre where actors wait to go onstage—was named for the soothing green walls that relieve eye irritation caused by bright stage lights. Dr. Deitzel confided that he has yet to find the "smoking gun," but he was kind enough to let us in on three promising theories that he categorizes as, in order of credibility, the "whistling bolo," the "flexible épee," and the "*basso profundo* whoopie cushion."

The Fiesole Freeloaders. Fiesole, Dr. Deitzel informed us, is the site of an important Etruscan amphitheater where many Greek playwrights opened their new works before taking them to Athens. (Etruscan audiences were generally maligned as being too provincial for the highly developed Greek dramas, but the real reason behind their often mystified reactions was their total ignorance of Greek.) Nestled in the lush, pollen-free Tuscan hills above Florence, the amphitheatre was famous not only for its lovely setting but for its luxurious dining facility, where local actors only too happily doubled as unpaid waiters when they were offstage. The only non-waiting actors were the has-been, "name" stars imported from across the Adriatic. As a method of keeping these stars both sober and in the theatre during performances, the management enticed them to the kitchen between scenes by offering them free food. Dubbed *pestos* by the chefs,

who had their hands full trying to keep some food for the customers, the imported actors favored the green pasta sauce for which the region was noted and often appeared onstage with strings of green still clinging to their chins. Thus the sauce became identified with the actors, and back in the theatrical quarter of Athens a job in Fiesole became known as "working the green room."

The Equestrian Misunderstanding. With the success of Shakespeare's Globe Theatre in the late 1600s, owners of other London theatres accurately perceived unprecedented growth potential and challenged the Bard for their fair share of the English entertainment pound. This time of heady innovation saw the introduction of twofers, seasonal discounts, and group rates. These marketing ploys were aimed at the groundlings, however, and held little significance for the Globe's tonier audiences. Shakespeare countered by catering to the well-to-do theatregoer, in the interest of reaping not only increased ticket revenues but higher grosses at refreshment and souvenir concessions, and came up with the concept of valet parking for carriages and horses. To meet the increased space and personnel requirements, he turned a section of the huge scene shop into a parking area and hired a staff of grooms to see to the equipage. Because the grooms stayed backstage with the actors until the show was over, departing aristocrats who were in a hurry to get home would bribe an usher to rush to the "groom room" and convey their requests for fast service;

these words, uttered in upper-crust accents unfamiliar to the uneducated ear, were interpreted by the staff as "grem rem" and eventually evolved into "green room"—a term that took hold and endured long after the failure of theatrical valet parking.

The French Farceurs' Undoing. The basis for this theory is the unhappy alliance between the French and humor to begin with. It seems the prospect of attempting hilarity so unnerved the French actors of Feydeau's time that, before going on, they were stricken with a virulent stage fright that caused them to come onstage green.

•　　•

"Please, sir. I desperately need money for food, but for the life of me I can't think of a single witty thing to say."

204

THE DANCE
GLASSBORO REVISITED
(1982)

[*Arcane Crotchet is the first and only permanent dance reviewer ever retained by our magazine. Miss Crotchet holds this position by dint of the enormous respect, not to mention abject terror, that she inspires in many here. When others have no time to keep up with their reading, their editing, their research, Miss Crotchet knows what there is to see, what should be seen, and what it's all about. Arcane Crotchet has the courage of her pretensions. The Glassboro Commemorative Ballet, held in 1982 to mark the fifteenth anniversary of the historic summit meeting, was hailed around the world as an event many hoped would thaw the strained relationship between the superpowers. Arcane Crotchet was virtually alone among dance critics in actually reviewing the performance.*]

THERE were three moments during "L'Après-midi d'un Huit en Ligne," Twilleth Carp's political *homage*, that launched me willy-nilly into a tropospheric nether region of thin air and rare gas. The dance took place outdoors at Glassboro State College, and its title— "Afternoon of the Straight Eight" —refers to an outmoded, esoteric, yet snazzy internal-combustion device favored by many automotive enthusiasts. Consequently, the ballet's performance included the obligatory array of unnerving clicks, honks, and *vrooms* associated with that species of postmodern noise art popularly referred to as car song. It should be no great *secret de critique*, then, that after a nearly four-hour safari down the New Jersey Turnpike amid charter buses en route to Atlantic City and trailer trucks en route to everywhere else, I was, and remain, ill disposed toward the sounds of the road. The hurly-burly was intensified by the presence of Ted and Carlotta Wussel, two balletomanes from West Hempstead, Long Island, from whom I had accepted a ride, thinking it less dear and more comfortable than public transit. I realize now that I'd have done better begging crawl space on the luggage deck of a Greyhound Scenicruiser.

The Wussels—whose jitterbugging Le Sabre wagon is adorned with a plaster cast (obtained through public-television auction) of Jacques d'Armoire's left foot hanging from the rear-view mirror, where it responded to every bump with a jerky relevé, of which I'm sure M. d'Armoire would not have been proud—insisted on stopping at an outpost called the Vince Lombardi Rest Area. In the center of this clearing was a Hot Shoppe establishment in which no one was able to provide me either with an apéritif or with conclusive support for my contention that this Lombardi was the same Lombardi who choreographed the first *pas du chien rouge*.

Upon arriving and, finally, locating the primitive grandstand abutting the downsloping lee in front of Hollybush, the college president's fieldstone hideaway, I was ushered—rudely prodded, actually—up to the precarious, topmost, splintery plank with nothing but a thin metal cross-brace by way of backrest. To make matters worse, the Wussels, from whom I was unable to escape, had seats next to me. So delighted were they with their presence at the dance (indeed, their presence at any dance) that they were ready to "bravo" themselves hoarse for an aerobics class.

The dance commenced scant moments after we sat down. I noticed that the performance was lit by fixed blue floodlights illuminating the grass with tight pools of light that, for some unfathomable reason, did not overlap. The troupe, which had obviously rehearsed in the full light of day, only gradually became aware that large sections of the playing area were pitch black. This was clear to me from the grunting collisions and cursed stubbings audible even over the prerecorded accompaniment. The dance was full of vigorous movement—the story, in fact, revolving around a series of mythic drag races—and the dancers kept veering off into the darkness. It was an evening so pathetic in its aspect, so abjectly barren of invention, so appallingly formless that today, a week later, I still have a rash. And yet there were those three grand moments. It is perhaps only because of them that my heart still beats.

Because it was staged in remembrance of the Johnson-Kosygin 1967 summit

conference, there is, of course, the temptation to dismiss "L'Après-midi d'un Huit en Ligne" as nothing more than a diplomatic gimcrack, akin to those much bruited Sino-American Ping-Pong competitions that seeped noxiously beyond the sports pages of our daily newspapers several years ago. The program notes weightily christened the evening's event "The Fifteenth Annum Glassboro Commemorative Russo-American Ballet Interproduction," which I'm certain will move at least one flip, phrase-making pundit to use "ballet diplomacy" as the lead for his next column. I, however, can think of no more heinous application of Gresham's Law than this mixture of dance and politics. The distinction between the cheaper and the dearer is profanely obvious. I cannot sit by and watch dance be trivialized. I consider it my responsibility to place the evening's performance aesthetics before its protocols. In fact, it is my moral obligation to lambaste this kinetic slag.

There is a hoary list of precedents for this maladjusted pairing, yet each time a dance has been commissioned to mark a historic occasion, the dance has lived on while the occasion is forgotten. Take, for example, Gaoleiter's classic, "Die Froggen Sind Kaput," commissioned to mark the end of the Franco-Prussian War, or Basque choreographer Lupe Elito's "Flan por Todos," which supposedly celebrated the now forgotten Spanish Civil War. Even Micky MacBobbi's oft performed modern suite "Flambé, Mon" had its début presentation at a place called Eniwetok the night before it was obliterated by a hydrogen bomb test.

THE Glassboro Dance was the brainchild of Undersecretary of State Hugh Evans Bedlow. Seriously dyslexic, he is the college's only undergraduate ever to receive a degree in dance, a major that was funded by his family and dissolved even as young Hugh was accepting his diploma. Though neither a crackerjack scholar nor particularly gifted in movement, he was gregarious and popular, and the Glassboro Tippy-Toers—the ballet club he founded—are still zealously practicing their jetés. After a summer at Rehoboth Beach, Bedlow entered the diplomatic corps, where his easy manners and family fortune moved him steadily along—until now. Sadly, Bedlow was unaware that while Lyndon Johnson, the President who actually attended the conference, was a Democrat, the present administration is Republican. Though he managed to secure enough bipartisan support and financing to mount the presentation, rumor has it that Bedlow is slated for posting to Beirut.

• •

"Henry just hasn't been the same since I had him fixed."

It was Bedlow's notion to express the spirit of détente by marrying unfettered American creativity to traditional Russian terpsichorean expertise. First convincing the iconoclastic, fuddle-brained Ms. Carp, he set about tirelessly petitioning the Soviets to allow their most riveting, charismatic dancer, Kolya Fyotglov, the chain-smoking lead male of the Azerbijan Ballet Collective, to dance at Glassboro. After months of compromise and arm-twisting, the Politburo finally agreed that Fyotglov could participate with one stipulation: because of the tendency among the greatest Soviet dancers to defect when on the same land mass as Carol Burnett, Fyotglov would spend his entire visit—*including his performance* —surrounded by a cordon of twenty fully armed crack Soviet marines, for whose transport, billeting, and per diems the production fund would be responsible.

Budgets were stretched even further when the noted aural-pain-threshold researcher and frontier-of-sound musicologist Elizabeth Swaddling elbowed her way onto the bill by claiming what she referred to as "my rightful cut" of all federal grant monies flowing into the Northeast. With allocations all but exhausted and only one dancer committed to the performance, Carp and Bedlow saved the day with a Yankee ingenuity that Andy Hardy would envy. First, Carp suggested she reëmploy recordings of the Beach Boys that she has used in no fewer than five dances in the past. Bedlow endorsed this plan, as he thought the group's *oeuvre* was a special favorite of the Secretary of the Interior, James Watt. It was also felt that the Beach Boys' quintessentially American lyricism would lend itself well to mythic themes like world peace. The use of recordings meant no union fees for musicians and, more importantly, a vast reduction in stage time for Ms. Swaddling, who had decided to perform by wailing Oriental halftone scales from *inside* a concert grand Steinway. (Oriental halftones occur between the notes of our Western majors, minors, sharps, and flats, and consequently figure prominently in aural-pain research, in which field Ms. Swaddling's career began.) The final pieces of the puzzle were Bedlow's gems. He proposed that the Russian marines be used as the set and that the Glassboro Tippytoers be pressed into service as the corps de ballet.

"L 'APRÈS-MIDI d'un Huit en Ligne" utilized the spirited running in circles and a little of the jumping up and down that are part of this corps' choreographic arsenal. Certainly the great Fyotglov, in a dual role, more than lived up to his name. As Jalopnik, one of the two drag-racing deities competing for the affections of the beautiful, veiled Shatila, third-world slum goddess, Fyotglov gave of himself with an exuberance hard to believe in a smoker. It was in his second and smaller role as a fume of exotic fuel that he surpassed the known extremes of the dancer's instrument. Rising from the exhaust pipe of his racer—portrayed with martial precision but no success by the Red marine entourage—Fyotglov actually, blithely, levitated and hung over the horizon, then somehow appeared to disperse into wispy snippets. Whether *trompe l'oeil* or actual magic, Fyotglov returned to earth with a clonk, landing

hubble-bubble into the crowd portraying his car and standing, rear to the audience, with his tights ripped and his Red Russian bottom exposed for all to behold. It was the first great moment of the evening.

Of the Glassboro Tippy-Toers not much should be said. Is it the province of the critic, one wonders, to comment in the area of psychological motive on the part of performers? "Where," I found myself asking aloud, "do those porkettes find the gumption to appear, in public, wearing leotards?" A young man named Glenn Urquhart was assigned the impossible task of dancing Moondoggie, Jalopnik's rival. Urquhart was game but, after running full tilt into the trunk of a stately but poorly lit ginko, was unable to continue, and Mr. Bedlow took his place in the cast with a descriptive narrative of Moondoggie's movements as they were supposed to occur. The presence of a suited man onstage yelling over the music created the mood of an army training film on insects of the night.

The second moment of piercing elation came during one of Ms. Swaddling's wailed interludes when the piano top fell with a deafening crash, silencing her for the rest of the evening.

A fable-like quality of story is the wool from which all-important balletic tales are spun. Moondoggie and Jalopnik's climactic race, upon which all depends, comes after about four hours of dance and two sentences of plot. The twist in the narrative here is that Shatila has a twin sister, Conchita, which didn't surprise me at all since I had long since confused Shatila with Jihan, who was really an exchange student who had wandered through the action on her way back to the dormitory. The *dénouement* produced little noises in my lower tract. The final race, danced by Fyotglov and explained by Bedlow to the plaintive bal-

lad "Don't Worry, Baby," was augmented with a flyover by the navy's Blue Angels, whose sonic booms re-created the ear-splitting roar of the dragsters, symbolizing the power of technology. The long, thunderous growl so shocked the totally engrossed Wussels that they leapt out of their seats and plummeted into the darkness behind our bleacher; my third and final moment of fulfillment. The performance was videotaped and copies are available (Corn EKG, 1409; $100), though the copies I've seen are almost all black with a scratchy noise on the soundtrack that sounds very much like crickets. The evening ended happily, I'm glad to report, as I rode back to town with the entire squad of Russian marines, who, after being offered chorus jobs in a national touring company of "The Best Little Whorehouse in Texas," decided to defect.

—ARCANE CROTCHET

•   •

Regional Theatre Falstaff

A REPORTER AT BAY

OFF-BROADWAY ORDEAL

(1972)

[*Grendel Pill has worked in so many areas of our magazine that Roger Devill calls him our utility infielder. Whether writing Talk pieces, fiction, portraits, or reviews, Grendel maintains a suave nonchalance and felicity of phrase that once prompted a fading Broadway star, disappointed by a negative review, to label him "a real lightweight." Nothing could be further from the truth. There is a grave, captious side to Pill's sensibility, as anyone who has seen him dress down a sluggish doorman or saucy waitress can attest.*

By the early 1970s, word of the burgeoning off-off-Broadway theatre scene reached Pill's home in Old Spice, Connecticut. Grendel was already sorry he'd missed the Living Theatre's triumphant return to these shores in 1968, but at the time he had no idea how to find the Brooklyn Academy of Music. In 1972, Pill promised Mr. Shwiz to call if he got lost, then sallied forth to investigate the brave new theatrical world of storefronts, lofts, and copious hair. His report, though surely the only piece of Grendel's to require the deletion of expletives, is among his best. For once it is possible to see the man's heart beating beneath the monogram on his shirt.]

As I am the sole Broadway critic who regularly dons black tie for opening nights, the smirks and giggles of my less elegant colleagues have become as regular a part of my theatregoing as the pricey mints I nibble during performances. Broadway's standard curtain time, once a sane 9 P.M., has rolled back first to 8:40, then to 8:30, 8:15, and finally (one hopes) to the present 8 o'clock, precluding the possibility of any pre-theatre dining more elaborate than a wolfed slice at Ray's Footlight Pizza on 45th Street. While street crime has not yet affected me directly (I assume it is my opera cape that puts the criminal element off its stride), I am regularly victimized by the importunate provocations of the theatre district's hucksters, panhandlers, and *filles de joie*. I mention these tribulations because I wish to make clear that covering Broadway for this organ is no bed of roses. None of these indignities, however, compares with what I have endured investigating the so-called "alternative" theatre. To whatever it is that these new theatres present themselves as an alternative is unclear, but they are surely not in the same league with Broadway's gilded and carpeted temples of Thespis in which I have spent so many charmed hours. Nay, off-Broadway is an entirely different sphere of wax.

Led by their director, trainer, spiritual avatar, and, for all I know, resident golf pro, Jerzy Kowtowski, the Kielbasa Laboratory Theatre of Poland arrived in this city several weeks ago to commence a State Department-sponsored tour. The event (I do not think it can be called a play) the troupe is performing on these shores is called "The Constant Fish," and it is chanted, whispered, shrieked, and belched in a language I assume is Polish. The plot synopsis and explanatory essays included in the program tell us that this version, based on a seventeenth-century Polish classic, has been whittled down, in the course of the company's customary seven-year rehearsal period, from a stately five acts with interstitial masques to a surprisingly endless thirty-seven minutes. "The Constant Fish" is a retelling of the Miracle of the Loaves and Fishes, with particular emphasis on the fishes. Apparently, this part of the Gospels has always held a strong fascination for the Poles, millions of whom live out their lives without access to their country's extremely limited Baltic Sea frontage. One is grateful for the program's exegeses, for the play is as incomprehensible as a legal brief and not nearly so entertaining.

Foreboding chilled me to the tips of my dress pumps as I entered the lobby of the Judson Memorial Church on West Fourth Street in Greenwich Village. In the cramped vestibule milled the too casually dressed, mostly young ticket-holders. Heavy aromas of cigarette smoke, incense, and patchouli hung in the calid air. When the entire audience, fully thirty-six of us, had arrived, we were ushered into a dank room whose walls were covered with black velours. Flush to the walls was a single row of wooden folding chairs. Because the room was lit only by the glow of a single candle in the middle of the open playing space, seating everyone took inordinately long. I stubbed a toe, reawakening to its former sensitivity a corn I'd nursed for months. Then I partially missed my assigned seat and placed one buttock on the chair next to mine; it collapsed and fell on top of the outstretched, immobile form of a nearly naked actor who lay artfully sprawled at my feet in a frozen apache dance of agony, nearly invisible for the gloom all around us.

Finally settled in ("settling in" is a relative term, and I strongly advise anyone intending to take in this or any other entertainment south of Fourteenth Street to bring a small cushion), I began to wonder if we were having a brownout, a surmise scotched when the candle was extinguished by the breath of someone in the darkness just beyond the candle's aureole. The room was pitch black. A cacophony of shouting and crashing began, a din that ended when a double row of overhead floodlights aimed directly at the slender perimeter of spectators slammed on. We squinted as one. "The Constant Fish" began.

Sturdy, athletic actors collided with each other violently, though whether affectionately or malevolently one could not tell. They ran around the room in ever-widening arcs. A couple fell to the floor and crawled. One strong-voiced young man yodelled while enacting his own disembowelment. At any rate, that is what I believe he was enacting. No props were used aside from some tattered rags similar to the mud-colored tunics, loincloths, and turbans sported by the cast. My mind wandered as my feet fell asleep. At various points in the performance, I was reminded of cavemen dancing, the Battle of Borodino, Orientation Day at Yale (where I went to college), frogmen penetrating the azure

of the Caribbean, some dry cleaning I'd forgotten to pick up, and the very large drink I would have the moment I got home. Droplets of hot wax sullied the lapels of my dinner jacket during the candlelit conga-line-like procession that ended the piece. The company's decision to omit a curtain call was wise. A Danish bootleg volume of unauthorized English translations of Polish lectures and manifestoes by Mr. Kowtowski was selling briskly in the lobby as I made a shuffling getaway on still dozy feet.

AFTER the brief but interminable en- counter with the Kielbasa troupe, I thirsted for something in the American vernacular, so it was with an eager spring in my step that I arrived at the tumble-down home of American Writers in Ear-nest (A.W.E.), which is currently pre-senting two new plays in repertory. Both display levels of writing and production talent that would be impressive in stu-dents at a vocational high school. The first, Rupert Geyser's "Dipstick Para-dise," is the sort of workmanlike, con-ventional family drama that prompted me to write, several years ago, "I'm getting awfully tired of these workman-like, conventional family dramas." This one unfolds in the auto-repair shop of Joe-Bob, a blustery but essentially de-cent fellow whose wife's death years ago left him with three children to raise. The children have flown the nest but are returning now that their father stands to lose his shop if he cannot pay off the gambling debts he has run up at a nearby jai-alai fronton. The eldest, Emmy-Lou, calls herself Edmund Laurel; she is a self-styled "modern woman" who lives in San Francisco with another woman and publishes a small weekly paper called *You're a Big Girl Now*. She seems to embody the author's voice, advising pacifism, strict organization of closet space, and daily prune juice, a litany of counsel heard dimly under the shrill babblings of the rest of the returning brood: Joe-Bob Junior, who operates a body shop in the next town and wages price wars against his father, and Sasha, at seventeen the baby of the family. She jets in from Gstaad, where she's been skiing with her husband, a wealthy Saudi who has not come with her because it violates his faith to speak with working people. There are recriminations aplenty as Joe-Bob admits to having been so grief-stricken at his wife's death that he ne-glected to teach his children to drive.

An extremely convincing set has been created, and the actors, under the direc-tion of the author, have been encouraged to behave with absolute naturalism. Per-haps this accounts for their long silence that opens Act II, during which a com-plete emissions inspection is carried out on a genuine vintage Studebaker and I, I am bound to report, nodded off, this time above the ankles as well as below. Had I not, I might have asked one of the Joe-Bobs out to Old Spice after the show to remount the rear-view mirror of my Chrysler.

RUTH Luther's "A Streetlight Named Gonzago" is something else again. Eschewing the hackneyed dramatic con-ventions of plot and character, Luther instead shows us a white man and a black man named, respectively, X and Y. X accidentally kills a supermarket delivery boy, an arrogant mulatto youth named Mirabell. Rather than dispose of the body, X and Y, who may be brothers or may never have seen each other before, use it as a floor lamp, screwing a 150-watt bulb into the fellow's mouth. Somehow it lights, and large worms made of black foam rubber fall from above. The two men stand back to back, walk ten paces and turn, then run into each other's arms for a spirited fox trot. Dream sequences, charades, and home-canning demonstra-tions appear, are graphically performed by four actors wearing tights, leotards, and a variety of hats. The play ends enigmatic-ally with a high-speed, nonverbal depic-tion of human evolution in which the entire cast participates. The development of the opposable thumb is among the evening's most successful moments. The play is set in a single-room-occupancy hotel with a large, wooden water tower in one corner. Sonny Tuffet is completely convincing as X, Clay Vessels less so as Y. Jesus Quiñones performs admirably as the floor lamp but has difficulties with his earlier scenes, when he must speak. Gadge McNabb, the director, has a predilection for keeping his actors behind furniture.

PERHAPS I'm listening to too much talk, I thought, as I waited in the cozy lobby of the Wonderspace Theatre on East 11th Street, sipping a thimble-size Dixie Cup of tepid apple juice while a bedraggled army of stagehands rushed in and out of the curtained-off auditorium with brooms, dustpans, and, ominously, a large bucket filled with gray water in which floated several large, dirty sponges. The hall was being readied for a wordless program called "Make Mine Mimes!" Happily I avoided the leak, although I did manage to catch the satin stripe of my left trouser leg on a protruding nailhead as I squeezed onto my eight inches or so of wooden bench. Hope springs perhaps less than eternally, but spring within my breast it did as I waited for the show to begin.

The luminous artistry of a Marcel Marceau fills the mind's eye with the sights and sound of a world so intensely imagined that we can forget we are actually looking at a man in black alone on an empty stage in a pool of light. Not so here. At no time could one forget one was watching mimes doing mime routines: peeling bananas, walking against the wind, pulling ropes, progressing from infancy to death, getting carried away by balloons, and more. The second half of the program consists of a playlet in which two virile young mimes fight for the affections of a winsome female mime who sits demurely to one side. The men soundlessly argue, fight, and,

exhausted, make up, only to find that their prize has slipped away with yet another mime. This is the sort of evening in the theatre that makes your bridgework hurt.

IMPROVISATION may be seen twice nightly, Wednesdays through Sundays, at Le Café des Deux Cafés, where a group called the Smarties holds the stage with what purport to be lighter-than-air sketches satirizing hippies and Texas oil millionaires (shades of Billie Sol Estes!), not to mention Vice-President Agnew and his clashes with his betters. After these painful skits have passed their hour upon the stage, the audience is invited to make suggestions that the Smarties will use to create

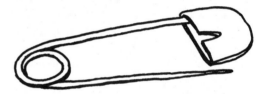

scenes "spontaneously." As I remarked several years ago at a cocktail party of which I remember nothing else, "Audience-suggested, improvisational comedy is dull, dull, dull, just as dull as dull can be." The Smarties do not alter my opinion. Here are a husband and wife, the latter the first female pope, arguing over their flooded basement in the style of Tennessee Williams; Estes Kefauver and the staff of a Chinese restaurant struggling to best each other in a race to the South Pole in the style of Rodgers and Hart; and, finally, this reviewer slipping out the door before the curtain calls, in the style of a rat deserting a sinking ship.

NOT all of off-Broadway is downtown, I reflected as I journeyed up to West 116th Street to the spotless grade-school gymnasium that is the home of El

Teatro Con Leche, a bilingual company dedicated to the promulgation of brotherhood through the presentation of Spanish plays in English and English plays in Spanish. Unfortunately, through some error of scheduling, I did not see Con Leche's English-language production of Lorca's plaintive tragedy, "Blood Wedding." Instead, the troupe performed "El Señor Roberts." While I could not grasp the reason for Ensign Pulver's sporting a matador's hat, I was never bored by this peculiarly Mediterranean view of life in the Pacific theatre. Even more exciting than the play itself was the search for a cab after it was over.

For a final sampling of off-Broadway fare, I selected the Dilettante Rep, a coöperative organization of actors and directors that performs in the lobby of a member's apartment building. This earthy, shoestring troupe believes in what it calls "Classics à Go-go"; that is, it takes old plays and does things to them. What's more, the plays they call classics are not necessarily familiar to anyone else. Dilettante's offerings this season include Nahum Tate's adaptation of "King Lear," "The Recruiting Officer," and a staged reading of "Gorboduc." The company's brochure proudly proclaims the last a New York première, neglecting to mention that the script had its out-of-town tryout in the sixteenth century. Dimly recalling having once seen, or perhaps read, Farquhar's "Recruiting Officer," I showed up for that. The play is a comedy about the bawdy peccadilloes that ensue when some randy recruiting officers arrive in a small English town, Shrewsbury or Shropshire, or possibly Shrewsbury in Shropshire. In the Dilettante's futuristic version, the military men wear outfits crafted, apparently, of aluminum; the women sport abbreviated tunics of the black vinyl more commonly seen on sofas in pediatricians'

waiting rooms. Flashlights are used as guns, spray-painted macaroni and dried lima beans serve as jewelry; there is a lot of juggling. Tenants passing through the lobby were included in the action until one, threatened by three players wielding yardsticks, threatened to call the police.

A sense of fair play prevents me from disclosing any of the names of the Dilettante members. They may yet work elsewhere, and this folly should not be held against them.

As I boarded the last train to Old Spice and installed myself in the club car, I pledged never again to complain about early curtains, talkative theatre-party ladies with big hats, or feisty matrons who make one ask three times for a program. I will feel grateful to be in a theatre that has a curtain at all, early, late, or not very clean. The raising of the curtain is one of the indicators that "Magic Time," as I like to call an evening in the theatre, is upon us. Most of the Magic Time in town, as of this writing, is to be found around the Great White Way.

—Grendel Pill

•

NOT TOO YOUNG TO ENTERTAIN
[from the Delaware Evening Sun]
The youngest parents of all time in the USA are Lindy Sue Linburg and Johnny Harris of New Lester, Colorado. At the age of 10 Lindy Sue became the mother of a 7½ pound baby boy. Johnny, the father, was 12. The cheese course should come after the entree. The value of cheese is that it helps digest all that has come before it. If your spouse is serving cheese before the main course, be kind to yourself and bring this information to his attention.

•

This prompts the observation that if we don't get a handle on some of this debt soon, we're going to get bounced on our own canards.
—*Ill. State Rep. William L. Butler.*

Duck! Duck!

School for Santas

[*From our first days, when staffers pooled their salaries to invest in Broadway plays, our magazine has been intrigued by the mechanics of show business. Originally, this meant articles about producers and playwrights. In the fifties, it meant Kenneth Myman's reports on European theatres, which suggested that without subsidy our own Broadway was doomed to become a wax museum for musicals. (He turned out to be right.) In recent years, it's come to mean glimpses of the profession's flotsam; ah, whither has fled the visionary gleam?*]

IT'S Christmastime once again, and the city is clogged with massed shoppers, vacationing students, temps helping out in department stores, Salvation Army Corpspersons and, of course, Santa Clauses. There's a Santa on every corner, it seems, distributing leaflets, hawking wares, collecting for charity. Of all the people who crowd the blocks around our offices this time of year, the Santa Clauses are by far our favorites. Their bright-red suits and relentless bonhomie embody both the cheery ambience of the season and, since street Santas are usually asking for money, commerce at its most hectic. Sadly, we no longer believe there really is a Santa Claus, so we found ourselves wondering where all the seasonal Santas come from. Asking one, a tall, thin, yellow-haired young man whose flowing white beard couldn't convince anyone that the face underneath was a day over twenty-five, we were directed to a rehearsal hall on West Fifty-fifth Street where an acting teacher who calls himself Noël Cadeau offers intensive training for street Santas.

Xanadu Studio is a large, poorly heated room with a mirrored wall opposite a dancer's bar. The other three walls are the pale shade of green believed to be gentle on the eyes. (Why anyone ever thought so is a mystery to us, but that's another story.) Two big windows with octagonal wire mesh embedded in the glass overlook the continuous holiday traffic jam. A far cry from a workshop with elves, we thought.

Three rows of red-clad figures faced the mirrors, in front of which stood a slight fellow in well-worn tan corduroys and a black turtleneck. Over his head, his right hand held a large bell; his left hand rested on the soft curve of an imaginary potbelly. He spoke crisply, not at all with the warm sonority we expected from a Santa Claus trainer: "All right, class, this is the basic posture. Hold the bell up high and let your other hand rest on your belly. Don't hook the thumb in your belt and let it hang there—that'll just make your belly droop when you take your hand away. Just a little light pressure around the midriff, like so. That's good, Bernie. You, too, Estebán. Get your left hand lower, Diane, you look like you're about to recite the pledge of allegiance."

As they practiced, we looked the Santas over. What a motley group! One was tiny, perhaps five foot three and *very* skinny, his padded gut almost bigger than he. A powerfully built black man, well over six feet tall with thick arms and chest, needed no padding to fill his costume, though his belly did not look in the least soft and pudgy; here was a Santa who would take no guff. All the Santas raised their right hands with bells properly in place, left hands on stomachs, and awaited their next command.

"The way you look ringing the bell is more important than the sound you make," coached Mr. Cadeau. "Remember, you're out in city traffic. People can hardly hear themselves think, let alone

"Support hose?"

•   •

pay attention to a little tinkling bell. They *will* notice, however, if you look as though you're ringing for the butler. Use the full arm, swinging from the shoulder, not just the wrist, and—stop that, Rob, no one wants to see a fey Santa. You look like you're drying your nail polish."

The Santa in question blushed almost the same color as his suit, then stiffened his wrist and swung his arm rigidly back and forth. "That's much better!" said Mr. Cadeau. *"Careful!"* But his warning was too late. A blunt, stocky Santa had swung his bell with such enthusiasm that he hit the Santa in front of him, a gawky, thin, nervous-looking Santa, right smack on top of the head. The gawky Santa staggered and broke ranks with the others. Mr. Cadeau was quick to use the accident as an example. "Not such big swings, everybody. You do that on Fifth Avenue, you'll find yourself under arrest for assault and battery. You're not sawing wood, remember. Keep the hand high and swing forward, then back, and forward, and back. *Good!*"

At three o'clock, Mr. Cadeau allowed his exhausted charges a fifteen-minute break, during which he retreated to a corner of the room where he kept a duffel containing a thermos of camomile

tea, a banana, and a foil bag of trail mix. As he refueled and rested, we asked how he'd gotten started in the Santa-training field.

"I'm an actor," he told us. "A few years ago I was a Christmas temp in Better Quilts at Macy's. Every day I'd walk to and from work, and I'd see all these Santas. Most of them looked so uncomfortable in their suits, and with what they had to do, that I'd get embarrassed for them. I looked over the six or seven Santas that Macy's had in the toy department. It was the same thing: tired laughter, no eye contact with the children, no body awareness of the false stomach. I told one of the floor managers that in three hours I could make the Santas look one hundred per cent jollier.

"Well, it worked. Our Santas pulled in kids, who pulled in their parents, who shelled out like crazy. I overheard one tyke tell his parents that he liked our video-game-department Santa better than the one in Altman's sports department. I figured that a lot of concerns might want to upgrade the quality of their Santas. I put an ad in *The Village Voice*, and now I've got three full classes of about twenty each. Usually, my two assistants take them through basic ho-ho-ho drills while I work with individual students on special problems. Some of my students are repeaters, semiprofessional Santas who come here to bone up on basics before the season starts. Most, though, are first-timers from the larger charities and department stores who're sent here by their employers. I charge a group rate.

"The next time you pass a Santa on the street, check him out. Is the beard centered, the voice placed properly, full and deep in the gut? Does he look like he's having fun? Do you think he knows if you've been bad or good? If not, he hasn't been through this course."

Mr. Cadeau excused himself and clapped his hands for the class to resume. The Santas, looking droopy, dragged themselves back onto the floor. We slipped away as Mr. Cadeau was explaining how to lift a child onto the knee without risk of hernia. We'd had no idea that being a Santa was such work.

Out on the street, we saw a Santa who had pulled his white beard away from his already bearded chin, so that it lay on his chest like a napkin. Spare change was causing a bit of a bulge in one of our pockets, so we gave it to the Santa and asked him why he'd pulled his beard so low. "What can I say? Scratches my face, man. Hey, hey, hey, give to Santa, show a little Christmas spirit, ladies and gents, let's give! Hey, hey, hey!"

"Shouldn't that be 'ho, ho, ho'?" we couldn't help asking, but we could not be heard above the din of traffic and passersby.

GOURMET ICE CREAMS

FRO-YO—A frozen yogurt concoction most frequently seen in sticky puddles on the upper West Side. No one knows where it's available or who makes it. Perhaps it falls from the sky.

RIFTENPOOFT—Thick and rich; after six hours on our table, it was still frozen solid. Pint containers depict cheerful families wearing lederhosen. Manufactured in the Bronx.

TOFATTI—The bland taste of tofu with all the calories of a double-scoop ice-cream sundae.

Especially good for those who wish to pretend they're dieting. Available in thirteen flavors, each indistinguishable from the others.

UTA HÄAGEN—Currently, the city's most expensive ice cream. Sold only in spoonfuls by street vendors dressed as kings.

ZORKENSPLETCH—Full-bodied and surprisingly bitter. After sampling, we discovered that it's an automotive lubricating jelly and not a frozen dessert. The name fooled us.

• • •

"Wipe your feet."

INTROSPECTIONS
TEA DANCES AND DESTINY
(1962)

[Bamford Nightingale's tender remembrance brought quite a lot of admiring mail. As a result, Miss Cinquefoil and Mr. Picketfence of Fact Checking organized a weekly class in ballroom steps that many of our staff still attend.]

L AST month, my wife and I were invited to chaperone a tea dance at our daughter's school. Tea dances have been called that since as least as long ago as my teen years, although when tea was last served at one is anybody's guess. A tea dance begins between four and five o'clock and is usually over by eight, early enough to assuage most parents' anxieties. "What a chance to see Spring's Awakening up close," I remarked to my wife after I'd eagerly accepted for both of us. She rolled her eyes and warily agreed to go.

We'd been asked to arrive at the school on the appointed Friday afternoon at three-thirty to receive instructions on how to keep an unobtrusive eye peeled for shenanigans. As we approached the upper East Side brownstone, I marvelled aloud at the idea that, within its impeccable confines, girls clean erasers and

"Keep the Trinitron! The way you make love, you'll need it!"

skin their knees and study and sigh rapturously over their dreamboats as girls have done for centuries. My wife yawned mightily, nodding, and reminded me that I'd thought the same thing last time we'd been there.

To enter the school, one climbs a short flight to the parlor-floor portal and rings the doorbell, which is invariably answered by one of a number of majestic women wearing basic black and pearls, absolutely smudge-proof lipstick, and perfectly coifed, unmoving silver hair. The Library, where the dance was to be held, is on the second floor. Its tables and chairs had already been removed and its large carpet rolled up by the time we arrived. For the next few hours, the Library would be used in the pursuit of a type of knowledge not to be found in all those thousands upon thousands of pages, I mused as I looked at the ceiling-high shelves, my reverie broken by my collision with a high-hat cymbal. Here, at the far end of the room, was a baby grand piano, a small drum kit (of which the high-hat I'd bumped into was a part), and, in its case, a huge acoustic bass, standing silently, ominously, like some leatherette sarsen stone of a contemporary Stonehenge, awaiting the musicians and their audience. The musicians, in powder-blue dinner jackets, were sitting on the other side of a large window, in the Librarian's office. They all looked up at the sound of the percussive discs toppling. One threw his cigarette down and rushed in.

"Ah, the drummist," I said, greeting the stocky fellow, who examined his cymbals carefully, grumbling and cursing the while. "Really sorry. When do the diversions begin—that is, when do you fellows start?"

"On forty-five, off fifteen every hour, mister. We start five-fifteen. And stay away from the instruments, do you mind? They're not toys." And so admonishing me, the chunky rhythmist was gone, returned to the camaraderie of his combo-mates.

S MALL, tidy Filipino women who work in the school's kitchen laid a large table with refreshment. Hefty nutted

cheese balls garlanded with Saltines, platters of butter cookies and sheet cake were flanked on one end of the table by a large bowl of punch, on the other by a fine array of sodas. An urn of coffee was provided for the adults. Loitering awkwardly, as we knew the young people would be shortly, we listened to the most elegant of the Basic-Black-and-Pearls ladies, who turned out to be the Headmistress, as she gave us our orders:

"Our guests attend some of the most expen—that is, exclusive—schools in New York City, so there is no reason to expect behavior less than proper, but there are rules that some of the boys may need to have pointed out to them. First of all, there is to be no unseemly comportment on the dance floor. I don't think you need insist on seeing daylight between couples, but if you think a couple is behaving with untoward intimacy, you need feel no compunction about stepping in. Also, discourage pairing off. Everyone should dance with several partners. Drinking, of course, is strictly off limits. Well, it's twenty to five. Will someone call in the girls?"

In they filed, eighth- and ninth-graders, among them our daughter. I've never seen so much clean hair in my life. The girls looked frightened. "Fasten your seat belts, ladies, it's going to be a bumpy night!" I called out, breaking the ice with a paraphrase of Betty Davis' quip in "All About Eve." Our daughter turned the color of an eggplant but said nothing. Neither did anyone else. Fortunately, at that moment the doorbell rang. Boys' voices floated upstairs from the foyer. The ceremony was beginning.

By five o'clock, the stately room was nicely peopled along one side with young gentlemen, almost all of them in blue blazers and brown loafers, and along the other with girls in tartan kilts or dark skirts and sweater sets. The boys spoke among themselves, pacing and shuffling in an elaborate charade of ease. The girls whispered, looked, giggled; a few sported amateurish stabs at makeup.

"How like young elk the boys are," I mused. "And the girls, even our daughter, so like young does."

"And I'm Bambi's mother," my wife said quietly, rubbing her temples.

Promptly at five-fifteen, the musicians took their places. Losing no time in proving their hepcat credentials, they began with a rousing instrumental version of "Louie, Louie." No one danced. Hardly anyone moved. Yet the music began to work its spell. After "Louie Louie," a Latinized medley of tunes from "My Fair Lady" had one of the Basic-Black-and-Pearls ladies tapping her I. Millered toe. The young people's hesitation seemed to me immensely poignant, and I wondered how long they could keep it up.

"How long, how long?" I whispered softly, inhaling deeply the scent of a perfume my wife had never used before. "Mmm, sweetheart, you smell lovely," I murmured.

"I beg your pardon?" asked the woman whose hair I'd been nuzzling.

In the hall outside the Library, I noticed my wife enjoying a cigarette by the water fountain. No wonder the perfume smelled funny.

Two girls boldly marched onto the dance floor and began a solemn lindy. Just then, the trio's rendition of "Theme from Peter Gunn" ended. After a long, awkward moment, the music recommenced, this time with a lively tune called "The Peppermint Twist." The melody's velocity threatened for a moment to overwhelm the pianist, but he managed to regroup and find the groove. There were scattered handclaps around the room, and some boys actually asked some girls to dance. Momentum began to take effect. I collared a young man standing next to me. "Let's ask someone to dance," I suggested unconditionally, and marched him over to where a B.B. & P. lady was discussing Latin cognates with a petite young woman whose cherry-red lips and heavily kohled eyes revealed careful study of Elizabeth Taylor's "Cleopatra" look. The young folk edged out onto the dance floor, while I squired the B.B. & P. lady and so danced my first Twist, my enthusiasm dampened only when I called over to my daughter to grab a partner and join the fun; she ran into the ladies' room instead.

The musicians, inspired by their young audience, played music as loud, pounding, and boisterous as a piano, bass, and drums can be. Most of the young people and a few of the chaperones worked up a great sweat. I felt I was witnessing one of those times in the lives of all men and women when, suddenly, they suddenly become suddenly, startlingly aware of the reality of women (in the case of men discovering this reality) and men (in the case of women). The quiet and deep truthfulness of this truth made me wistful even when a fistfight broke out be-

"Do you do windows?"

• •

tween two of the boys who, it turned out, had been swigging Robitussin all evening, and again when one of the girls was caught sneaking a cigarette in the stairwell. Happily, these disruptions were all settled by the time I dragooned students, parents, and teachers alike out onto the floor for a rousing, Twisting singalong of "Hit the Road, Jack" during which the Headmistress fell on her bottom and I bruised a disc. By eight o'clock, the students were gone, the cleaning up had begun, and the musicians had packed up and left. We headed home, too, our daughter off to some friend's house for a post-mortem.

IN the elevator up to our apartment, I sighed, put my arm around my wife and wondered aloud, "What was it H. G. Wells said: It's a crime that youth is wasted on young people?"

"That's not quite it, and it was Shaw, not Wells. Jesus, I've got the migraine again."

And so she had. One more reason why Shaw was right, I thought, climbing into bed next to my wife, who was lying very still, trying to clear her mind as she waited for the phenobarbitol to take effect. I was asleep before Paar came on.

—BAMFORD NIGHTINGALE

THEATRE AROUND TOWN

CHARTS—Pie graphs, comparative studies, and other visual aids serve as a backdrop for this bouncy, frothily entertaining look at the world of business statistics. Original score by Jacques Prell and Lee Iacocca. (Bartles St. Jaymes Theatre.)

'CISCANS AND LOLLARDS —This bumptious musical is based on the fourteenth-century feud between Oxford's Franciscan Brothers, whose library was closed to the public (which was illiterate for the most part anyway, the abbots argued) and the Lollards, who believed in the ontological necessity of open stacks and lending cards. The score, by Andrew Void Schlepper and Tim Lice, makes one grateful that the synthesizer was not available to medieval composers. The show's finale includes the currently popular "Buboes Become You," which lingers in the mind long after you wish it had gone. John Dextrous directs the Royal Avon Company of Swindon with his usual itchy flair (lots of men in cassocks up and down the aisles, for one thing). John Nappy's elaborate set, modelled after Oxford's Bodleian Library, fills the mezzanine and part of the lobby as well as the stage, demonstrating yet again that American investors go soft in the head when they hear English accents. (Neil Pieman Theatre.)

EL GRANDE DE RC COLA—A brief (eighteen-minute) cabaret purporting to take place in a sweaty San Diego bistro. Two inter-missions. Flat. (Theatre in the Ground.)

THE JEWEL AND THE RESTLESS—In David Mammy's new play, a marriage deteriorates into confusion, bickering, and divorce because of the couple's inability to make head or tail of an incomprehensibly English-accented series on PBS. Mammy has much to say about love and relationships in the age of electronic media, but his arguments cannot match in theatrical impact the profound wonderment he clearly feels at Alistair Cooke's perpetual tan. Spencer Chablis and April Snapper perform very well under the direction of Bob Fungus, as do Vincent Fritata as the neighbor and C.O. Jones in the small role of a Chinese restaurant delivery boy whose hands are briefly visible as he passes the couple their dinner order through the doorway from the hall. (Tertiary Stage.)

THE SPICE RACK—The third play in Sam Sheepskin's trilogy about a garage sale he had last year. Synthetic and marginally entertaining, thanks mostly to the somewhat offbeat casting of John Houseman as a teenage girl with a severe speech impediment. (Théâtre de Trop.)

YOU'RE AN IDIOT—Musical based on the works of Dostoevsky, with an unexpectedly jaunty score by John Cage. The title role is portrayed by Sally Struthers, who does a competent job of playing an incompetent. (Granny Smith Forum.)

CHAPTER NINE

FOOTAGE
AFOOT

Film

*T*HE *magazine is only two years older than the talking picture, but for most of our readers cinema long lurked in the tawdry half-light of popular art—too present to ignore, yet beneath notice. For them, Pauline Zeal's arrival at our magazine was an event equal in historical significance to the outflanking of the Maginot Line and the collapse of the West Side Highway. No more would our movie reviews be lost in the back of the book, among memoirs of obscure childhoods, poetry translated from the Russian, and tiny ads. Miss Zeal took over the department from Grendel Pill, who quit the post immediately when he realized that the people whose work he was evaluating onscreen were not actually present in the theatre ("Why should I waste my time if they aren't even there?" he apparently shouted at Shbop). Her first column served notice to a drowsy readership that here was a voice that would not be silent, even when it had nothing to say. In 1968, her review of "Bonnie and Dud" rescued a sleeper with a broadside of explication that, in a scant nine thousand words, drew analogies between the film's saga of two bloodthirsty, sexually aberrant hooligans and the works of Sidney Kingsley, Vermeer, Bela Bartók (but only early Bela Bartók), and the Swinging Blue Jeans.*

Miss Zeal is one of the most formidable members of our staff. Though unquestionably feminine, she possesses a set of manners and a vocabulary of blue words that would not be out of place at a Friar's Club roast. Her battles with Mr. Shnurk are legendary. She is the only person currently with the magazine—or ever at the magazine, for that matter—to call him by his first name, or what she claims is his first name ("Wimpy"). Shratz, accustomed to working with more malleable writers, was at first quite at a loss with Miss Zeal. Now he simply sneaks out of his office and hides in the Library when he sees her coming. Miss Zeal, for her part, notifies Mr. Shooth in advance of any unspeakable words in her copy so that he can avert his eyes when he gets to them.

Calvin Chitterling's appearance in this chapter is a fluke. His consuming interest, so to speak, is food, and in pursuit of treats he has travelled all over the country, eating and writing, writing and eating. When at home, he divides his time between his typewriter and his restaurant, Bud's Boîte & Barbecue.

CITIZEN KALE

(1984)

[This is the article that was later expanded to even greater length for publication in "The Citizen Kale Coffee-Table Book," an oversize volume of truly impressive heft.]

THE protean-*auteur*, the wiggy moviemaker in a Rootie-Kazootie hat with a hand-cranked camera, is an image embedded in our minds as subtly and permanently as the heavy-drinking reporter with a press card in his hat or the stage-door Johnny waiting for a chorus girl, flowers in hand; they are the stuff of our dreams and they all come from the movies. This idea of the all-purpose man of the movies had some validity in the silent era, when it was routine for one person to write the scenario, play the lead, and direct the damn thing. Those guys were snap-pop, hit-and-run technicians: wham, bam, three reels in the can. For them it was an act of practicality as much as ego. Scenes never loitered, and the pictures had an *outré* specificity that nobody knew was art. Chaplin and Keaton did it all because nobody else was around. Today, Woody Allen, Mel Brooks, and a few others still do it, but with them you always wonder who's minding the camera while the *auteur* is playing the scene.

Now Hollywood, with its unfailing sense of proportion and overkill, has put another slug in the gun and made the protean-*auteurs* of the past look like lug-a-beds. In I. Kale's "Citizen Kale," you know you're in Art-land right from the start, when you hear the sound of the Panavision camera under the titles—the first of many self-conscious, onanistic references, or maybe it's a mistake. You can't really tell, because the eighteen-track overlapping sound was recorded on good Nagra equipment but with discounted THC8000B tape purchased at the Thrifty's drugstore on Ventura Boulevard in Sherman Oaks. The result, as any film student could guess, is so muddy that you think Enrico Caruso and Alexander Graham Bell are in a shouting match recorded at Magno Sound by the middle-period Bob Altman.

"Citizen Kale" isn't bad, but good or bad isn't the point here. If you want laughter or tears or any of the other traditional movie honks, you're in the wrong Bijou, because with this picture, the protean-*auteur*ist school has transcended emotion, come of age, and gone feminist. Kale, who until now has been an overvoiced if occasionally effective filmmaker, has, as they say in the back room at Le Dôme, laid out the lines and chopped them fine. She's written, directed, acted, produced, photographed, designed, and—in the iciest, hot-pop move since Marlowe turned left off Cahuenga onto Ivar—written all the reviews. The reviews are distributed to the media and reprinted on milk cartons along with the missing-kid ads. If the results are mixed, there's still no denying that *après*-Kale the Yalu has been crossed; the elephants are over the Alps; good golly, Miss Molly, there's no turning back. The cinema of the twenty-first century has just sailed in through the window on the side of a half-gallon carton of skim milk. No American director working above the level of the ABC after-school specials will be able to go back to the old wait-and-see-what-the-critics-say school of filmmaking. The

"Look! Wretched refuse!"

• •

studios wouldn't touch the movie, natch, but now they're all jockeying for cassette rights and foreign distribution. The picture was financed by a consortium of West German banks, Thai rice tax shelters, and a lot of overextended American Express gold cards. It's distributed domestically by the Pas de Beurre Jamming and Packing Company.

The release of "Citizen Kale" is as electric a moment in cinema as the first performance of "Le Sacre du Printemps" is in music or the time the great Slovak outfielder Elmer Valo was struck by lightning during a game at the old Shibe Park in Philadelphia. The picture is occasionally exhilarating but maddeningly stuffed with the sort of fake-humble, woman-of-the-people metaphysical digressions that seem to afflict the very young and the very mature. In the end, the picture itself, if not the ideas it promulgates, is really more of the same old flossy, Pepto-Bismol, me-too existentialism tricked up in a prankster life-of-the-party style. It reminds you of the early Kerouac as done by Lily Tomlin before she could handle his Céline imitation of a cranky old fart on Parents' Day at an offshore medical school.

That's not to say this thing isn't hip; if anything, it suffers from near-terminal with-it-ness. The plot, with its attendant reviews, reflects the old *auteur*ist conundrum of style versus substance as it chases the true authorship of an appallingly vast number of columns about movies that appear as regularly as the flu in an overwritten magazine, influential out of all proportion to its intrinsic worth. Like Citizen Kale herself, the magazine is running on near-empty, getting by on style and remembered triumphs. It's the movie loon's age-old question: What is style and what is substance in what Godard, in one of his more playful moods, called "*le* truth twenty-four times a second"? The detective angle—who wrote these things and, more important, who reads them?—is played out against the story of Kale's life. Kale plays herself as an adult. At first you think the performance is right; then, the more you watch, the more convinced you are that she's outside the character, looking down her nose at herself. But that starts to feel right when you realize two of the sub-themes of the critiques, if not of the picture itself, are Kale's inability to correct the universe and her resulting self-contempt.

The mystery plot is supposed to keep you going. A movie-review major from the U.S.C. film school is trying to parse all the columns, but it's really only a bunch of cuts of this pasty-faced kid in various libraries reading back issues of magazines. It's forced and tentative, and you keep thinking the kid ought to go outside and get some fresh air. The reviews he reads are seen in a Slavko Vorkapich-style montage of the articles; the words fill the screen and you get the idea that the reviews are like phone conversations with a really smart friend, unpretentious but tenaciously right and full of common assumptions that don't have to be explained. Who actually wrote the columns, however, is a question as fundamentally dim-witted as who wrote Shakespeare's plays, or did Big Mama Thornton's recording of "Work with Me, Annie" predate Georgia Gibbs' recording of "Dance with Me, Henry," or what. The problem is, it's obvious that no one person could have written them all. Like the putative author of these endless columns, you can't figure how or when this movie is going to end. Even as it wears you down with its fizzy erudition, it assaults you with a barrage of "only connect" I.Q. points. Still, it's good for a few laughs.

A guy I know, a screenwriter who used to be hot, says it's all some film-school fantasy. Who cares about a movie about a movie reviewer? But that's wrong; it's a great subject precisely because of its self-consciousness. It's a "Tristram Shandy" for an age of viewpoint-mongering, when the main reason most people go to the movies is to have an opinion.

The central ethos of the damn thing is a sort of combination platter of Mr. Natural and Freddy Ayer, filtered through the Arthur Waley translation of "The Book of Genji." The yarn, what retro studio executives call the front story (that is, when they're not redecorating their offices from the Memphis Collection catalogue), starts in the thirties and moves in a linear progression—shockingly so—into the present. It's about the daughter of Old Man Kale, a Russian-emigré chicken farmer in Petaluma, in Sonoma County, who works his way up to being a gentleman rancher before the Depression creams him. When he goes belly up, young Citizen Kale retreats into the movies and the local boys. The father becomes a Republican, an insatiable womanizer and adulterer just as the daughter becomes a voracious reader and movie nut. Neat. Then, when you think this is going to be another meditation on the meaning of the modern West, filled with pickup trucks and dusty roads, and disguised as a daughter-leaves-home-to-find-herself story, Old Man Kale dies and young Citizen Kale, showing strains of the family excess, starts marrying and divorcing and making her way in the world. She uses what at the time were called womanly wiles, mostly sewing, cooking, and eyelash batting, to endear herself to the Petaluma male power structure, probably in an attempt to connect with her dead pop. Later, as a critic, she'll learn to use the unexpected adverb and the unlikely sociological detail as weapons. All this is done without a conscious nod to Freud, but old Sig's cigar looms over the proceedings any way you snip the

tip. Form and content get all skewed in a pranky, comic-book way, as if all those kewpie-mouth, chicken-foot dorm bull sessions had been put through a Cuisinart to make a giggle-babble, pop-mush picture of what it means to be smarter than anybody else, with nobody to talk to but feed salesmen and randy roosters, and eventually not to give a damn about it.

Not a bad hook for a picture, but with I. Kale herself playing it all, you get the idea that her real task is not patronizing the form. The rhythms seem self-conscious, and young Citizen Kale is such a tabula rasa that you feel snookered by the structure, fleeced by a good mind applied to bad movies. The culture disappoints her, just as her father did, and by extension you feel let down, too. It's as if Pär Lagerkvist had taken a part-time job writing up the veal orders at Lobel's.

A FRIEND of mine who used to be a studio executive tells me that Kale, in her earlier pictures, sometimes played some of the smaller parts, too. According to my friend, she did it in disguise; but if you look closely, he says, you can see her as the beggar woman in "Red Kales in the Sunset," as the tweedy dominatrix in "God and Man at Kale," and as a peripheral monster in the early "Kales from the Crypt." The point is, she also played the leads in those pictures. Whether she did it for budget or for ego is finally less interesting than her technique. She used a blue-screen-and-animation combination developed at the old Disney by the team of Shamus Culhane, the Pluto specialist, his colleague Ub Iwerks, and the great matte artist Albert Whitlock before they squabbled over the lunch menu at the Disney commissary. Blue-screen and matte work were set back by at least a generation.

If nothing else, "Citizen Kale" means you have to look at Kale's other pictures in this look-Ma, no-hands protean-*auteur* light. The musicals "Kale House Rock," "Kale, Kale, the Gang's All Here," and the smaller political pictures like "Kale-Safe," which were regarded as simple *auteur*ist works, have to be re-reviewed in the protean-*auteur*ist light. It was always there, but you couldn't tell.

After Old Man Kale's death, the narrative takes a weird leap. You go from the chicken feed of Petaluma to a chicken-feed art theatre in Berkeley in what I guess is the early fifties. It's hard to tell because this part was shot on short ends of refrigerated Eastman Color 5247 and 5249 raw stock to give it a documentary feel and then developed at Le Drugstore using a one-hour, double-soup system (to keep it grainy) instead of at Movielab or Technicolor. The result is murky.

As Pudovkin showed in his little-known 1913 kineto-social experiments, if you keep the camera close enough, long enough, eventually the audience will sympathize with Rasputin. In "Citizen Kale," even though you get a movie critic who is either going to a flick or writing about one, you still like her, probably because you spend so much time with the bitch. It's like "Psycho," where you wind up hoping Tony Per-

kins will get away with it because once everybody else is dead he's the only one you've got, or the early Bob Dylan of "Subterranean Homesick Blues," where you're amazed he can remember all the words, no matter what they mean.

THE action picks up after young Citizen Kale leaves the chicken coops and heads for the fleshpots of San Francisco and New York, but there's a definite loss of inner life. For Kale, doing Schopenhauer one better, the first twenty-one years are text and the next forty-odd years are commentary. In San Francisco, she writes program notes and does a radio show about the movies. Husbands and lovers, including an avant-garde porno filmmaker, come and go, but Kale keeps critiquing everything in sight. Back home with the chickens she was always telling her birds what she thought of them, mostly that they were chicken feed, and now she's doing the same for the movies, except you know that she's really criticizing/understanding her dead father. When she's cooking you don't care, you're even interested, but still a lot of the time you think it's going to take forever to get to the end.

There's a daring cut in the third reel, right after sprocket hole four hundred and eighty. Up till then Kale has been played by an anonymous urchin, possibly a hologram of a computer-enhanced model of the youthful I. Kale herself. She steps onto an elevator in some creaky office building on Forty-third Street in New York, and when she gets out nineteen stories later she's thirty-eight years old and played by Kale for real. As an adult dame with very little of the chicken farmer's daughter about her, she's now a noisy woman in a bright-red, low-cut dress who keeps clanging her bracelets and telling people she's hip and that she knows Norman Mailer. At first you think the character is going to turn tedious, but damned if she doesn't charm you and damned if she isn't really as hip as she claims. The real mystery in this thing is how she does it.

There's a secondary surface mystery, but it doesn't amount to much. She has four disciples, called Kalites, and they stand in for sons or maybe lovers. Each one tries to be her clone, aping her opinions and her fizzy-pop-highbrow style. Each one uses the second person singular and lots of contractions and tries to write columns that are even longer than their mentor's. Each one is trying to get Kale to help him get a job as a movie critic on a big paper. One of them (they're all so interchangeable, you're never sure which) turns on her and becomes a sort of apostate Kalite, buttering her up at screenings and then, when she's gotten him a job, taking subtle jabs at her in print to show his independence. It's a recapitulation of the chicken-farmer's-daughter-leaves-home theme.

The big Kalite scene is played out in a restaurant that's meant to be Florent on Gansevoort Street, but they couldn't afford the location insurance so it's actually a well-designed set. Over a meal of Sole au Malaise Europa, she tells one of her acolytes that she's arranged for him to teach film theory at some tedious college in the Philippines; the quid pro

quo is he's supposed to arrange for an honorary Ph.D. He accepts the offer and then nothing more is said about it, but you know he's doomed. "Citizen Kale" doesn't follow up on this plot thread. Maybe Kale is saving it for the sequel.

You know this thing is flawed from the start, but in a way that still keeps a lot of it interesting, moment to moment. It's the triumph of this picture that it makes something as essentially dopey as reviewing movies seem important. Despite the moral bankruptcy and parasitical nature of the occupation, while you're watching the meandering plot curlicues for the film's five-and-a-half-hour length, the whole world seems like a movie review. At its best, movie reviewing is raised to a level of social and aesthetic criticism that it can't support. It's the high-wire act of art disguised as commentary. Not bad and not chicken feed, if you know what I mean.

—PAULINE ZEAL

• •

LETTER WE NEVER FI—
Dear Animal Lover,

The spider monkey you see here is the star of Good Morning America, the Today show, the Tournament of Roses....

The Animal League
223 Alhambra Ave.
Morristown, New Jersey

IN AN APE'S VALISE
The ear cavities of the Sumatran orangutan are so large and accommodating that they are often used for fast-food storage in case of emergencies.

—*Zoology Today.*

We can't hear you, we've got a banana in our ear.

I ATE IT AT THE MOVIES

(1956)

[Calvin Chitterling sent this little-known piece to us when he was fourteen years old; clearly, the child was appetizer to the man. It is unique among Calvin's works in not having been anthologized until now.]

IN MY book a full stomach is guaranteed by the Constitution, and that's why people who think television is going to knock off the movies are just dumb. At our house, for instance, everybody is too busy with antenna strategy or vertical-roll fear to think about a good viewing snack. In fact, when we were all glued to the McCarthy hearings, my mom didn't even find it appropriate to restock the lazy Susan with the minty white things with red stripes or the wrapped-up brown things with goopy middles that she reveres because they're "imported." (It's always bothered me that if European children are starving, as has so often been brought to my attention over, say, a pile of lima beans, their parents could be so heartless as to *export* their precious, life-giving supply of brown goopy stuff.) Occasionally, my mom will put out a bowl of grapes, but not very often. Like an army living off the wild roots and berries of the terrain, I'm left with the same old copper bowl of walnuts and that nutcracker that's good for making extremely loud cracks so that everyone turns around and stares. What's left after this process looks like an exploded hand grenade, so I always end up throwing the whole thing out anyway.

No, on considered reflection, I would have to say that television doesn't come close to an afternoon at the Ascot, the

Rialto, or the Lux. The two or three hours of nonstop movie eating are just the beginning, like hitting the beach. You also have to take into account benefits like what it is you eat, how much you can eat, how you eat when you eat, and even that the movie might be O.K. Obviously, there's a lot to consider here, and I've spent a lot of time at it. Every time I go, I'm reminded how important movie houses really are. I can't think of many other places that have marquees. The theatre marquees in our neighborhood are big, curvy jobs with lots of neon. Some have different-colored sidewalks underneath them. There's nothing like a blinking "Bijou" or "Orpheum" to set my mouth watering.

I usually go to movies in the afternoon, right after lunch. I approach the theatre as others take the Constellation to Rio, even allowing myself a tricky mambo step or two between the ticket booth and the uniformed usher who tears my ticket in half. Across the lobby, the candy counter beckons like Jeanette MacDonald. Good movie food often causes me to fling open my arms and burst into song. When you come from the bright sunlight into the dark theatre, the counter is the only thing you can see. Bathed in a pool of yellow light, it's a centrally located oasis of reliable happiness. Not too long ago I found myself at the Calderone, anticipating a ten-cartoon medley followed by "To Hell and Back." After the newsreel, I sat through all of "Love Is a Many-Splendored Thing," a really mushy movie, expecting the cats, mice, and soldiers to follow. Mom found me still sitting there, in stunned disbelief, waiting hopelessly through a second viewing. (She often gains free admission in order to get me home in time for dinner.) Having bitterly learned that it's clearly a case of *caveat emptor*, I have trained myself never to enter a movie theatre without first asking the booth lady if they're trying to sneak in a showing of "Love Is a Many-Splendored Thing" before I give her my quarter.

THERE are some all-purpose movie-food rules I've developed. Build around popcorn. Movies are the land where popcorn is king, and no movie should be watched without buying some. Even if you've had enough or you don't like it, it's good to use as trade bait or to share instead of something more valuable like Sno-Caps. Buttered popcorn is O.K.—it's pretty neat when they put the butter on—but I go for unbuttered if it comes in a bigger container. I don't like the kind that comes in a closed box, because you can't carry it to your seat in your teeth; you've got to carry it in your arms, which you may need for bulk cargo. I always back up the first popcorn with a chocolate, a taffy, a caramel, or a gel. Straight nuts are taboo on the first round because it's impossible to get enough soda on one trip to get you through a second salty item, and that might cause you to blow the timing of your second trip with a water-fountain emergency. Movie seats are built so that you run into some problems if you don't plan. If you're in the middle of a row and have to get past other kids' knees, you can be an easy target for big kids in the back who throw stuff. The whole idea of the movies is to get settled in.

Put your coat on a seat next to you so no one will be close enough to try to glom a handful of Raisinettes or ask you for a bite of your Charleston Chew. Anyway, I especially like a mixed-chocolate chewy on the first round—Milk Duds, say, or Pom Poms, or maybe Rollos. There are also some really first-rate gels that are good early, like Spearmint Leaves, Dots, Jujubes, and Twizzlers. Some gels become too big a production; they can take up too much time and make your jaws really tired. Turkish Taffy has that problem, although it's sure a good trading buy.

MOVIE hot dogs are undistinguished. They come in two major categories: the pronger and the roller. The pronger type is stuck lengthwise on a metal prong that rotates on an axle in a small glass box. The axle is run by a little electric motor the same size as the one in my Gilbert erector set. When you order one, the lady opens a little glass door and either stops the motor or tries to grab one on its way by. Either way, you're not guaranteed the dog of your choice. Candy-counter ladies hate hot dogs with a passion. Candy-counter ladies hate hot dogs so much, in fact, that no matter how much pressure is applied by theatre owners to "move the franks," they have conspired to discourage the world from buying them. Even the second type of hot dog—the roller, in which the dogs lie heating between sets of hot, rotating metal pipes—hasn't eased the situation. Candy-counter ladies who are otherwise patient, encouraging, or completely preoccupied seem to turn on you if you so much as scan the dog selection for a crisp one (there never is). I've often gotten responses like "We're all out" or "The machine's broken" when I'm standing right there, watching it rotate and whirr away! One lady even asked, "What, are you trying to give

Rowlin B. Stones

"I'm blowin' this pond, Ma. I'm gonna show 'em all. I'm gonna do it for Dad. I'm gonna play that violin like it's never been played before."

•   •

me a hard time?" Even my friend Mrs. Whorshower, who works at the Valentine and is always good for fascinating tidbits of candy-counter info ("Try the Goobers—fresh today") remains mute on the hot-dog freeze-out. Sometimes I think the problem is cultural.

Hot dogs don't go with movies. They go with baseball games.

Bon Bons come five to a pack, with a picture of each one on the side of the box. Bon Bons are ice cream and can melt. If you get them in the first round, you have to eat them first. Eating Bon

Bons is a progressive experience. The first one is hard and too cold to bite into, and the last one is soup. As they get softer, they get more difficult to eat. At first the chocolate shell cracks, but then, as you slide them out of the box, they become less like sweets and more like hand lotion. Unbearable levels of stickiness can mean an emergency water-fountain trip, and if you've gotten your Bon Bons on your second trip, a quick *third* trip can create really hostile attention toward you and even speculation that you're on your way to the bathroom to vomit. I usually give Bon Bons a wide berth.

Some movie food is designed for endurance. Certain types boast lots and lots of little pieces that you can eat one at a time or shove in your mouth in huge handfuls till both your cheeks bulge. Other types have dense consistency for enduro-chew. Still others have outer layers that need to be sucked through before the serious eating can begin. When you combine these qualities—lots of pieces, enduro-chew, and suck-thru layer—and add the fact that most movie food leaves over thirty-three per cent of itself in your teeth and gums the first time through, you begin to realize that you've got some real supersnacks here. If I'm going for straight endurance, I might grab Black Crows, Good and Plenty, Jordan Almonds, Root Beer Barrels, or Jaw Breakers.

Movie candy bars cost more than candy-store candy bars, but they're bigger, which is important in the movies. I like to get at least one bar per visit. Candy bars travel well, and if you forget you bought them you get a real treat the next time you wear the coat. I love looking at the display case and seeing them lined up: Zero Bar, 5th Avenue Bar, Mr. Goodbar, Mounds, Bit O Honey, 3 Musketeers, Sugar Daddy, Mary Jane, Clark, Payday, Chunky, Heath, Pep-

permint Pattie, Broadway Bar, Baby Ruth, Milky Way, Reese Cups, Mason Mints. Once I was taking my time deciding, looking over every bar in the stand, and without glancing up from her magazine Mrs. Whorshower said, "Isn't America great?"

I just sighed and shook my head. "I don't know which to pick."

"Go with the Goldenberg's Peanut Chews. I had one a minute ago, and it was just right."

"I was kind of leaning toward the Chocolate Babies or Necco Wafers."

"Suit yourself," she said, getting up and turning away. "You could get them both."

WHEN it comes to movies, I would agree with the critical maxim "More is better." When Hollywood unveiled "the epic," I was more than pleased. Now all I have to do to find out which movie to see is find out which one

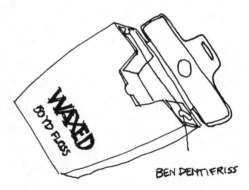

BEN DENTIFRISS

in the neighborhood has an intermission. They don't seem to have as many double features as they used to, and besides, you can't always count on a second feature not being a mush movie. Mush-movie titles can be very misleading, like "The Burning Hills" or "Not as a Stranger." They try to make you think they're monster pictures. In my opinion, Hollywood's missing out on a lot of candy-counter dollars by not doubling some of these epics. I sometimes lie in bed at night and think about pairing up, say,

"Alexander the Great" and "War and Peace." They both have enough dull stuff between battles to stay well stocked, and they both have lots of guys who get it in the neck. Although the Macedonians didn't have cannons, the French didn't have chariots or shields. On the downside, I thought Henry Fonda's hat looked kind of stupid. And if he was Russian, how come his name was Pierre? Biblical pictures can be O.K. if they have good miracles. "The Ten Commandments" didn't really have any good battle scenes, but the Red Sea closing in on Yul Brynner was first-rate, I felt. Overall, though, desert pictures make me too thirsty. It seems to me that the best movies are the ones you can think about as you're walking home. I like to slowly replay all the different parts of them, kind of put myself in the place of the hero and wonder what I would have done in his situation. That usually gives me enough time to finish off a slice of pizza before I hit the front porch.

—CALVIN CHITTERLING

• •

MOVIES

BEVERLY HILLS CPA (1955)—Wally Cox stars in this expertly crafted vehicle that was a 1955 Oscar nominee for lighting. The plot is little more than a series of opportunities for Cox to do his patented Little Guy routines: hemming and hawing, straightening his tie, lunching on a tuna sandwich at his desk. In the film's most memorable sequence, Cox convinces a toothsome Shelley Winters that she would save much more by doing the short form. The director/screenwriter of the film, Victor Bombelle, went on to do some wonderful industrials for Westinghouse. (Failia; all seats co-op for evening shows.)

BRINGING UP BABA (1979)—Satyajit Ray's drama about one of his homeland's most beloved teachers and mystics. As usual, Ray made the film with an economy that approaches the impoverished. A full third of it was shot with no film in the camera, and comprehension depends on reading notes which are supplied to alternate ticket holders only. This director's characters are most effective when they say the least, and this was probably the quietest movie ever made until Ray's 1982 adaptation of Feh Mehta's autobiography, "Me-Ji." In Hindi. (Bombay Talkie Place.)

CHANGE AT JAMAICA (1980)—Fendeckman's haunting, lyrical epic about a Long Island broker obsessed with punctuality. Filmed entirely on location in Massapequa, Massapequa Park, Amityville, Copiague, Lindenhurst, and Babylon. A painful, memorable experience. Subtitles. (Bleak House Cinema.)

GRENADA, MON AMOUR (1984)—A surreal, black-and-white film, skillfully directed by Klenny Blabes, about the trauma endured by a young woman whose dental training at an island medical school is interrupted by the American invasion. Romantic, gauzy scenes of the woman surfing, sunning, and making inlays contrast sharply with the deprivations suddenly forced upon her: thirty-six hours without hot water, no place to cash a check, an endless wait at the phone booth to call her family in Grosse Pointe. The film's unusual score, performed entirely with dental tools, was composed by the rock musician Stink. (Theatre Debris.)

INCENSED (1944)—Obscure Bogey and Bacall mystery thriller. With Peter Lorre as the suspicious night watchman, John Garfield as the callous chauffeur, Robert Mitchum as the bewildered pilot, Dorothy Malone as the trusting hatcheck girl, Cary Grant as the drunken professor, Alice Faye as the mysterious countess, Dana Andrews as the clinic supervisor, George Sanders as the friendly inspector, Ingrid Bergman as the deluded showgirl, Leo G. Carroll as the doting but despised uncle, Horace Heidt and His Orchestra, others. (Loews Sixpack.)

I SEEK DEATH (1973)—Mujupoppy, who brought an all-Mexican cast to Belgium to film O'Hanrahan's novel of romance and deceit in colonial New England, serves up a smorgasbord of clashing filmic styles. Apparently he feels strongly about something, but we're not sure what it is. (Blechman.)

BOOKS NOT SO BRIEFLY NOTED
GENERAL

TV TIME: 1001 OF THE BEST SHOWS EVER, by Jill and Bub Everett (Quickie; $54.50 cloth, $54.50 paper). It's not our custom to peruse books devoted to a medium we scarcely acknowledge; still, this volume is not without historical interest. A sampling:

Dreamboat (episode 323). Ethel Merman has Mickey Rooney's baby. Wee-wee the Chimp objects. Dolly Parton and Carol Channing go at it in a vat of Glo-Coat. It's Dolly by a country mile.

Skylight Zone (episode 16). Young married couple find themselves trapped in an uninhabited town where time has stopped. Their child turns out to be a Martian who tries to change his parents into slave robots by feeding them mushrooms ostensibly grown for a school project. Everyone turns out to be very tiny and part of the contents of a little girl's toy chest, which she closes with a bang at the end of the show.

I Love Juicy (episode 1,234,678,921). Juicy and Methyl decide to teach the boys a lesson when Juicy discovers Panstick on Dickie's ocarina. The boys retaliate by graduating summa cum laude in plasma physics, Texas Southmost College, class of '61. All is set right in a scene involving a cranshaw melon, a recording of "Downtown," and a .22-long rifle.

SMUTTERINGS, by Cornelia Heavings (Harrowing; $14.95). Generally, we prefer our gossip a little more *al dente*. In real life, Miss Heavings is even witchier than the scheming admiral's wife she portrays in "New London," the long-running television series about the seamy side of the submarine business. Miss Heavings shows a real flair for mysterious pronoun reference and even gives Dostoevsky a run for his money in the confusing-use-of-nicknames department. It is also refreshing to come upon a show-business autobiography without self-serving backstage vignettes from the subject's early days in rep. Miss Heavings instead concentrates on her more recent past as a prostitute who "only took money for it before dinner." With some illuminating photographs of the most unlikely people (what's Jacques Lacan doing here, anyway?).

•   •

Claire de Goon

[Law enforcement is a subject rarely addressed in our pages, as it tends to upset Mr. Shwat. Still, I cannot but feel that the subject of the following Talk story speaks for all of us—or, at least, for me.]

CLAIRE works weekends at the Oxford movie theatre as a matron in the children's section. She wears a starched white suit and low pumps, and carries a flashlight. Monday through Friday she's a school-crossing guard. She likes to say that though during the week she directs traffic with a whistle, a stop sign, and a Sam Browne belt across her chest, it isn't until the weekend that she really gets to *enforce*.

"I brook no truck," says Claire, defining "truck" as any behavior that infringes upon someone else's viewing enjoyment or any behavior she just plain doesn't like. "In a movie theatre, you have to act fast. There's no time for niceties or explanations. People may say I'm too rough, that I act like the cop, judge, and jury, all rolled into one, but they don't understand there's a gray area here. What if an important part of the picture is going on, one of those Mac-Guffins or maybe a *dénouement*? You can't ask the projectionist to rewind the picture and play it again just because one noisy apple causes a disturbance. We got a schedule here. People are waiting outside for the next show. I say move that noisy apple out as fast as you can."

Before becoming a matron, Claire worked briefly as an usher at Yankee Stadium. She liked the job, but her stately beam impeded her ability to move between the narrow rows with the necessary alacrity. The darkened movie theatre setting allows her to isolate offenders in the searing arc of her flashlight. And if she is called upon to move between the rows, it is always at a determined pace with her steely-eyed stare locked onto her hapless prey. "In a corporal encounter, always go for the ear," she advises. "An ear yank gets 'em to their feet in a flash. You can pull 'em out of the row, up the aisle, and out the exit just like

• •

BROTH

you were throwing away a bad fish."

We spent a recent Saturday afternoon with Claire in order to watch her technique. As the kids filed in before the show started, she stood in the aisle behind the seats and explained to us how she prospected for potential troublemakers. "First thing you look for is a kid who knows a lot of other kids. A kid goes down the aisle, he's waving or pointing, laughing, or yelling at some other kid that he's a 'spaz,' you watch to see where he sits. You know it's gonna be a hot spot. They want to socialize, they should stay on the block. They want to see a movie, they keep the mouth shut and the butt in the seat." As if on cue, a mop-topped redhead sauntered down the aisle, working the crowd like a politician. With a hatch-rattling basso that stopped traffic and turned heads, Claire shouted: "You wanna play games? I'm ready!"

We asked Claire if she felt it was fair to single out the young man before he'd actually done anything wrong. "You want fair," she answered with some visible agitation, "you join the Little League. Over here, it's 'an ounce of prevention.' What I just did was establish presence. Now every kid in the section knows I'm here. If they've been here before, they know I don't give second chances." We then asked if she meant by this that children were ejected on first offenses. "Second chances," Claire answered, emphatically, "are for shadowboxers and organ recipients." We didn't really understand this response, but, as the show was starting and the children were quiet-ing down, we didn't query it.

As the movie played, Claire made intermittent trips up and down the aisles bordering the section, rhythmically clapping her flashlight into her open palm and continuing to "establish presence." Between trips, we learned from her hushed monologue that she enjoyed working the seven-day "grind" and that she felt days off were for "lollygaggers." In a personal aside, she informed us that she had been married once, although soon after the ceremony "the man actually attempted to put his hands on me." After she fended him off with a double boiler and he subsequently returned to consciousness, the couple was estranged.

Toward the middle of the movie, things started to heat up. On the screen, Charles Bronson had just knocked a supernumerary cold with one remarkable punch. This sent shock waves of improvisational, imitative behavior through the section, giving it the appearance of a bubbling tar pit. Claire managed to snare three popping-up punchers *in flagrante delicto*, and in a trice they were back out on the pavement. A fourth won an appeal to return to his seat for his coat and, once free of her clutch, sprinted back down the aisle, yelling "Yo, matron" at the top of his lungs. The formidable Claire bunched her girth for momentum and gave chase, but she proved no match for the nimble youth, who ran her ragged before diving kamikaze-like for the emergency fire doors at the side of the theatre. His final colorful comment, though unprintable, left the

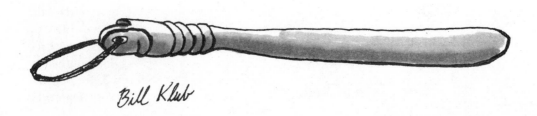

Bill Klub

Claron Burr

"I don't care how much you paid for it. It looks like a cat."

•   •

entire children's section abuzz with admiration. It seemed to us that Claire was defeated, yet she returned to her post like a general who has lost a battle but won the war. "Once you weed out the ringleaders, it's like getting the mother wart," she confided.

Events proved that she knew her game. There were only four more calls for direct action: two girls smoking cigarettes; a "hairy motha" contest, in which the boys tried to outdo one another in volume as they screamed the phrase "hairy motha"; a very young man who appeared in the aisle with no clothes on; and a creditable (to our ears) Donald Duck imitator who repeated all the film's dialogue with inappropriate and unprintable additions.

The Donald Duck imitator turned out to be none other than the redheaded suspect Claire had pointed out before the show began. No doubt the reason for his popularity (Claire was soundly booed as she led him out) was his facile ability to make funny noises. Even we found him quite amusing, although Claire reminded us of the importance of decorum in all things.

"They think just because they're kids they're allowed to make noise. Well, that's not the way the world works. Maybe I'm not too popular, but it comes with the job. Maybe when these kids grow up, they'll remember me and keep their goddamn mouths shut. There are enough know-it-all jerks around already."

All we could do was nod.

•   •

MOVIES

LITTLE SHOP OF HAIRCUTS (1982)—Cult film based on the cult musical based on the cult film. Ticketholders not costumed as members of the film's cast become objects of scorn and ridicule to everyone else. Shown only at midnight. (Lowest Astor Piazza.)

ONCE UPON A TIME IN SECAUCUS (1985)— Sergio Pontoon uses the history of American meat-packing as a metaphor for capitalist expansion and the hyperdevelopment of free market trade in a deliberately overblown, Baroque romance whose apocalyptic ending will cause you to leave the theatre thinking you smell pig's blood. Desi Arnaz has never given a finer performance than he does here. In Italian. (Cinema Blasé.)

101 DONATIONS (1975)—Animated Disney classic about a PBS fund-raising drive run by squirrels. First-rate family entertainment. Vincent Price supplies the voice of the tote bag. (Trivoli.)

OUTWARD BOUND, PART TWO: FIRST BLOOD (1977)—In the first reel or so of this brief but intricately cut bloodbath, a group of enthusiastic weekend outdoor types embark on a rugged, four-day trek in the North Woods of Maine. Leading the group is a taciturn, muscular Penobscot Indian called Chief Boat Moc. "For the next few days," he says, "we'll all be living as if the Indians had beaten the white man." What follows exceeds the campers' wildest expectations or desires. They are led over waterfalls and up cliffs; they are charged by a rabid moose, attacked by killer bees. The lone survivor vows never to go anywhere less civilized than the Bronx Zoo. We leave Chief Boat Moc a happy man, preparing to protect his beloved ancestral lands from the encroachers we may expect in parts three through who knows. (Cinema Jehoshaphat.)

THE PERSECUTION AND ASSASSINATION OF JEAN-PAUL MARAT AS PERFORMED BY THE INMATES OF THE ASYLUM OF CHARENTON UNDER THE DIRECTION OF THE MARQUIS DE SADE, PART II (1983)—Lifeless sequel. Subtitles. (Criteria Oneplex.)

PETER PETER PUMPKIN EATER (1981)—Tube Hoper directs a grim, dank, nasty retelling of the Mother Goose saga. In homage to Godard, cinematographer Hiroshi Tetejecki bathes everything in overpowering bright light, causing the fine cast, headed by Robert Vaughn, to squint throughout. Subtitles. (Cinemxyztplk.)

THE RUSSIANS MUST DIET (1986)—Action adventure featuring Stallone, Schwarzenegger, Norris, and Bronson as an élite team of cold-blooded nutritionists out to prevent détente. Sequel already completed. With Lee Marvin as Saunders. (Pigfield.)

TENDER IS THE HORSE (1967)—Fendeckman's controversial second film. Originally panned by critics as neither tender nor about a horse, the film contains no dialogue and shows nothing but a grainy, black-and-white close-up of a man's nose (Fendeckman's?) for three hours and forty-six minutes. Now, almost twenty years later, it's clear that the critics were right. Subtitles. (TKO National Twin.)

THE
VIRTUOSO
LISTENER

Music

*D*URING *our magazine's early decades, the great music of the day was heard onstage and in clubs, not on the scratchy, brittle records that had only recently come onto the market. Our first editor, Rant, was thoroughly uninterested in music aside from a lingering fondness for military bands, a taste probably picked up during his army days. Still, a magazine that celebrated New York could hardly ignore the cascades of melody pouring from theatres, clubs, speakeasies, and radios all over town. Shav, our second editor, is a trained musician who for several years led his own Las Vegas (New Mexico)-based band, Charlie Chon and the Chopsticks. Even today, he is said to play piano at family gatherings, pounding out old tunes like "Hottentot Potentate," "Wait 'Til the Sun Shines, Nellie," and "Fever" until well past 11 P.M. while his sons, Walrus and Albion, clap their hands in accompaniment. Today, we report on more musical events than ever before. Sadly, McPhumpher's article on Javanese gamelan music could not be included in this chapter; owing to a tiny disaster in my office, involving a rabid truffle-hunting boar, all 691 page proofs were savaged beyond repair.*

SOMETHING YOU RUN ON

(1980)

[*A memory: A beautiful spring morning in 1952. I have just shown up at work. The door to Shwet's office is open. Inside are he and Whitey Bassinet, both of whom have clearly been up all night working. Bassinet is in collar and shirt sleeves; Shvitz has not even unbuttoned his vest. I draw closer. Bassinet is trying patiently, slowly, and certainly not for the first time to explain what a "moldy fig" is. Later, Shriff teams up with Bassinet and E. J. Kohrvette, both fine musicians, and, on hurriedly rented instruments, the bouncy trio regales us all at an impromptu office party in the hall.*]

KLAVE Drayman is back. After a self-imposed exile of seventeen years, during which he played not a note in public, Harold "Klave" Drayman, the near legendary trumpet player, the man whom the curator of the Smithsonian Classic American Jazz Collection repeatedly addressed as "Occupant," is performing again, playing concerts, playing clubs, playing benefits and political dinners, playing everywhere. For so long only a name in yellowing programs and crumbling newsprint, Klave Drayman is suddenly as ubiquitous as pocket lint.

When he left the scene in 1963, he had established a reputation as an individualist and an innovator. Over the years his *oeuvre* had developed a prismatic quality; depending on which facet one shined the light, different colors appeared to predominate. His youthful work, for example, had an ice-blue, feral, trumpet-as-weapon attitude about it. He would characteristically attack the melody in short, choppy bursts, making frequent leaps of a twelfth or more, skewering each phrase as if he were angry at it, playing the punctuation rather than the words. Not so in his later periods: listen to the warm yellow bath he gives the ballads on his last completed album, "The Soul of Empire: Gilbert & Sullivan & Klave" (Flotsam, 9107SK). All languid slides and fat, honeyed whole

notes, he celebrates the childlike, petulant tonality of Poor Little Buttercup's mannered lament, leaving out huge chunks of melody, suggesting how unnecessary they are to one who *will not be rushed*, and even though he has only reached the fourth bar by the time the rest of the band arrives at the end of the second chorus, we have no sense of incompleteness, but rather a feeling of having taken a leisurely walk through a world inclined to be hasty. Perhaps this was the musician pointing toward the long, nomadic excursion upon which the man was about to embark.

I visited Klave Drayman at his apartment on East Eighty-fifth Street. It is a cheerful place with sprightly patterned wall coverings, Oriental rugs on shiny wood floors, comfortable chairs, and a good view of the East River. There is a Delacroix print on one wall and what looks to be a bare canvas (except for an illegible signature) on another. In the southeast corner of the living room, at one end of the large picture window, is a black baby grand piano piled high with music, books, and manuscript paper. One notices with some surprise an almost total absence of memorabilia, the sole exception being a framed photograph of Billie Holliday above the bar. The inscription reads, "Klave, Baby—Don't let it get to you. Love, B." This is probably a

"They sit in every year on Django's birthday."

●　　　●

reference to the critical response accorded Klave Drayman's 1948 album called "Blues à la Modal" (Boptone 16), in which, among other experiments, he essayed a version of "Gloomy Sunday" using only major chords.

I had been admitted to the apartment by Klave Drayman's agent, Martin Scheisskopf, a short, animated man, balding with flecks of gray, and possessed of generous arched eyebrows that give him a perpetual look of surprise. Using a cellophane-tipped toothpick from the remains of his club sandwich, he was chasing down a recalcitrant string of bacon that seemed to have lodged itself somewhere around the second upper-left bicuspid. Between stabs, he told me:

"Klave will be right out. Have you met him before? He's a beautiful guy, isn't he? I used to call him from time to time, when I could find him, tell him, 'Klave, it's time already, people want to

hear you play, they want to know what's going on with you.' He's very independent, though. Very independent and very sensitive. A beautiful guy. *Gotcha, you son of a bitch!*" (This last to the bacon.)

Klave Drayman emerged from the hall to the bedroom, looking a little too rumpled to be beautiful, but after seventeen years welcome just the same. He seemed larger than remembered, as if imbued with an extra hide, a carapace compounded of renewed purpose and incipient melodic joy. His face holds an inexplicable interest, its ample flesh consorting comfortably with strong bones and honest teeth. It is a face that might have been made for L. L. Bean: serviceable, no-nonsense, red plaid. His eyes are grape-green with just a trace of gold, but they metamorphose into more of a calm brown when he opens them. He no longer sports a pencil mustache, and his unadorned upper lip, with the scar that is the badge of his profession, seems to push out a little pugnaciously, as if to say, "If you think *that* was good, wait till you hear *this*!" Louis Armstrong once told him he had big ears, and although it was almost certainly a compliment (among jazz musicians, "big ears" means the ability to hear and respond to everything being played around you), Klave Drayman admitted to me one night several weeks later that he'd always had a nagging doubt, because he does, in fact, have very big ears. His shoulders involuntarily hunch, an act born of a lifetime spent standing in front of a microphone and trying to will his body into the perfect projectile to load into and fire out of his horn. He carries his medium-sized (five-foot-nine) frame with equal parts bravado and stealth, as if he were the prime sparring partner for the middleweight champ; he's a good fighter, but in the end he's the one expected to take the punches.

H E walked over and we shook hands. Scheisskopf bounced up and announced, "Klave, I've got to check on the limo and some other stuff. There's sandwiches in the refrigerator. I'll be back around five. We'll leave at six." He said goodbye to us and went out.

"Where are you playing tonight?" I asked.

"Long Island," Klave Drayman said. "North Shore Center of Israel. It's a wedding, actually, but I told Marty what the hell. To me it's just a chance to play in front of people. I missed a lot of chances. Not that I have any regrets. I had a dog when I was a kid. One summer we went away and forgot about him. He died, starved to death. Ever since then, I try not to look back. My father was a genius, a visionary. When he was growing up on the lower East Side, he had a pushcart. All the other peddlers sold ices, pickles, stuff like that. He sold tax shelters. Never unloaded one.

Nobody had any money, and there were no taxes to speak of anyway. But what an idea, seventy years ahead of its time. Now he would probably be a millionaire. My mother had a Victrola you had to wind up and a bunch of Caruso records. I liked them O.K., but one day an uncle gave me some records of a guy named Ray Ticonderoga and his Dixieland Rhythm Stampeders. I played them over and over. I couldn't get over how bad they were. Those guys couldn't play at all. But then I started sneaking into Merriman's Dance Emporium on Fourteenth Street, and I got religion there, man. They had the best, everybody. Louis, Duke, Bix, Red, Skeets, Duff, Klaus, Fweet, they all came to Merriman's. That's where I heard Fats Leviathan jamming with the great slide clarinettist Rusty Johnson until noon the next day. I got my first horn right after that, and I started practicing whenever I had time."

"North Shore Center of Israel. Is that in Manhasset?"

"I left home for good sometime during the Depression. I couldn't afford to keep my own group together, but I'd get work from time to time in different bands. I was always searching around for a style I liked. Some guys wanted you to play the same way every night; I couldn't handle that. I got fired one night in Kansas City by a big, ham-handed piano player named Weldon Meat, who liked to tell people he was descended from African royalty. I told him it must be the biggest descent since Lindy landed in France. During the war I did USO tours with all the Hollywood stars. Bing Crosby liked me. He taught me a lot, gave me a whole new insight into the melody and the way to approach it. 'Keep the melody in mind,' he said. 'Don't forget it.' I still come back to that."

"Great Neck? Port Washington?"

"After the war I ran for a while with

Bird and Diz, played with Monk some. We had some good times, played some good music. But you could see people falling into camps, lining up in one bag or another. I didn't have a flag. I was making records by then, but they all sounded different. I'm fascinated by the tonal possibilities in the tiniest fragment of sound. One year after I cut out, I only played F-sharp, the whole year, man. Just F-sharps. Of course, it limits you in some ways, but it really frees you up in others—rhythmically, for example. Then about five years ago I met Reebo Fype, and he opened up whole new worlds for me. It was a tragedy about him; he was the freest spirit and the most, you know, *adventurous* musical soul I ever met. [Reebo Fype, the avant-garde gypsy cornettist, suffocated to death trying to play the cornet by placing the bell of the horn over his nose and mouth and sucking the sound out of it. At his funeral, Klave Drayman reportedly played, in the conventional manner, an improvised recessional based on Adams and Strouse's "Put on a Happy Face."] Reebo taught me more than anyone else. He *knew*, man, about music and about life. About a week before he died, he told me, 'A hill is not necessarily something you have to get to the top of. It may be only something you run on very tilted.' That's when I started thinking about coming back."

"Can I ride out in your car?"

"Sure, no problem. You want a sandwich?"

Six of us traveled out to what, in the event, proved to be the *South* Shore Center of Israel in Massapequa. The driver, Scheisskopf, Klave Drayman, and I were joined by two of the three sidemen for the evening's gig, Shorty Prokoffiev and Serge Bubbele. Prokoffiev is a pianist of considerable range who has lately divided his time between accompanying a select group of singers he admires and working on a jazz opera he is composing based on the life of Sy Syms. Bubbele was the bassist for Woody Herman's Herds Nos. 271–304. He has a thumping, exuberant style that can occasionally overpower a small group, but which Klave Drayman likes to use to advantage, creating a delicate petit-point horn counterpoint to the roiling athleticism underneath. The drummer, Cecil Packer (who would join us at the hall—he lives in Freeport), has played on three of Klave Drayman's albums (including the controversial "Animals Cry When You Hit Them," Superfluity-31) and is a good complement to the rest of this rhythm section; he plays with great authority, but he stays out of the way of the more flamboyant personalities. The ages of the quartet range from Prokoffiev's fifty-three to Klave Drayman's sixty-seven (though he could easily pass for sixty-three or sixty-four). They have played together many times.

The "all-purpose" room at the South Shore Center of Israel had a small carpeted riser at one end with a piano, a much more extensive drum kit (including five ride cymbals and six tom-toms, three of the wafer-thin electronic variety) than Packer's (Packer's drums and Bubbele's bass had been brought separately by van), a bank of synthesizers, and a jumble of sound equipment, cables, and signal-enhancing paraphernalia. A man in a tuxedo who may have been looking askance at our dark suits or may merely have had a bad stuffed mushroom explained that Klave Drayman's quartet would be alternating forty-minute sets with a group called Dead Buckets of Scum, whose principal member was the bride's younger brother. This established, the musicians tested the microphones perfunctorily, played about thirty-two bars of a medium-tempo blues, and repaired to a tiny room offstage to eat and to attend to their small, individual pre-gig rituals.

At eight-thirty, the musicians took the stage together. Klave Drayman stood at the edge of the riser until the others were settled, then walked leisurely to the center microphone and nodded, smiling to the audience. There was scattered applause. Packer counted off a vigorous two bars, and the quartet launched itself into the curiously underperformed Harold Arlen classic, "Scrod for Breakfast." It was immediately evident that this night Klave Drayman had hit the ground running. His register transitions were seamless, his tone was warm but not too wet or gunky, and his phrasing was confident and informed with wit. He stated the main theme—a simple, unembellished quarter-note phrase— with just enough rhythmic quirkiness to suggest stumbling, and then suddenly landed decisively on an F-sharp that he held over a long series of chords to which it seemed frequently irrelevant but which somehow seemed to fall into line. Then, having established who was boss, he played a series of bright, *parlante* sixteenth-note runs—scrod running?— and passed the baton triumphantly to Prokoffiev.

From such a happy beginning, the set progressed easily, effortlessly. The second tune was new to me, a bouncy piece of (Shorty) Prokoffiev's called "Clothes Make the Man," and the quartet gave it a coruscating, playful read-

ing. In the ballad that followed, Alec Wilder's stunning "I Was There Early, You Took a Cab," Klave Drayman played a lyrical, sad-but-unsentimental, stark-white solo that captured perfectly the particular synthesis of private loneliness and public discomfiture which is Wilder's forte. ("Klave Drayman," Wilder has said, "plays like you'd like your toast done: brown and crispy, but not burned.") And so it went, on to the energetic finale, Klave Drayman's own "Go Back for a Long One," in which Bubbele took a torrid solo, his long fingers whipping and hammering the strings into vibrant life, the phrases alternately coiling and springing around the heart of the beat. This seemed to inspire Klave Drayman as well, because his playing on the last chorus was some of the finest I have heard from him. Notes exploded from his horn like passengers from a rush-hour subway train, erupting, cascading onto the platform, pushing, shoving, spitting, running for the shuttle, missing the 6:14 to Hartsdale and lining up six deep at the bar of the White Rose. The audience—that part which had stayed, the younger members having withdrawn to the parking lot to take drugs and await the onset of the Buckets—applauded enthusiastically. The musicians bowed and left the stage.

Much later, riding back to Manhattan after what all agreed had been a *coup de maître*, I asked Klave Drayman, "What's next?"

"First, I think, a shower," he said. "Or a hot bath with a little rum stirred into it. I like the way it makes me smell. When I was twenty-five, I went out on the road playing fourth trumpet for Benno Flosseur's big band and I met a girl in Seattle who smelled exactly like oatmeal cookies. I would get hungry just talking to her. Smell is very important. Sometimes I look out my window at, you know, Queens, and I think about

248

what we're doing to the air and everything, and I wonder if it's all worth it. I mean, why make music for a smelly world? But then I get in a groove like we had tonight and I feel like I'm playing for the first time, not, like, *really* the first time, but with that kind of enthusiasm. It's the enthusiasm that's so important. The enthusiasm and the smell. And, of course, the music itself. There's always something new you can discover when you play. One more small step. It's like a labyrinth, but they've given you a sonic road map."

I thought: Reebo Fype was right. Klave Drayman is still out on the road, still running. And still very, very tilted.

—WHITEY BASSINET

BOOKS NOT SO BRIEFLY NOTED
GENERAL

THE DURHAM LEGACY, by Nils Bountyman with an introduction by McCreary Steinman (Val-U Bookettes; $1.25, Dynelle). A very selective and somewhat obsequious biography of Cas Durham, the man sometimes credited with inventing the genre of semiclassical music. Mr. Bountyman seems only sporadically aware of the world outside Durham's chosen musical field. Although Durham was the first to orchestrate rock-and-roll compositions for use in shopping malls, bus terminals, and halfway houses, Bountyman incorrectly credits him with actually writing the classics "Satisfaction," "Stone Soul Picnic," and "Ugi, Ugi, Ugi." Even more irksome is Bounty-

man's (Durham's?) insistent lumping of the two genres—semiclassical and orchestrated rock and roll—under the same aegis. "What Now, My Love," "The Pizzicato Polka," and "Lara's Theme," though vastly popular, certainly do not belong to the rock idiom. Perhaps Mr. Steinman, who is at least nominally responsible for the curiously phrased introduction ("I first laid my two eyes on a guy called Cas Durham for a nice lunch with my lawyer at their office"), could teach Mr. Bountyman the difference between a beguine and a shuffle.

P. J. PROBY: TIGHT PANTS, BIG CITY, by Phillip Norml (Gear & Fab, Ltd.; $19.95). During P. J. Proby's heyday (October, 1964, through May, 1965), his records rose as high as number six on the British charts. For three consecutive weeks, he had records in the top one hundred in Great Britain, the Benelux, and Japan simultaneously. Phillip Norml's prodigious (700-plus pages), well-researched biography is a worthy successor to his "Two Lads and a Van: Peter and Gordon in the North Country." In addition to providing a detailed account of Proby's life and career, Norml puts the lie to the assertions of Hugh Constant-Reamer and others that P. J. Proby was the notorious "eighth man" of the Philby, Burgess, Meredith, Wilson, Pickett *et al.* spy scandal, establishing beyond doubt that Proby, on the one occasion that he actually fell over Anthony Blunt in the dark, did not recognize him. Illustrated.

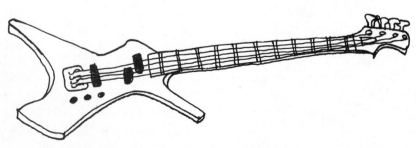

PORGY MAKES THE MET

(1985)

[How we all admire Wanerd Torper! Week after week, it seems, he makes the rounds of the recital halls and the festivals, separating the wheat from the chaff purely, his admirers believe, for the sake of seeing his name in print.]

HINDEMITH described the act of composition, for him, as a process akin to reconstructing a landscape perceived completely, but very fleetingly, during a flash of lightning. It seems safe to say, however, that composers do not necessarily look before they leap, figuratively speaking (and sometimes quite literally: Art Tatum's breathtaking plunges from the top to the bottom of the keyboard were legendary; although one does not tend to think of the blind pianist primarily as a composer, any jazz musician improvises extensively, if often tediously, and is, when so doing, composing just as surely as was Bach when writing a chorale prelude).

Did Gershwin, in choosing the story of Porgy and Bess, set out to write a grand opera with piquant jazz overtones? Or did he set out to create a new genre—jazz opera in the truest sense? The evidence overwhelmingly indicates that most composers are not always sure where a new work will lead them, or even where it will end up beginning. The two mighty E♭ major chords that form the portal through which we enter the *Eroica* symphony are not present in Beethoven's earliest sketches; he added them, no doubt, when he realized that the basic tonality of a symphony whose opening theme slips out of that tonality after a mere four seconds (3.7 seconds with Toscanini conducting) needs all the help it can get. Beethoven himself, it should be noted, was known as a spellbinding improviser. "I take my hat off to him," wrote Albrechtsberger to a friend who ran an apothecary directly across the street from the home of Mozart's washerwoman. "He really plays up a storm." The fact that Albrechtsberger's hat size was almost identical to Beethoven's has led to speculations among certain modern scholars that can only be described as silly, ridiculous, and beneath consideration; I will address these speculations in the future. Mozart's washerwoman, by the way, was not only still alive in 1798; she was still working for Constanza and keeping her mouth shut about who finished the Requiem.

Nowadays, people tend to associate improvising exclusively with jazz and baroque music, but the seeds of Western improvisation were sown, it is now believed, by the great early fifteenth-century English composer John Dunstable. Indeed, many if not most of the significant developments in jazz have had their roots in England, from the birth of George Shearing (like Tatum, a blind pianist, but considerably whiter) to that of Charles "Charlie" Chaplin, whose song "Smile" was Nat "King" Cole's biggest hit ever. The chauvinism of Americans when it comes to jazz is perhaps more understandable than it is defensible: let us remember that the first conductor ever to perform at the site of Benny Goodman's legendary 1938 Carnegie Hall concert was a Russian—Peter Ilyich Tchaikovsky.

Does jazz belong in the pantheon of truly lasting music? Several considerations have kept this question in the forefront of thorniness for decades. Serious lovers, often referred to as "buffs," and practitioners of jazz insist that improvisation is a *sine qua non* of the genre, although to most listeners the presence of certain textures and rhythms is enough to justify the sobriquet "jazz" (as Edward Ellington, who had the habit of pretending that his given name was "Duke," put it—I quote from memory— "It doesn't mean much if it doesn't have that swing"). Assuming that improvisation is indeed integral to what the jazz pianist/educator William ("Billy"— these people cherish their informality) Taylor has called "America's classical music," it may be that the inherent impermanence of improvised music has militated against durability, although my colleague Whitey Bassinet has pointed out that the development of jazz has coincided almost exactly with the development of sound recording, with the result that jazz musicians have had access to a kind of permanence that earlier improvisers—Machaut, Frescobaldi, Buxtehude, Handel, Bach, Mozart, Beethoven, and Schubert, to name a few; Josquin, Gibbons, Carissimi, Scarlatti, Haydn, Hummel, Mendelssohn, and Schumann, to name a few more—simply did not have. Nevertheless, the question of greatness vis-à-vis jazz remains murky and will not likely be resolved during this century.

I want to make clear that I was just kidding about Mozart's washerwoman clamming up about who completed her late employer's Requiem—she was visiting her family in Gratz when Mozart died, and knew nothing about anything. A little joke, in the words of the Latin poet Tertius, "never hurt anyone." Mendelssohn agreed, and said so to his mother.

Gershwin's place in the musical firmament is an odd one. It is difficult to imagine any educated person, asked to list the three greatest composers in the history of Western music, hesitating over the names of Verdi and Elliot Carter, but that third slot is a tough one. Can it *really* be given to Peter Maxwell Davies at the expense of Mozart or Pachelbel? As fine a composer and as engaging a personality as Max is, or are, it cannot be denied that some of his works teeter on the brink of an untoward intelligibility that the vulgar may applaud, but that time will perhaps file away in the "cheap shots" drawer. Verdi, of course, was no stranger to intelligibility, but that's different.

There are those, of course, who resist —with vehemence—the suggestion that *any* contemporary composer deserves to be mentioned in the same breath as the titans of yesteryear; a simple reminder that even Adam de la Halle (c. 1240– 1287) was once a contemporary composer should serve to silence these reactionaries, but it won't. Things take time, and some things take more time than other things. It is hard to believe that Eugene Ormandy could say, as late as 1951, that he found the music of Brahms "virtually incomprehensible," nor *should* it be believed, since it isn't true.

The other side of the coin, what composers have thought about their audiences, is a more complex question—too complex, in fact, to be gone into in a review of this nature. But what the hell, I'll do it anyway.

Even while professing indifference to, and even disdain for, their audiences, some of the haughtiest composers have, in private, expressed a desire to be accepted. Yet these same composers have seemed, at other times, to go out of their way to avoid acceptance. On the one hand, Schoenberg once admitted that "There is nothing I long for more intensely than . . . to be taken for a better sort of Tchaikowsky, or . . . that people should know my tunes and whistle them." (How do you like, I cannot resist asking, *them* apples?) On the other hand, composers have been known to withhold

Allegro Furioso

•   •

from publication pieces that later became (and that in all likelihood they suspected might become) their most popular works: Mendelssohn's Italian symphony and Saint Saëns' "Carnival of the Animals" are cases in point. One is used to thinking of Guillaume de Machaut as a man impervious to criticism, even if one has always suspected that his oft-quoted remark, "I do not care a little pea what all the world is thinking, when that I am able nevertheless always to compose myself," has been the victim of inadequate translation; indeed, as Barryl

Surd convincingly demonstrated in his doctoral thesis at Slippery Rock State College, the translation is more than misleading. Mr. Surd leaves no doubt that the fourteenth-century French idiom "to care not a little pea" was actually a chivalric "code phrase" that would be more accurately translated as "Th–th–th–that's all, folks!" This obviously throws new light on things; we're talking now about a very different kettle of fish. (A touch of the colloquial here and there can be as effective in prose as in music; it allows the reader to harbor the harmless illusion that he or she is on the same intellectual level as the author.)

Musically speaking, many of the great composers of the past were equally at home in the colloquial and more rarefied regions of their art: Schubert improvised endless waltzes at parties, Bach family gatherings were characterized by the spontaneous invention of quodlibets (the combining of songs or themes from different sources), and the recent discovery at Pseudon of several manuscripts attributed to Orpheus himself indicates that the legendary lute-picker's Dithyramb II, $\pi \, \epsilon \nu \, \tau \omega \, \text{ov} \rho \alpha \nu \omega$ ("Pi in the sky"), was not only the first song in history to employ the musical form abcc, but, in fact, the original model for "I've Been Workin' on the Railroad."

In this century, however, the gulf between "entertainment" and "art" has widened. Haydn wrote the Austrian national anthem, and Queen Victoria sang Mendelssohn songs from memory; it is hard to imagine Elliot Carter writing anything that Ronald Reagan would be able —or, for that matter, caught dead trying—to sing, especially at the top of a ball game. Attempts to combine popular and classical musical genres have become more self-conscious—"Third Stream," the 1960s shotgun marriage between classical music and jazz seemed

particularly forced. Doctrinaire dodecaphonists like Rolf Liebermann were sabotaged by the fact that nobody, as Hindemith was the first to point out, can improvise within the twelve-tone system, and Gunther Schuller—a streetwise but classically trained New York musician who played with many of the top names of "be-bop" and "cool" jazz —was handicapped by two facts: 1) his primary instrument, the French horn, has never been regarded by *anybody* as a very hep (to use the vernacular) vehicle for jazz, and 2) he married a woman from Fargo, North Dakota.

In restrospect, earlier attempts at fusion, scorned at the time by both jazz and classical musicians, seem to have been the most successful, if longevity can be considered a valid yardstick for success, and, let's face it, that's exactly what most people consider it. Darius Milhaud's score for the 1923 ballet "The Creation of the World" is often cited as the first instance of symphonic jazz despite the fact that John Alden Carpenter's 1922 score for the "jazz pantomime" "Krazy Kat" was a real toe-tapper. Stravinsky's "Ebony Concerto" is an indisputable, if minor, masterpiece, the opinion of the members of Woody Herman's band notwithstanding. In the long run, "authenticity" of style has not proved to be important, and the twenties and thirties now look like the Golden Age of classical/jazz cross-pollenization.

Which brings us to the subject of this review, and one of the current season's most talked-about operatic events: the first performance at the Met—half a century after its composition and decades after its consensual acceptance as a genuine American cultural artifact—of George Gershwin's opera-in-spite-of-it-self, "Porgy and Bess." Alas, a lack of space precludes any discussion of this interestingly flawed production.

—Wanerd Torper

Rocking Reds

[Mindful of the intimate relation between culture and politics, we had our Talk reporter at this unpublicized first result of the Gorbachev-Reagan cultural exchange agreements.]

RECENTLY a young friend of ours with a taste for rock music attended a party at the Golden Blini, a large nightclub in the Brighton Beach area of Brooklyn. The party was being held to welcome a new group from overseas. Here is her report:

Chivago is absolutely the hottest band to come out of the U.S.S.R. in *years*. Usually Russian music is so draggy, like all that classical stuff they play at funerals and parades. And their pop stars have always been the tackiest. I mean, who was Dean Reed anyway, but a folkie who couldn't make it Stateside? *Chivago*'s different. They play really loud and fast, and you can dance to them. Their drummer calls himself Yuri L. (All the guys in the group use their last initials over here because, they say, no one here can pronounce their last names anyway.) Yuri has a hook instead of a left hand; the rumor is that he lost the hand in a student riot, even though his official Tass biography says he lost it in a tractor accident when he was a boy. The other guys in the group are Sergei O., the bass player (round and dark and cute, with a big beard and mustache), Mikhail N., valve trombonist (small and blond and ferrety, with a wispy goatee and a beret that he always wears, even indoors), and Anatoly Y., who sings and also plays an electrified balalaika (very short, balding, always wears a suit several sizes too large). It's the balalaika and the trombone together that give the group its unusual sound.

The party kicked off *Chivago*'s first American tour and the simultaneous release here of their album "Collective Funk-Boogie." It's been a smash all over the Eastern Bloc despite the chronic vinyl shortage over there and the fact that there's no MTV.

The Russian state-owned record company has a special distribution deal with International Harvester to market the group here. *Chivago*'s hoping to shake up the States the way they've shaken them up back home! "*Da*, we're really bad," Mikhail N. assured me as he nervously toyed with the trombone mouthpiece he wears on a leather thong around his neck ("Is bringing good luck to group as whole"). I asked the group's manager, Fyodor Gojkovic (slim, thirty-sixish, wearing a suit several sizes too large for him), where the guys will be going on the tour. He said they were doing clubs and small halls in Dayton, Milwaukee, Louisville, Ypsilanti, Ann Arbor, Cincinnati, Evanston, Charlotte, and Florence (South Carolina). "Is fine start, no?" Mr. Gojkovic asked, but before I could answer the band started playing on the tiny bandstand at the end of the room. What a sound! It was as if Luther Vandross had met the Moiseyev Folk Dancers! They played their signature tune, "Please to Love Me," followed by a searing blues they're not allowed to perform back home called "Kabul Mess-Around," a forty-five-minute jamming rave-up of "Devil with the Blue Dress On," and a couple of others. We were all dancing and clapping by the time

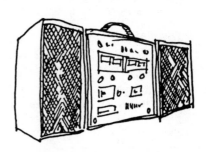

they finished, and then there were little glasses of vodka and all the buttered rolls you could eat. I went up to Anatoly Y., the balalaika player and lead vocalist, as he stood by the buffet and filled the pockets of his extra-big suit with rolls to take back to his motel room, and told him how much I enjoyed their act.

"Is true good rocking music no longer flies only stars and stripes," he said. "Man, when I'm playing and singing on my ax, I'm getting down as freely as any cool cat from the States, no?"
Da!

BOOKS NOT SO BRIEFLY NOTED
GENERAL

LA PETITE POULE, by Cissy De Mico (Tarpaulin; $22.50), is a steamy biography of the famous Parisian chanteuse Celestine Poopée, "the Little Chicken." Poopée spends the early part of her life in the engine rooms of a succession of tramp steamers where, her ample bosom bound, she pretends to be an able-bodied seaman. All the while she sings songs of her own composition in a deep, throaty voice in order to convince her shipmates of her maleness. In 1924, she meets Jean-Baptiste Barrault, a professional *Savat* fighter (they kick) on the run from the Foreign Legion in Rabat. He ships on board under an assumed name and pulls the same watch as Poopée. She falls madly in love with him and, without revealing her true sex, croons love songs to him for three months until he attacks her. She deftly sidesteps his onslaught, but his momentum carries him into a rotating turbine and he is blinded for life. Poopée leaves the ship and grows wealthy and famous performing the songs she composes for him. She cares for him lovingly until his death, although she never succeeds in convincing him that she is a woman.

AMONG THE NEW RECORDINGS (1928)

"BAKE THAT CHICKEN PIE" AND "HARLEM, HERE I GO (AGAIN)"—Bill Blackbird Anderson with Roscoe Mueller and the Blackamoors. Two of the season's best dark ditties and not haphazard. (Oreo-Phone 62751.)

"TEN YEN A DANCE" AND "LAMPPOST LULLABY"—Mickey Moore and his Bohemian Orchestra. Two resounding interpretations played *con fuoco* and not in the manner of local bands. (Beechwood 45789.)

"HALL OF MIRRORS WALTZ" AND "PRENEZ MON HOMME—S'IL VOUS PLAIT"—Celestine Poopée, a chanteuse we admire, brings considerable avoirdupois to these two Continental chestnuts. (Mecca Un-Deux-Trois Cats Sank.)

"HONEYMOON FOR STRINGS" AND "CARTAGENA KITTY"—Bobby Boyer with The Travelling Salesmen of Song, Boyer's Bobcats. A convincing pitch with musical interpolations from the stage epic "Piece-Goods on Parade." (Rictus-Sardonicus LSVDB-1000.)

"HYENA HACIENDA" AND "THERE'S A CARIBOU FOR EV'RY LIGHT ON BROADWAY"—Monty Snarls and his All-Dog Band. Canine doings with a nice stretch of a-cappella rhapsodizing by The Whistlin' Pup. (Milkbone 72463.)

"MY YIDDISHE CAPON" AND "UNDER THE PESACH MOON"—Menasha Luftmensch and the Mandelbrots. Second Avenue stuff with a deft bit of wailing by The Vaudeville Cantor, William Witherspoon. (Piltdown 43892.)

"OH, LADY LADY!" AND "A.E.I. AND OH, YOU KID"—Eeeny, Meeny, Minny, and Moe, The Salt and Pepper Boys, bring their usual enthusiasm to a couple of nifty ones from "Life Begins at 8:42, Approximately." (Cuneiform 𓂉 𓂀 𓏤 𓂸 𓃾 𓅓.)

"PLEASURE MAN" AND "BACKCOMBING BLUES"—Big Mama Bergdorf. Hefty interpretations with nothing of the lighthearted about them. Songs from the "Plantation Picturebook" series. (Cuttlebone 34761.)

"THAT NIGHT IN CAIRO" AND "ZIGGURAT FOR TWO"—Eugene Immermann and The Lava Ladies. A torcher and a novelty fox trot from the balladeers of the U.S.S. Fabulash. (Burnoose 06942.)

PORTRAITS

BROWN STUDY (1985)

McCreary Steinman

[*Kenneth Myman's leisurely, probing portraits of show business legends, of which this is probably the finest, take us beneath the accretions of fame and success that cling like barnacles to his subjects. Not all of them thank him for it. We are obliged, however, to thank Steinman Enterprises Limited for the right to quote from McCreary Steinman's lyrics, without which the reprinting of this article would not have been possible.*]

A MAN so old he looks like an actor in bad age makeup shuffles downtown on the sunny side of Central Park West. He is held erect at his right elbow by a fashionably sweat-suited, retired member of the Los Angeles Rams. Attending his left side is a former Miss Ohio, now a registered nurse in a maroon cape and winged cap, and carrying a state-of-the-art paramedical tote bag. In front and in back, surly, square-jawed men in pin stripes and snap-brim hats scan the high windows and rooftops warily, their hands never far from the Uzis just inside their custom-vest pouches. Crawling along curbside is a Bugatti ambulance equipped with klaxons, wet bar, and a senior attorney from the firm of Hilliard, Bentsen and Peckfliesch.

The old man stops at the corner, gruffly pulls his elbow free, and takes two leaden steps on his own toward a street hot-dog vendor. He orders one with mustard and onions. The vendor, unshaven and obsequious, spears one of the floppy ochre tubes, beds it in a stale bun, and, with a twisting flourish, drapes it in watery yellow paste. Then he ladles on a small pile of limp onion strings in an inexplicably reddish sauce. McCreary Steinman, the man who has written more pop standards than there are keys on a piano, accepts the hot dog from the vendor and says, "If I couldn't eat a hot dog, I wouldn't care if I dropped dead." He takes a bite large enough to include a combination of all the dog's constituent parts and chews methodically, looking blankly into the middle distance, stopping momentarily to forefinger an escaping strand off his chin and back into his mouth. The procession collectively holds its breath. Steinmen stops moving entirely, teeters for a moment, then makes a noise like a back-hoe uprooting a section of ancient water main. There is a mighty expectoration. The bite rockets back at the vendor's chest. The old man's face turns the color of a western sunset as his medical team whisks into action. Within seconds, the Bugatti is screaming its way up the cordoned-off Park Drive toward Mount Sinai Hospital, just as the senior attorney is handing the stunned vendor a summons and complaint along with a word to the wise that he would do well to settle out of court.

Not only does this miraculous tunesmith recover within hours, but his forthcoming composition "If I Couldn't Eat a Hot Dog," arranged by Mel Cosner and performed by Lawrence DiCarl, is unveiled in DiCarl's gala opening two weeks later at the Claudius Dome in Atlantic City. The vendor does settle out of court and is now a wholly owned subsidiary of the ever-expanding Steinman empire.

IT HAS been calculated that a Steinman song is performed or broadcast somewhere in the world every twenty-three seconds. In response to his worldwide popularity, Steinman has commented, "If there were ever such a thing as true world peace, I could buy a new apartment from what those commie kishkas owe me in royalties." Songwriters often take a back seat to their songs in the public eye, but over the years Steinman has sought to reverse this tendency by a vigorous public-relations effort. Though he funds a scholarship program at Brooklyn Law School, appears at both Shea and Yankee stadia to sing the national anthem as often as they will offer him free tickets in return, and has tirelessly attempted to buy controlling interest in the city's offtrack-betting operation in order to rename it McCreary Steinman's OTB, his tunes clearly have a larger life of their own.

All this began at the onset of the Gay Nineties, back when Alice Hlavn, a high-kicking, star-struck, teen-age chorine, succumbed to the illicit advances of Oklahoma Fuzzy McCreary, the King of the Cowboy Troubadours, backstage at the New Casbah Theatre in Trenton, New Jersey. The Cowboy Troubadour came to a sad end less than a year later at the hands of an irate San Francisco tavernkeeper, having never made an honest woman of the unfortunate Alice. Abandoned by her family, Alice faithfully named her new son for his errant sire. Several years hence, on the eve of the new century, Alice wed Sol Steinman, who had invented the industrial miracle of the age, the Inverted Steinman Bobbin. Grudgingly, young McCreary accepted his new stepfather's name and so became McCreary Hlavn Steinman.

McCreary had been a difficult boy, making a bad adjustment to the arduous life out of the theatrical trunk. Though music was for him a daily presence, he showed neither interest nor aptitude in it, exhibiting a fastidious antisocial streak that precipitated a bevy of brushes with the law. Had his life not been so peripatetic, he certainly would have earned himself substantial incarceration, but because of his mother's vaudevillian travels he was never in one town long enough to become a repeat offender. This all changed with the entry of clothier Steinman. The inverted bobbin had effectively halved the time it took to hem both shirtwaist and tunic. Steinman Shirtners Inc. underbid and outproduced all

comers during the Spanish-American War. A popular ad of the time showed Teddy Roosevelt about to charge up San Juan Hill, exclaiming to his executive officer: "I wouldn't dare charge without a Steinman shirt on my back."

The war made Sol Steinman a millionaire, and as a result he wore the familiar Rough Rider brown tunic and jodhpurs every workday for the rest of his life. Every night before retiring he idiosyncratically charged his valet with the same order—"Lay out my browns for the morning, St. Clair." The brown military uniform was to become the symbol of a music-business success that remains unparalleled in all the annals of Tin-Pan Alley.

Sol's largesse elevated young McCreary from the sink-or-swim school of the

• •

JEOPARDY FOR IDIOTS

SHAPES PANCAKES COME IN	THINGS IN YOUR POCKET	LETTERS AFTER "W"	YOUR ADDRESS	TOOTH-BRUSHING DEVICES	YOUR NAME
$100	$100	$100	$100	$100	$100
$200	$200	$200	$200	$200	$200
$300	$300	$300	$300	$300	$300
$400	$400	$400	$400	$400	$400
$500	$500	$500	$500	$500	$500

ZEITGEIST

streets to the fanciest finishing schools in the Northeast, where for the first time he was exposed to the sophisticates and aristocrats of his generation. He absorbed what he needed behaviorally and was facile at languages and sports, but he made no lasting friendships. His rebelliousness caused him to be bounced from one institution to the next.

It was during his brief attendance at Princeton University that the first signs of his true calling emerged. While he was watching a slapping bout between two dining clubs, a dimly remembered two-beat rhythm came into his head and he found himself moved to stand and sing a fight song that he made up as he went along. It is today lost forever. Steinman himself claims not to remember a word and the witnesses to the event are long gone, but it was enough to inspire the losing side to rally and win the day. It was also enough to inspire young McCreary to leave school once and for all. He moved to a garret in Hell's Kitchen, where, close to the Tenderloin strip of music publishers' row, he would begin to fulfill the destiny in his genes, imprinted there by a callow young "hoofer" and a worldly western yodeller. Although Alice was secretly pleased, Sol felt it was the final betrayal, a jealous payback from a long-dead rival.

This was 1917. America was becoming caught up in a furor of war fever. Steinman had an appointment to meet the comedy double Cockburn and Levy, who needed some incidental tunes for a series of review sketches they hoped to break in at a small theatre in Sheepshead Bay, Brooklyn. On his way to their rehearsal hall in the east Eighties, Steinman stopped to watch a parade of soldiers on Fifth Avenue. "Those funny-looking helmets stuck in my head," he says now. "To this day, they still look stupid to me. I don't know why the Germans didn't break up in laughter when they saw

them. Probably because the German helmets looked stupid, too. Or maybe because everyone was too busy laughing at the French helmets." For whatever reason, preoccupation with his stepfather's uniform or the fact that the helmets really did look stupid, Steinman, with the help of the long forgotten comedy double, was inspired to write his first revue, "Soup-hats on Parade." When speaking of his early collaborators, he says: "They really didn't contribute much—an intro here, a piece of business there—nothing that survived." In any case, Steinman's was the only name that appeared on either the program or the copyright when, a month later, "Soup-hats" opened to lukewarm notices. What saved the revue was its signature song, "We're Puttin' On Our Browns," which was reprised three times and never failed to stop the show. The folks left singing it, whistling it, and humming it, and, as the nation's involvement in the Great War grew, sheet-music sales went through the roof. Today the chorus of the song is familiar to everyone; less so, the verse:

> We're follying Black Jack Pershing,
> Steamin' fast across the sea,
> Leavin' Ma and dearhearts pining,
> It's the A.E.F. for me.
> For we're puttin' on our browns,
> Feedin' Gerry to the hounds,
> Pullin' the Frogs' fat from the fire
> 'Cause we're puttin' on our browns.

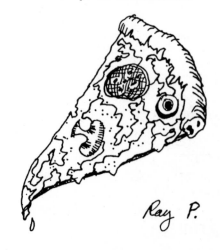

Ray P.

Oddly, as McCreary Steinman's fortunes rose, Sol Steinman's plummeted. Though the Inverted Steinman Bobbin was patented, other innovations created an intense rivalry in the garment business for Uncle Sam's First World War uniform needs. Steinman Shirtners Inc. won precious few contracts—some naval officer's dress togs, but that was about it. As the United States' entry into the war became more likely, Sol had bought up all the brown and khaki wool stocks he could find. Cash-poor and overstocked, he did what he could to lay off as much as possible, but the competition, bitter from almost twenty years of what amounted to a Steinman government monopoly, squeezed him hard. It was around this time that young McCreary took to visiting home in an ostentatious white suit, humming his hit tune and lighting his cheroots with dollar bills. In his 1936 autobiography, "An American Shirtner: My Life as Sol Steinman's Valet," St. Clair Kelway wrote:

McCreary Steinman, with the smashing success of his first song, 'We're Puttin' On Our Browns,' was held in high esteem by those generals and admirals concerned with enlistment rates. Young men signed up in scores and ran into battle with the song on their lips. It would have been nothing for the embittered stepson to wield a small influence with these generals when it came to dispensing uniform contracts. To do so was both in his character and his interest, as events bore out.

It has certainly never been proven that McCreary Steinman manipulated government buying decisions. What is clear, however, is that he benefited from them. As the screws tightened on Sol, McCreary made overtures through his mother to bail out the beleaguered manufacturer. At first the elder stubbornly refused, claiming he would go under before accepting the help of his wife's love-child. But Sol Steinman had a practical, businesslike regard for both his company

and its employees. He had not the heart to see all those helpless "sewing-machine girls" become unemployed or, worse, go running into the arms of the burgeoning I.L.G.W.U. Sol accepted his stepson's offer, and, in return for financial considerations, McCreary Steinman set the style for all his business dealings to come. McHlavn Music Corporation, McCreary's new company (changed to Steinman Enterprises Limited in 1967), gained controlling interest in Steinman Shirtners Inc. before the end of the war. Oddly coincident with the acquisition came an unexpected windfall of government contracts, and the company's profits once again skyrocketed. But now Sol Steinman was a company manager on an employee's fixed salary. Needless to say, when the turnaround came, he did not get a raise.

With the war finally over and the company in his pocket, McCreary Steinman was in a position to hand-pick unknown Irish tenor Miles Tweed to showcase his next big hit, a ballad in waltz time called "Foldin' Up Our Browns":

Foldin' up our browns,
Paintin' crimson our hometowns.
Shovin' 'em back in the closet drawers,
We're foldin' up our browns.
For now, for now,
Foldin' up our browns, for now.

From the end of the war until well into the Depression, Steinman's songs were not, strictly speaking, love songs. This was an early period of voice finding, and, since he was barely into his twenties, his sentimental revelations, when they showed themselves at all, were rather adolescent. It was not until almost 1930, when he had some emotional history behind him, that his lyrics took on a deepening, knowledgeable romanticism. Steinman himself, in his "An American Songwriter: A Self-Retrospective," refers to his first ten years' work as "songs of misfortune, songs of determination, songs of adversity, and songs of laudation."

On the heels of "Foldin' Up Our Browns" came a second Milo Tweed rendition, this one a tip of the hat to the introduction of daylight-saving time called "Impolite at Twilight." The lyric was still light and direct. Steinman's next two successes were more darkly ironic. "The Influenza Credenza," about the 1919 epidemic, was sung by the husky, operatic songbird Carmen Pickerel, while the 1920 prohibition ditty "Highball, Pie-in-the-Skyball" was recorded by noted socialite Horace Van der Topp as a kind of highbrow talking blues.

Little by little, Steinman began to replace his stepfather as family patriarch. He forced Sol to expand into a line of high-fashion short skirts. Sol, a prudish moralist when it came to fashion, decried the move as the ruin of the company, but McCreary turned out three songs in support of the latest flapper rage: "Lovely Leggy Peggy," "Skirtin' Disaster, 'S Curtains for Me," and "Your Knees Make Mine Weak." Popular music and popular fashion have always travelled hand in hand. Both the songs and the skirts were smashes. McCreary could do no wrong. Meanwhile, he had moved back into the family man-

"He called Gounod a hack."

sion. Tensions between the two men increased, trapping Alice in the middle. Sol, in uniform, stormed out to the office early every morning, leaving McCreary still abed from his late-night Broadway carousings. But when McCreary installed an office for himself complete with piano and copyist down at Steinman Shirtners, Sol, losing his last refuge, fought back like a wounded tiger. Retaining the celebrated Boston jurist Edgar Travailian, Sol marched forward into the fray of litigation. McCreary parried onslaught after onslaught and in the process gained an enduring respect for the efficacy, not only of the right to one's day in court, but of the threat of that day in court as well. Tabloids of the day were full of pictures of the fabulous trials that McCreary attended religiously with a new companion on his arm, the black-haired, music-hall rug dancer Miranda May Marley. Miss Marley, bedecked in breathtaking parure of diamond-encrusted tiara, earrings, and choker, wore arrays of furry animal pelts from the neck down, usually with one or more of the heads still attached. She never took her hands out of her jewelled ermine muff, causing editorial speculation that she was hiding everything from an engagement ring to a pearl derringer to razor-sharp, reptilian talons (she always wore gloves in her act).

To finance his legal attack, Sol had found it expedient to go to the highest echelons of organized crime's loan-sharking operations. As the trials dragged on, not only was more and more money needed, but more and more return was demanded by the mob. Sol Steinman was a proud man. Alice had many times begged him to call off his suits, but by then he was in too deeply. He began to gamble. Like most beginners, he did well at first but then began to lose disastrous sums. When finally at a point where a court victory simply meant handing over his company from his stepson to a pack of gangsters, he, late on a December evening in 1924, uncharacteristically asked St. Clair for a fresh set of browns and marched out into the night. It is assumed that he confronted gang kingpin Georgie "Dutch" Klibber with a defiant refusal to pay back his debt. His riddled remains were found several days later in a locker at the Weehawken ferry slip.

McCreary has always claimed that his next great hit, "Rat-a-Tat-Tat Tango," recorded again by the sultry, dramatic Miss Pickerel, was no more than a response to the pervasive openness on the part of Gangland in general during prohibition. To those who accuse him of writing the song as a musical gloat, he does not respond. He attended the funeral with his mother, who never again appeared in public. (Though unsubstantiated, it is believed that after Sol's death the mob tried to collect his debt from McCreary and that McCreary resolutely gave up nothing, threatening the mob with a rash of negative songs. In the past fifty years, Steinman has survived a number of life-threatening "accidents" that insiders claim were Mafia-sponsored; hence his rigid personal security.) Within a week, McCreary Steinman and Miranda May Marley were married. Alice was, of course, conspicuous in her absence. Although the nation was tapping its toes to Steinman's biggest hit yet ("Spoonin' to the Croonin' on the Radio," a tribute to the new medium's popularity), the deepest valley in the young songwriter's career was about to begin.

The character of the Steinman household had changed drastically. After Sol's death, St. Clair vanished (surfacing again as a writer and noted theatre critic in the late thirties). Alice fell ill now. Most important, the new lady of the house, Miranda, threw off her furs to reveal the ambition of a Roman courtesan.

Given to a gamut of physical excesses, she nightly destroyed heirlooms and daily replaced them with exorbitant knick-knacks that even the staff thought hideous. McCreary, preoccupied with his mother, remained unaware of his bride's tasteless indulgences. He took to waiting on his mother hand and foot and even wrote a song called "Mother's Eating in Her Room Again Tonight." It was his first commercial failure. Soon after, Miranda's jealous behavior became vicious as she took to getting elsewhere the attention that was lacking at home. Gossip columnists led their copy for weeks with stories of her latest infidelities as well as the real meaning of Steinman's comeback blues hit, recorded by Bryce Whitehead (the only black he used until the string of Raynique Wilde hits in the fifties), "Quit Yo' Slatternly Ways." The marriage ended on Black Tuesday in 1929, prompting Steinman's famous quote: "If you have the choice between marrying a beautiful woman or buying Kennecott Copper at sixty bucks, take the stock. At least you can use the certificates [as toilet tissue]." Steinman had one more hit in New York, "Chowline Chowder (Made from Parsley and Soap Powder)," before moving to California with its new "talking" pictures and a new era in his life.

AT a time when New York City meant music, music, music, it is odd that McCreary Steinman was out of town. Radio, Broadway revue, vaudeville, and the recording industry were eating up songs at an unprecedented rate, and they were all staunchly New York-based media. Although Jolson had claimed we had as yet heard "nothin'," the movie as a purveyor of popular music had not yet hit its stride. Almost forgotten in the early thirties, Steinman was to be, more than any other individual, responsible for the rich tradition of movie musicals. The

bandleaders came running to him. On a recent late-night Ted Burkheim talk show, long-retired bandleader Flaxie Nurmnersberg confirmed this, saying, "I'd've as soon performed a set without a McCreary Steinman tune as without my trousers."

Steinman was adept at the incidental love song that bore no relationship to the plot but was somehow undeniably cinematic. Barton Lang, who made a career out of playing the sincere romantic co-star to the antic shenanigans of the immortal Schnook Brothers, sang Steinman tunes in sixteen successive pictures, each one a smash hit, including "Don't You Look a Sight," "The Face I Behold," "Eyes of Bliss," "A Vision in My Arms," and "I'll Be Seein' My Seaplane Sweetie on the Sea of Romance." Says Lang, "To this day, people just have no idea that they were his songs because he hid that famous Steinman touch behind the camera. He wrote songs for the close-up."

Indeed, Steinman was so out of touch with the public that he appeared as the mystery guest in 1935 on the radio game show "Mists of Time." After his identity was revealed, he played a brief medley of his early hits and actually spoke and sang over the airwaves for the first time. His most famous comment on the show was a segue he used over and over between songs that is now rightly attributed to him in "Bartlett's Familiar Quotations": "And then I wrote. . . ."

During his years on the West Coast, Steinman took assiduous care of his mother, who thrived on the warm climate and was rejuvenated by the technical hurly-burly of moviemaking. She loved to sit quietly at the back of the soundstage and watch the dancers go through their routines, holding her breath when the director finally yelled, "Action!" She once said of filmmaking that every scene was like a little opening night. It was Alice who first befriended

Helen Hart, a young girl singer from New Mexico ("I must have a weakness for that Western drawl," Alice said later). Helen had a big, wide, pretty face, hair the color of straw, and the trim, short figure of a palomino. She also had a booming, happy voice that President Roosevelt once said was "enough to make the Depression go away—at least till the end of the song." Helen Hart soon became the second Mrs. McCreary Steinman. The late thirties were a happy, quiet time, and the family grew. Daughter Sally was named after Sol at Alice's insistence, and, as the storm clouds grew over Europe, McCreary felt more energetic than he had in years. When war finally broke out, it was only natural that Helen should record what was to become Steinman's biggest smash ever:

World War Two,
The world is turnin' blue,
Folks are wearin' frowns,
And they're lookin' for their browns.

Out of the mothballs,
At the back of the drawer,
The Krauts forgot their lesson,
They're a-beggin' for some more.

So we're puttin' on our browns,
Like we did one time before.
Hey, Ma, let out some inches,
'Cause we're goin' back to war.

The family returned to the East Coast and threw themselves into the war effort. Steinman was put in charge of Washington's Office of Adverse Popular Senti-

"After our daughter stopped, Donald took it up. So I'm having him killed."

ment (OAPS), where he was responsible for lines like "loose mouths sink scows" along with the coining of the term "jangle" to refer to a short promotional song.

Helen's famous publicity shot, showing her dressed in her signature buttressed shorts, bunting mantle, and soup-hat, made her one of the war's most popular pinups. She travelled fearlessly

from one war zone to the next to entertain the boys, once even parachuting into Messina less than a day after the 3rd Army had "dug in." She often said, "After my girl Sally, I love my boys." But when the DC3 that was carrying Helen and the Slats Silverman band vanished over the Sea of Marmara (Slats stayed behind in Brindisi), it was not just "her boys" who were plunged into despair. The *Life* photograph by Yakov Biaritz of McCreary and Sally in tears after the news of Helen's loss symbolized the grief of the whole country and now hangs in the Petterford Museum for Black-and-White Art.

Since the Second World War, Steinman has unfailingly turned out at least one new smash per year. Now, though, his career is far more accessible to the public

in general because his songs are invariably introduced as either "the Steinman classic" or "the latest Steinman gem." His third attempt at matrimony, to former Pennsylvania senator Martha Carlisle Johns, ended amicably but after only a year. Daughter Sally is now a speech therapist in Yonkers, New York, married to an insurance executive. She and her husband have three children and they guard their privacy.

Steinman today, at ninety-three, is clear-eyed and defensive. Rumors still occasionally surface in the more outrageous tabloids, describing his enduring Rabelaisian capacities, but it seems clear that these allegations are nothing more than attempts to boost circulation. The longer Steinman lives, the more of an institution he becomes. His own favorites are still the songs he refers to as "my patriotic ditties." He shied away from the Vietnam conflict as a musical venue, siding briefly with the counterculture ("My Hairy Honey"). He is reported to have widely experimented with hallucinogenic drugs at the time, but his song "Drippy Face Downer" suggests that he only heard about them from someone who actually knew very little. Lawrence DiCarl's recording of "Ugh, War!" was his last non-love song until "Cool Blue Water in My Hot Brown Boots," about the recent incursion into Grenada.

Steinman has the uncanny ability to be whatever people want him to be. Politicians from both parties claim him as their own. Young or old, yuppie or hippie, he enjoys universal inclusion. His rhythmic commentary on the American condition has for generations caused us to pause for a moment and turn up the radio, just a little. We are all, its seems, aware of him. He claims he not only will see his third century but will still be writing songs. To those who scoff, he says "I'll sue you from my grave."

—KENNETH MYMAN

SUITABLE SPOTS

BLARNEY ROCK, Eighth Ave., at 55th St.—
Overweight longshoremen humming Scott
Joplin nightly. No need to call in advance;
the dinner special is always London Broil.

CHEZ SLIM, 110 Living End Ave.—The menu
here boasts "Japanese, Continental, native
American cuisine." The real surprise comes
when your order is served: it's origami.
Specially trained chefs fold paper and use
wax, plastic, and a few "seclets of the
Olient," as owner Toyota Cavendish jok-
ingly calls them, to create perfect but inedible replicas of the dishes on the menu.
Specialties include mesquite-infused chèvre,
Langoustine tails with monkey-flavored butter, and stuffed peas. The daikon slivers
served while you're waiting are real. Reservations suggested. All credit cards. Dancing permitted, but bring your own music.

JIMBO'S, 786 Third Ave.—A spiffy and
friendly old-world alehouse that, as of this
writing, is on fire. Prompt service.

MARIO'S HOUSE OF FOOD, 985 Eleventh Ave.
—Black-and-white photographs of Italian
ices adorn the walls of this eclectic, unpretentious establishment. Waiters in white
T-shirts with the sleeves torn off present a
roster of the day's specials in a singsong
voice. Wandering minstrels stroll among
the diners, stopping only to finish leftovers.
Try to get a table as far from the continuous horseshoe game as possible.

KASA KLAUS, 911 E. 62nd St.—This intime
little *boîte*, hard by the coronary resuscita-
tion unit of Bellevue Hospital, boasts a first-
rate kitchen. Specialties include Battered
Shrimp, Insalata Insulin, Lamb to the
Slaughter, and Cornish Hen à l'Irrevers-
ible Coma. The stage show varies from
night to night; the entertainment includes
the host's impressions (David Niven, Curt
Jurgens, and Queen Victoria are his most
successful) and the hostess' musical challenge to mud-wrestle any woman in the
house, two falls out of three. If you're sitting in the first couple of rows, ask for a
lobster bib when they roll out the mud pit.

TAKEE OUTEE, 45.8 Grand St.—Working out
of renovated Fotomat, Yim Yow and his
dedicated staff of six prepare the city's most
unpronounceable dishes. Service is quick,
although the meals served seldom match
the orders. Luckily, they're good.

THE TEXAS HOLE, 2,003,416 Madison Ave.—
The loud, raucous, and smoky atmosphere
here is the perfect counterpoint to the serv-
ings of leathery, inedible cuts of charred
beef. The live music is nonstop, and harmonica player Willie Langdale is said to
have never left the place since he arrived
seventeen years ago. Waiters frequently de-
mand more money than is indicated on the
menu. Firearms suggested.

TOM'S CAFÉ, 4511 Second Ave.—Continental
cuisine with a twist: only men named Tom
are permitted to dine here. Call maître d'
Tom for reservations if you're named Tom.
There are more of you in this city than you
think.

TOM TOO, 18 Bleecker St.—Operated by the
owners of Tom's Café, this less formal version of the original admits Tims on slow
nights.

AFTERWORD

*A*ND *so my work is finished.*

Yesterday the staff bade me farewell with a small party. Crepe-paper streamers decked the hall. Miss Featherduster and Mr. Kumquat from Fact Checking prepared their justly famous petits fours. Pauline Zeal showed up with a fruited Jello ring, the words "Goodbye, Eustace" spelled out in miniature marshmallows around its top. In a small ceremony during which our editor, Shwond, made a toast in my honor (at any rate, he raised his glass and moved his lips), my venerable Royal typewriter was affixed to the Library ceiling, from which it now dangles alongside Densely's bowtie, Rakk's hairbrush, Bimbo's railroad cap, Quite's hoe, Thumper's joy buzzer, a Ray's pizza crust, and the other mementoes enshrined there. McPhumpher had prepared what he called "a small valediction." Unfortunately, during a brief, unexpected moment of demonic possession, I ripped the hefty sheaf of pages from his hands, dashed into my office, locked them in one of my recently emptied file cabinets, and swallowed the key.

I am not bitter.

My plans for the future are vague. I. B. Single has invited me down to Key West for some sport fishing and "to take a load off." I have thought of retiring to the family seat in Patch Pocket, Rhode Island. Probably, I shall remain here in New York, in the squalid little flat to which my career has consigned me.

I am not bitter about the years I've spent here, although that we have never had a masthead has always pained me. I would have liked knowing the names of my bosses. But Runx and Shplat, for reasons known best to themselves, conspired to keep our work uncredited. And so, anonymous lives were spun out in this, our ghastly warren of offices, designed (in the sort of bizarre economy that made Rezz such an embarrassing tipper) by our chairman of the board, Hardly Truox.

Despite the indignities, I will miss the role that I, through the magazine, played in affording millions of readers much that is excellent in writing and drawing, as well as some of the best sleep they've had in years.

No, I am not bitter. I leave with memories: Thumper and the Indian newcomer, Feh Mehta, sneaking into each other's cubicles after hours to move the furniture around; George Steinway, Bruno Beetlebrow, and Stanislau Lemon winning the round-robin wheelbarrow race four years in a row at our Annual Contributors' Day Sherry Party; visiting DePinna's with Chauncey on a Sunday afternoon, when the store was closed, and trying on a top hat. It has been a full life, after all. One would have preferred a little more recognition for all one has done, but then the dandy who symbolizes the magazine isn't named, say, Ross or Shawn, is he?

OUR APPENDIX

SNOOZE
THE BEST OF OUR MAGAZINE

Conceived and created by
Alfred Gingold & John Buskin
for WURDZ, INC., and Big Al
Enterprises, Inc.

Alfred Gingold—*editor*
John Buskin—*executive editor*

David Kaestle—*designer*
David Vogler—*associate designer*

Sally Kovalchick—*project editor*
Lynn Strong—*copy chief*

Charles Kadau—*contributing editor*
Joe Raiola—*contributing editor*

Cartoon parodies conceived and written by: John Buskin, Pamela Buskin, Alfred Gingold, Charles Kadau, Joe Raiola.

Cartoon parodies drawn by: Warren Sattler, Elaine Lee and James Sherman, John Buskin.

Reviews, Listings, and Newsbreaks written by: Arthur Boehm, David Buskin, John Buskin, Alfred Gingold, Charles Kadau, Joe Raiola.

• •

Foreword, Commentary, and Afterword written by Alfred Gingold.

CONTRIBUTING WRITERS

CONTRIBUTING ARTISTS

Cartoons

Warren Sattler:
27, 28, 41, 44, 48, 50, 56, 62, 77, 91, 98, 109, 122, 133, 138, 153, 163, 167, 190, 198/199, 203, 206, 217, 218, 221, 226, 236/237, 260, 263.

Elaine Lee & James Sherman:
17, 23, 24, 35, 61, 68, 73, 112, 159, 181, 215, 244, 251.

Sattler, Lee & Sherman:
171, 233, 239.

John Buskin:
19, 65, 81, 105, 115, 140, 175, 208, 257.

All chapter openers drawn and inked by Elaine Lee & James Sherman.

Feature Art

Elaine Lee & James Sherman:
109, 185, 195, 255.

John Buskin:
130, 135, 143.

Spot Drawings

John Buskin:
15, 20, 21, 22, 25, 39, 43, 47, 58, 59, 67, 71, 78, 82, 84, 85, 95, 100, 111, 117, 119, 128, 147, 157, 164, 168, 169, 173, 183, 200, 228, 229, 231, 234, 238, 248, 253.

David Vogler:
53, 93, 94, 97, 144, 147, 179, 196, 197, 205, 207, 210, 212, 219, 247.

Susan Cohen:
154, 160, 187.

Alfred Gingold:
258.